The
GOLDEN CLOAK

The
GOLDEN CLOAK

ANTOINETTE WITHINGTON

An Informal History of Hawaiian
Royalty, and of the Development
of the Government During Each
Reign Under Steadily Increasing
Foreign Influence

Mutual Publishing

ISBN 0-935180-26-5

First Printing, 1986
Second Printing, 1996
Third Printing, 1999
3 4 5 6 7 8 9

Cover design by Julie Matsuo

Mutual Publishing
1215 Center Street, Suite 210
Honolulu, Hawaii 96816
Ph: (808) 732-1709
Fax: (808) 734-4094
e-mail: mutual@lava.net
www.mutualpublishing.com

Printed in Australia

To

PAUL

Foreword

Long before Captain James Cook anchored his vessels, the *Resolution* and the *Discovery,* off Waimea village early in 1778, the Polynesian culture and a monarchial form of government had been firmly established in the Hawaiian Islands. Descendants of a people believed to have migrated from the Caucasus, men with vision—and the courage to follow it—left their homes and, through the centuries, sailed their open canoes across the great unknown ocean from island group to island group. Sailing north from Tahiti, they discovered the Hawaiian chain and here they remained. Generation after generation of these sturdy Polynesians was born before Captain Cook arrived to open the Islands to the outside world.

How Hawaii has become a commercial and educational center merging the Occident and the Orient is history of epic proportions. Across its pages, leaving their imprint as landmarks of change, move Polynesian gods, kings and queens, explorers with their charts, missionaries and their children, and those, seeking their fortunes, who drifted to the Islands as flotsam from the sea.

Any history of Hawaii, however informal, can readily become a cumbersome affair by reason of Hawaiian proper names (many of which begin with the letter "k") and special terms. It is the purpose of this book to approach Hawaiian history through a magnifying glass—emphasizing those trivial happenings and minutiae of detail usually ignored by proper historians and making note, in their proper sequence, of those events which historians have considered epoch-making. However, it should be recalled that modern scientists have long had a great respect for the microscope as an all-revealing instrument. But to utilize the informal, microscopic approach to history entails the use of many personal documents. Existing records of Hawaiian history, unfortunately, employ such a variety of spellings for single terms that the technical historian could well lead his reader into a morass of confusion. For example, papers relating to Hawaiian history throughout the past century and a half have a single meaning, yet employ different spellings, when they use such words as "taboo," "tabu," and "kapu." Kamehameha II, whose given name was "Liholiho," is often referred to in old documents as "Rihoriho." These same documents refer to Hawaii as "Owhyhee." Kamehameha, himself, is often, in old manuscripts, called "Maihamaiha." The present volume has of necessity made considerable use of old papers and has quoted them accurately, with the single exception of the fact that, for the ease of the reader, it has unified certain multi-spelled Hawaiian names or terms.

In writing of these early times in old Hawaii, the accepted foreign terms relating to royalty are generally used. Old Hawaii did not know such words as "king," "crown," "prince," and "princess." These terms came to Hawaii through British influence. Even today, among Hawaiians of the old school, Kamehameha is referred to as "The Great *Alii.*" All members of the Hawaiian nobility are known as the *"Alii."* The insignia of the reigning chief was not a throne and a crown but a red feather girdle and a cloak of yellow feathers.

To the Hawaiian, history offers no more illustrious a personage than Kamehameha the Great, whose statue stands in the heart of Honolulu, backed by the territorial buildings and facing Iolani Palace, the official residence of later kings and queens of Hawaii. On his statuary likeness Kamehameha wears the symbol of his royal office: a feather cape. (It has been said that the feather war-cloak of Kamehameha occupied nine generations in the making. The feathers, of a bright yellow hue, are exceedingly small and delicate. Little clumps of such feathers grew above and below the black tail feathers and on the thighs of each bird— the *mamo.* If the labor expended on this cloak could be estimated, its nominal worth would be found equal to that of the most costly gems in the regalia of Europe at that time.) The statue's cape is freshly gilded annually on a day set aside in Kamehameha's honor. Then, throughout the year, the golden cloak of the Great *Alii* glistens in the sunlight— token of old Hawaii and the days of its recorded monarchy.

Although this book attempts to offer an informal history of Hawaii through the collective biographical sketches of its chief *alii,* the picture would not be complete without reference to three friends of old Hawaii as it stood at the threshold of modern civilization. Two were aliens on Hawaiian shores and one was a Hawaiian on alien shores. Their impact on present-day Hawaii was immeasurable. Because of John Young, the government of Hawaii, as well as its trade and commerce, took on new ways. Obookiah stands as a spiritual connecting link between old Hawaii and New England, a tradition which has been continuous and unbroken to this day. The economy of Hawaii is today based essentially on agriculture; its beauty as a tourist center is attributable in no small part to the riotous flora that is everywhere. Hence, it is appropriate that Francisco de Paula Marin, one of Hawaii's "first" farmers, should be accorded his rightful place in this history.

On completing the book, I wish to express sincere appreciation to all those who have in any manner opened the doors of the years that I might glimpse and feel the true spirit of old Hawaii. I would give especial appreciation to Capt. Frank L. Pleadwell, M.D., U.S.N., retired, to Mr. J. Garner Anthony, and to Dr. Paul Withington for their critical reading of the manuscript. To Mr. Norman J. Wright I am grateful for editorial assistance in getting the book ready for publication.

To Mr. Walter F. Dillingham I owe special thanks for a photostat copy of an original letter written by John Young. To the late Mr. Walter R. Coombs, Deputy Supreme Council Scottish Rite of Hawaii, I am indebted for providing me with the records of the masonic history of His Majesty, David Kalakaua. For a photostat copy of an original letter written by Obookiah, I offer my thanks to Miss Bernice Judd, librarian of the Missionary Children's Library, and to Miss Ethel Damon, historian and author of missionary history. To Rev. Henry Judd, professor of Hawaiian History and the Hawaiian Language at the University of Hawaii, I express my appreciation for his careful interpretation of Hawaiian lore. For the same reason, I am deeply indebted to Dr. Kenneth Emory, anthropologist at the Bishop Museum. To the librarians and their staffs of the Library of Hawaii and the University of Hawaii Library, to the Library of the Bishop Museum, and to the Territorial Archives, I acknowledge and tender appreciation for their long continued attention to my work. To Miss Maude Jones, custodian of the Archives, and to Mrs. Clarice B. Taylor, authority on Hawaiiana, I owe thanks for their critical reading of the manuscript. It has been the fine and interested cooperation of these friends who know and love Hawaii that, in the end, has made the present volume possible.

ANTOINETTE WITHINGTON

June 11, 1953
(Kamehameha Day)
Honolulu

TABLE OF CONTENTS

PROPHECY

Part One

THE BEGINNING

Chapter I

*"A red star like the falling rain
is red when the light shines through
it."*

On a certain night a great storm, such as had not been known for years, broke over the island of Hawaii. It was in the late fall when storms could be expected, but the ferocity of this one created great concern among the people. Driving wind and rain as well as crashing thunder and terrifying lightning, which were almost unknown in the Islands, rocked the kingdom.

It was on this stormy night in Kohala that a man child was born to a high chief, Keoua, and his wife, the high chieftess Kekuiapoiwa, the niece of Alapainui, the king of Hawaii. Even the stars foretold his coming, so tradition tells.

The Polynesian astronomers watched the sky continually for signs and portents. When a new scion of a chiefly house was born, it was customary to select a star rising in the East, which would be used in astrological predictions as to the future of the young prince. But on the night when Keoua's son was born a strange star appeared in the heavens over Kohala.

The star was called *Kokoiki*—"a red star like the falling rain is red when the light shines through it."

The astronomers prophesied that the princely child born that night would be a great chief, greater than any chief in the Hawaiian Islands, and that he would crush all other chiefs who stood in his way. Because of this prophecy there was jealousy among the high chiefs and their clans. Keoua, fearing his child would be kidnapped from his home, took every precaution. As soon as the baby was born he entrusted him to a high chief, Naeole by name, who swiftly and silently, with the child in his arms, ran to the high mountains where a retreat had been arranged with a nurse waiting to receive the baby.

It was not long before the nurse saw two strange men coming up the trail. Rightly suspicious that they were seeking the hiding place of Keoua's son, she quickly hid the baby behind a roll of Olona fibre, from which she had been weaving. Finding no indication of the child's presence, the men passed on.

Modern astronomers have been greatly interested in the traditional facts concerning the strange star, *Kokoiki*. They say the description of the celestial visitor denotes that it was probably Halley's comet, which more than any other comet has figured in legend as an omen of great and terrible events. Their records show that the comet passed the sun in March, 1759, and that it was also observed in Germany in 1758 on the night before Christmas.

Students of Hawaiian astronomy have long been interested in the details of the legend of the appearance of a new star on the night of the birth of Kamehameha, and have sought to explain and to identify it. One study made at the Bernice P. Bishop Museum in Honolulu resulted in a paper presented before the Hawaiian Historical Society by Dr. Maud W. Makemson, assistant professor of astronomy at Vassar College, the closing paragraph of which reads as follows:

"From all these considerations it does not seem unreasonable to suppose that the keen visioned Kilohoku (Hawaiian astronomers) sweeping the sky vigilantly from their temple platform in North Kohala, in the crystal atmosphere of the tropic night, caught sight of the new object in the familiar configuration of the stars, which appears to have been Halley's comet. And, through the accuracy of the account which they gave which has come down by word of mouth, perhaps by rock carvings, we are now able to suggest a date for the birth of Kamehameha the Great, namely, November-December, 1758, which, curiously enough, agrees with the evidence of other lines of research."

So it is, through tradition and through science, that the birth date of Kamehameha is supposedly established.

It is not difficult to visualize the setting in which Kamehameha was born and reared. Snow-capped Mauna Loa looked down upon the ocean as it does today. Mauna Loa, the old volcano, destroyed the land as it has done for centuries, and, in the cracks and the crevices of the gray lava, nature replanted the verdure and the bloom. From the trees of the dark forest men built their swift canoes, and, as their fathers had done before them, they traveled long distances on the sea. They erected their temples, worshipped their gods, and obeyed the taboos which were a complicated code of laws that were, in effect, religious ordinances. High chiefs sought control of lands as men are doing now and for the same reason. Ambition was the keynote of the songs their retainers sang.

When Kamehameha reached young manhood he went to live with his half-uncle, Kalaniopuu, king of the island of Hawaii, who was engaged in a lifelong war with the king of Maui, Kahekili. Although his uncle was somewhat unfortunate in his war, history says, "The young prince, Kamehameha, distinguished himself in these campaigns as a brave and skillful warrior." But the stage upon which Kamehameha made his first entrance into the civilized world was the deck of a British ship.

Captain Cook had anchored his squadron in Kealakekua Bay off the island of Hawaii on January 17, 1779. King Kalaniopuu made a formal call upon the Captain. He took with him a number of attendants, including Kamehameha. Officers of the ship were impressed with the personality of young Kamehameha. It was noted that he was a favorite of the old king, and that he appeared to direct the interview with Captain Cook. One of the officers, Lieutenant King, wrote on January 26, 1779, in his record: "Among the chief attendants of the king was Kamehameha, whose hair was now plaited over with a brown dirty sort of paste or powder which added to as savage a looking face as I ever saw. It however by no means seemed an emblem of his disposition, which was good natured and humorous, although his manner showed somewhat of an overbearing spirit, and he seemed to be the principal director of the interview."

Throughout Polynesia it was the custom to cover the head with a paste to bleach the hair, which was an accepted fashion. Often only a strip of the hair, bordering the face, was bleached. This produced a very striking effect. Kamehameha, being especially interested in his appearance, probably followed the fashion of the South Seas, and, if it added to his savage look, that, too, may have pleased him. He was at this time around twenty-five years of age, and, perhaps, the Beau Brummel of his set.

King Kalaniopuu was then an old man. The following year he decided to settle the matter of the succession in his kingdom. He called the council of chiefs together in the landlocked valley of Waipio on the island of Hawaii.

There was once a *heiau* (temple) and a "City of Refuge" in the valley. In those early days the ancient gods of old Hawaii kept their watch. It was here that the chosen chiefs came to counsel with the king. One can see them coming down the trail, their rich brown bodies reflecting the changing lights and shadows of the sunlight and the shade. The high chiefs in their brilliant feather cloaks and helmets, their faces clean cut and strong, tell the history of their people. Hawaiian chieftains were outstanding men with the dignity and bearing of their rank.

As the council assembled, three young chiefs of the royal house formed the center of interest: Kiwalao, the King's son and heir presumptive to the throne; Keoua Kuahuula, his younger brother; and Kamehameha, half-nephew of the King. It was a dramatic moment when the old king, Kalaniopuu, announced the final decision regarding the succession. Kiwalao was to have the red feather girdle, the symbol of kingship, as he was the son of the reigning chief. Kamehameha was made the keeper of Kukailimoku, the war god of the kings of the island of Hawaii.

To the assembled chiefs the King's decision may have seemed prophetic. To them Kamehameha's understanding and comprehension of war was surprising. The older chiefs may have talked of this among themselves. The boy was the son of the stars. The prophecy made at his birth might prove true.

DRAMA

Chapter II

*"Let the aged men and women
and little children lie down in safety
on the king's highway."*

—KAMEHAMEHA

IF HAWAIIAN HISTORY is to be understood, it is essential to know something of the importance of the gods which the people worshipped and which played an important part in the detail of their lives. There were numberless deities in the religion of old Hawaii. Every man had his own *akua,* the god which was believed to preside over the occupation or profession which he followed. Images were made from wood or stone to represent these deities. The people believed that the spirits of the gods lived within the images. The war gods of the kings wielded a powerful influence over the men of war. These images were carried in every battle before the kings. They were designed to strike terror to the hearts of the enemy. Grotesque and terrible, with eyes made from *kukui* nuts, dark and shining, with centers of mother-of-pearl, giving the impression of movement, with open mouths filled with shark's teeth and the teeth of dead warriors, and with heads covered with red feathers, these images were awful enough to terrify any warrior who believed in their power.

Kamehameha must have known how great was his inheritance. The very meaning of the name of the war god, Kukailimoku, was "to conquer." The King had given Kamehameha the greatest honor. The door of opportunity opened before him.

After Kalaniopuu closed his council of chiefs at Waipio, he left at once for another part of the island, hoping to control a rebellion which had sprung up in that district. The leader of this little war was captured and killed. His body was carried to the *heiau* dedicated to the war god to be sacrificed.

The sacrificial ceremony was supposed to be performed by Kiwalao, as representative of his father. But while Kiwalao was making the preparations for the ceremony, Kamehameha suddenly picked up the body of the dead chief and laid it on the altar in the *heiau* and proceeded to perform the ceremonial rites himself. Historians say that Kamehameha may have reasoned that, as keeper of the war god and of the *heiaus* dedicated to it, this was his privilege, but many of the warriors did not think so. There was great consternation and excitement among the chiefs.

There had been jealousy between Kamehameha and Kiwalao for some time. Kamehameha's high-handed action intensified this. The King, fearing his nephew would be killed, advised him to go away until the excitement had died down. So Kamehameha, taking the war god with him, retired to his own lands in Kohala.

Two years went by and the old king, Kalaniopuu, died. This was in 1782. Kiwalao became the king. He was at once joined by his uncle, his father's brother, Keawemauhili, an ambitious chief of the very highest rank, who hoped for great returns for himself when, as was the custom following the death of a king, the lands of the kingdom would be divided among the chiefs or won through civil conflict.

David Malo, the Hawaiian historian, gives a vivid account of the ceremonials performed at the death of a king. A shallow grave, about a foot deep, was made ready. The body of the dead ruler was first wrapped in banana and taro leaves, then placed in the grave and a light covering of soil laid on the top. A fire was then built the full length of the grave; this was kept burning for ten days and ten nights to hasten decay. During this time a *kahuna* performed continuous ceremonies. After the body had become decomposed from the heat of the fire, it was removed and the flesh was scraped from the bones. The bones were then carefully arranged, those from the right side of the body placed together, as were those from the left side. The long bones of the arms and legs were stained a dark red, the insignia of kingship. They were tied together and wound round and round with strands of human hair. The bundles of bones were wrapped in royal black *tapa,* and the skull was carefully laid on top. The skull was completely encased in the *tapa* which so closely followed the outline of the head that it was as smooth as though it had been pasted.

A strange ending to the fire ceremony shows the thoroughness with which the Hawaiians did their work. The flesh which had been scraped from the bones was also wrapped in black *tapa,* and on a night of the god *Kane,* when spirits were supposed to walk abroad, every light was extinguished and perfect silence settled over the village. During the black-out, the sacred bundle was carried out to sea and buried in the deep.

After the time of mourning for the King had passed, Kiwalao, with his brother, Keoua Kuahuula, and, accompanied by his uncle and a large retinue of chiefs and warriors, sailed in his double canoe, carrying the bones of his dead father to be placed in *Hale o Keawe* at Honaunau, the burial place of the kings of old Hawaii.

When Kiwalao reached Honaunau, he was called upon by Kamehameha. Kamehameha met his cousin with all courtesy and together they wailed in memory of the dead. After this was over, Kiwalao spoke very frankly to his cousin. He said to Kamehameha, "Where are you? It is possible that we two may die. Here is our aged uncle pushing us on to war. Perhaps you and I alone will be slain. Alas for us two."

For two years Kamehameha had been living quietly in Kohala, improving his lands, building a watercourse which may still be seen today, making a landing for canoes, and in every way laying a foundation for the future. In the meantime, a group of important chiefs from Kona, knowing Kamehameha's ability as a warrior (one of the group having been his instructor), and also knowing his power to make and hold friends and to inspire men with great loyalty and devotion to himself, persuaded him, in case of coming war, to be their leader. This he agreed to do.

The day following the funeral rites of the old king, Kiwalao announced from the platform of *Hale o Keawe* the last will and testament of his father, King Kalaniopuu. This but verified the decision which had been made by the king's council at Waipio. It did not, however, please the chiefs from Kona. War clouds began to gather.

The system of land tenure in old Hawaii was a feudal system. The king owned all the land, at least in theory. The practice was to divide the land among the high chiefs and they, in turn, allotted lands to retainers, receiving from them the larger share of what the land produced. But at the death of a king the situation might be entirely changed. When a new ruler came into power, he and his counselors were privileged to set up a new regime.

Kiwalao, the young king, was not especially strong of character. While he had appeared friendly to Kamehameha at the time of the funeral (and historians say that he asked that Kamehameha might be remembered when it came to the division of lands), he was later persuaded by his old uncle to so divide the kingdom that he and his favorite chiefs would receive the important share, robbing Kamehameha and the Kona chiefs of much of their most valuable property. This situation, to the men from Kona, was insufferable. They exclaimed, *"Ua aho o kaua."* ("It is better to go to war.")

There followed one of the greatest battles in Hawaiian history: the Battle of Mokuohai. Thousands of men, including Kiwalao, the king, lost their lives. The "City of Refuge" at Honaunau was filled with the women and children of the contending warriors while the battle raged outside.

Kamehameha's party was victorious. This war changed the entire political set-up of the island of Hawaii. Instead of one kingdom over which Kalaniopuu had once been ruler, there were now three small kingdoms. Keoua Kuahuula escaped to become the king of the district of Kau, and his uncle became the high chief of the district of Hilo and a portion of Hamakua. But to Kamehameha came the great reward. Through battle he had won the larger section of the island.

As time passed there were many skirmishes between the opposing forces—Kamehameha, with his stronger army, continually adding to his domain. As he cruised along the coast watching for every opportunity to strengthen his position, an incident took place which gives a closer insight into Kamehameha's character.

A party of five fishermen was about to land, having returned from a night's fishing. Kamehameha saw them. It being the custom for a high chief to take what he pleased, he pushed his canoe ahead, thinking to intercept the fishermen and to take from them their fine nets. The fishermen were retainers of Keoua Kuahuula, cousin of Kamehameha, and, seeing Kamehameha's fleet of canoes and fearing an attack, they hurried ashore. Carrying their heavy nets and paddles on their shoulders, they started inland. Kamehameha jumped from his canoe and chased after them.

One man, carrying the heaviest load, was a little behind his companions, and Kamehameha soon caught up with him. He shook the fisherman and tried to wrench a net from him. The man did not strike in his own defense and managed to keep the net. While the scuffle continued, Kamehameha's foot was caught and wedged in the coral rock. This gave the fisherman the chance to get away. Kamehameha grabbed a rock and threw it with such force that it shattered a young tree behind which the fisherman had taken refuge. At this, one of the men carrying paddles laid his load down, keeping one paddle to use as a club. Not knowing who Kamehameha was, he struck him over the head with such force that the paddle was splintered into pieces.

It was the custom of old Hawaii that, if there was trouble between two men, no one was to interfere; they were to be allowed to fight their own battle. But Kamehameha's men, seeing the situation, came to his assistance. He had been felled to the ground. They carried him to a canoe and took him to the home of a friend where he lay between life and death for several days. His men wished to follow the fisherman and to punish the man who had struck Kamehameha, but he gave orders that the fisherman should not be punished in any way. He later asked that he be brought to him. The man crawled into his presence expecting to be sentenced to his death.

The historian, Dr. N. B. Emerson, gives the story of the interview between Kamehameha and the fisherman. When Kamehameha recognized the man, he ordered him to sit down. Then he said to the man who had struck him,

"Are you the man who struck me on the head?"

"Yes, I am he," was the reply.

"You gave me but one blow, did you?" asked Kamehameha.

"Yes, but one."

"Why didn't you strike me a second time?" Kamehameha demanded.

"I thought one blow would suffice to kill you," the fisherman boldly replied.

There was a pause, then the King resumed:

"You are a soldier. I had flattered myself that I was to be the one to do the hurting, but it turned out that I was the one to be hurt."

Then Kamehameha said:

"I was in the wrong in making the attack. My *kahu* (teacher or instructor) used to tell me that violence and robbery should be punished with death. If I live I will make a law against robbery and violence and lay on it the penalty of death."

Kamehameha dismissed the man telling him to go to his home in peace. He not only forgave the injury done to him, but he presented the man with lands which he retained all his life. He became his most devoted friend. Tradition tells that when (in later years) he learned of Kamehameha's death, he took his own life.

It was many years before the edict of the "Splintered Paddle" was actually put into words. But Kamehameha lived and taught the principle which the law contained throughout the remainder of his life.

Kanawai Mamalohoa

The Law of the Splintered Paddle

"Let the aged men and women and little children
lie down in safety on the king's highway."

At the close of the campaigns which gave Kamehameha his first notable victories on the island of Hawaii, political changes were taking place on the other islands. The king of Maui, Kahekili, was making rapid headway in the race for supremacy. He, too, dreamed of an empire for himself.

The king of the island of Oahu suddenly died, leaving his son to succeed him. This did not please the ruling nobles of Oahu, and they soon set the son aside and chose a king who they thought would better suit their purposes. This king also proved to be a failure. The situation was well known to Kahekili and gave him an advantage. He invaded and conquered Oahu, and moved his court to that island, setting up his residence at Waikiki.

A few years of peace settled over the Islands. Kamehameha and other warring chiefs took this opportunity to re-establish their forces, which had been greatly reduced through war and disease. A terrible epidemic of measles had attacked the people of the Islands. It is claimed that more than three hundred bodies were carried out to sea from Waikiki in one day.

It was around this period that the great fur trade of the northwest coast of America was opened to the world. The expedition of Captain Cook, the English navigator and discoverer, who lost his life in Hawaii, had pointed the way to an important development in trade in the Orient by way of North America. England, France, and Spain sent their merchant ships to America to purchase furs which could be exchanged with great profit for silks, ivory, spices, and tea in the markets of Canton. These ships, one by one, cast anchor in the waters of Hawaii. Some of the ships wintered in the Islands, their officers and men becoming closely associated with the native life of the people.

Captain Cook's expeditions not only opened the avenues of trade to the Orient, but also the minds of the Hawaiians to the knowledge of firearms. When the foreign ships began to arrive, the native chiefs, including Kamehameha, were only too glad to give their produce for guns and ammunition.

Among other foreigners who came with the trading vessels were two English sailors, John Young and Isaac Davis. These men had been left by Captain Metcalf on the island of Hawaii. Kamehameha, realizing their knowledge of ships and of navigation, persuaded them to join his army and to assist him in his campaigns. He also acquired the support and allegiance of a very important chief, Kaiana, from the island of Kauai.

This chief, Kaiana, had made a voyage to China as the guest of a captain in the Northwest-China trade. Kaiana was a handsome fellow, with features finely cut, brilliant eyes, and a commanding personality, and he dressed in English fashion. In Canton, he was warmly received by the English community and had, altogether, a fine time. It was upon his return that he accepted the offer of Kamehameha to join his staff, probably realizing that Kamehameha was on the way to greater power which he, Kaiana, might like to share.

It was in the spring of 1790 that Kamehameha again entered the area of war. Kahekili, king of Maui, had remained on Oahu enjoying his new home in Waikiki. Kamehameha was waiting for just this opportunity. In the absence of Kahekili, he invaded the island of Maui. One of the bloodiest battles of Kamehameha's time was fought and won by him. The setting was the beautiful Iao valley. So many men were killed in this battle that their bodies filled the small river which flows through the valley to the sea. The battle was given the name of *Kepaniwai* (the damning of the waters).

It is said that the assistance of John Young and Isaac Davis, who managed the guns of Kamehameha in the battle of Iao, was a great factor in his success. Another important factor was the strange and unexplained renewal of friendship between Kamehameha and the old chief, the uncle of Kiwalao and Keoua Kuahuula, from Hilo, who allied his forces to those of Kamehameha in the Maui campaign.

After this battle, Kamehameha made a visit to the island of Molokai especially to see the widow of his half-uncle, Kalaniopuu, who, some years before, had made him keeper of the war god. He found the high chieftess so sick that she lived but a short time. Before she died she gave into Kamehameha's charge Liliha, the young widow of Kiwalao, and their infant daughter, Keopuolani. This baby princess was a very important child. She held a high rank as an *alii,* higher even than that of Kamehameha. From babyhood she was carefully guarded and she was especially trained for the high position she would be expected to occupy. (Reaching young womanhood, she became the wife of Kamehameha and the mother of his two sons, Kamehameha II and Kamehameha III.)

While Kamehameha was on the island of Molokai, he laid some new plans of procedure. He sent a messenger to Kahekili, the king of Maui and Kauai, carrying two symbolic stones, one white and the other black, offering him peace or war. If the king returned the white stone, it was equivalent to making over his kingdom to Kamehameha without battle; but if the black stone came back, Kamehameha would prepare for war. The King answered that when his body should be covered with the black tapa, then Kamehameha could take possession of the kingdom without battle. Black tapa, a cloth pounded from bark and dyed with a mixture of soot and water, was used as a burial wrapping for the remains of dead royalty. Sacred to the *alii,* it was soft and pliable and somber, suited for its purpose. Since it was considered ill-omened to speak directly of one's death, the words "when my body is covered with the black tapa" were often used, as Kahekili used them here, euphemistically. This Kamehameha accepted for the time being.

Step by step Kamehameha had been gaining ground, but he was far from the realization of his hopes. While he believed in himself, he believed still more in the gods of his fathers. He sent a messenger to a famous *kahuna* (prophet) of Kauai, asking what he should do to attain the high command of the island of Hawaii. The reply was that he should build a great *heiau* for the war god, Kukailimoku, at Kawaihae, on Hawaii. So, with anticipation, Kamehameha returned home to begin this great project.

The Hawaiian temples of the higher order were usually erected on a mountainside overlooking the sea. The temple which Kamehameha built at Kawaihae was served by the priests of the highest rank. Histories describe this temple as an "irregular parallelogram two hundred and twenty-four feet long and one hundred feet wide, with walls twelve feet thick at the base and varying in height from eight feet on the upper side to twenty feet on the lower side. The entrance was a narrow passage between two high walls, and the interior was divided into terraces paved with smooth, flat stones."

Within the enclosures were thatched houses used for the care of special images, one especially dedicated to the war god of the king. There was a high altar of stone guarded by huge images. This was the altar of sacrifice where the bodies of high chiefs who had been killed in battle were sacrificed to the war god. There was also an obelisk of fine wicker work, within which the oracle was stationed when the king should come to consult him. Around the outer walls were many great images carved from wood or stone.

The modern mind cannot comprehend just what the building of the great temple meant to Kamehameha. Chiefs and commoners alike took part in the building of this *heiau.* The hillsides were a camping ground for thousands. Kamehameha, himself, it is said, carried stones for the walls.

In the meantime, Keoua Kuahuula again started on the warpath. He was furiously angry when his old uncle had joined Kamehameha in the battle of Iao. He invaded his uncle's district of Hilo and killed the old chief in battle. Keoua Kuahuula, younger brother to Kiwalao, then marched on to Kamehameha's lands and destroyed property. Word of this was soon carried to Kamehameha. He was obliged to give up temporarily the building of the temple.

Kamehameha met Keoua Kuahuula in several skirmishes and drove him out of the Hilo district. Keoua Kuahuula with his army, in three divisions, started homeward to Kau. They traveled by way of the volcano Kilauea. While encamped there a severe earthquake took place. One division of the army got safely away. The middle division followed but was overtaken by a terrific explosion from the volcano, one of the few explosive eruptions in Kilauea's history. An enormous quantity of black sand and cinders were thrown to a great height and came down in a destructive shower for many miles around. The third division of Keoua Kuahuula's army escaped, but when they went forward and reached those who had gone before them, they found the people of the middle division all dead. Some of them were still standing, others were clasped in each other's arms, while still others, who had been running, were left in the very positions they held, completely encased in ashes and cinders from the volcano. Their footprints can be seen today.

Foreign ships had been supplying the Hawaiian chiefs with more and more ammunition, and several foreign men had joined the chiefs in their battles. Kamehameha, in order to meet an attack from Kauai and Maui, prepared a large fleet, including several double canoes armed with guns, and, with John Young and Isaac Davis in charge of the artillery, he fought and won the first great naval battle in the history of Hawaii. The Hawaiians call this naval war the "battle of the red-mouthed gun." Following this battle, Kamehameha returned to the completion of the *heiau* at Kawaihae.

Although Kamehameha had not been able to control Keoua Kuahuula's invasions, he believed that he held the final victory on Hawaii in his own hands. His next move was one of diplomacy. There are different versions of what took place, but, according to accepted tradition, Kamehameha sent two of his high chiefs to see Keoua Kuahuula and to invite him to come to Kawaihae and meet him "face to face."

The chiefs approached Keoua Kuahuula with every formality and courtesy due his high rank as the king of Kau. They gave him Kamehameha's message and urged him to return with them to Kamehameha, saying, "You two will be the rulers." Keoua Kuahuula was pleased, and evidently believing the invitation was one of friendliness on the part of Kamehameha, he decided to accept it. He assembled his retinue and, with all the splendor of his court, he accompanied the two chiefs back to Kawaihae.

History cannot tell what was in the mind of Keoua Kuahuula, but the fact that he rearranged the seating in his canoes before reaching Kawaihae denotes that he was not confident of the outcome of his visit to Kamehameha. He took into his own double canoe with himself the chiefs who would be suitable companions to die with him.

As Keoua Kuahuula's canoe neared the place of landing, he said to his companions, "It looks stormy ashore; the flight of the clouds is

ominous of evil." Standing on the platform of the canoe, he observed
the scene. On the shore stood Kamehameha, resplendent in cloak and
helmet. With him was the high chief, Keeaumoku, his prime minister.
Surrounding them were armed warriors. On the mountain side was the
new *heiau*, finished and complete, ready to be dedicated to Kamehameha's god. It would not have been strange if Keoua Kuahuula's courage failed. But he called to Kamehameha in pleasant greeting, "Here
I am." Kamehameha replied, "Rise and come up here that we may
know each other."

As the canoe touched the beach, Keoua Kuahuula sprang ashore. Men
closed about him and about his canoe. Then, suddenly, the old chief,
Keeaumoku, threw his spear and killed Keoua Kuahuula. The body of
the dead king was carried to the *heiau* and there sacrificed in the dedica-
tory ceremonies of this new temple to Kukailimoku, the war god.

The death of Keoua Kuahuula cleared the stage for Kamehameha
and gave him the sovereignty of the island of Hawaii. The big island,
torn by war, settled down to more peaceful living. Kamehameha studied
his people and his dominions with a long look forward. Foreign ships
were arriving in greater numbers. Kamehameha gave them all a cordial
welcome and supplied their needs. He became personally acquainted
with the captains of these vessels, and he was not slow in learning the
intricacies of trade. One captain, in his records, speaks of him as "an
acute trader and a match for any European in driving a bargain." But
while Kamehameha was shrewd, he was also honest. On one occasion,
when an English ship had run aground and had cast overboard 90 ingots
of copper to lighten the vessel, Kamehameha ordered his men to dive
to the bottom of the ocean and salvage the copper, which they did.
Instead of keeping the metal as his reward, he inquired of an Englishman as to what would be done in England in a similar case. He was
told that one-eighth was considered a fair salvage. He counted out
twelve ingots and returned the rest to the owner.

It was at this period (1792-94) that Captain George Vancouver
arrived in Hawaii. During several of his voyages of exploration for the
British government, he wintered in the Sandwich Islands. Fourteen
years earlier he had visited Hawaii as a young officer with the expeditions of Captain Cook, who had so named the Islands in honor of his
patron, the fourth Earl of Sandwich. It was at that time that he first
saw Kamehameha. He tells in his *Voyages* how surprised he was to find
Kamehameha so changed from the most savage-looking person he had
seen among the Hawaiians to a man of "cheerful and sensible mind
combined with generosity and goodness of disposition."

Kamehameha first made an informal call upon Vancouver, taking his young queen, Kaahumanu, and her retinue, and John Young with him. The Captain was much impressed by the beauty of the Queen, whom he judged to be about sixteen years old, and by the conduct and appearance of all the members of the royal party. Before they left the ship he gave presents to them all. To Kamehameha he presented a handsome scarlet cloak trimmed with gold lace, which pleased the King very much. Kamehameha put the cloak on at once and walked about to the delight of his people, who stood by to admire him. The mirrors on the ship, placed opposite each other, delighted him, reflecting, as they did, his entire royal person and attire.

The following day Vancouver received a grand state visit from the King. Vancouver writes: "The squadron was made up of eleven large canoes, arranged so as to form an obtuse angle. The largest, in which Kamehameha was, had eighteen paddles on each side. It headed the procession, guided by orders of the king, who regulated the maneuvers with great skill. The fleet paddled around the vessel in a slow and solemn manner. Then the ten canoes were ordered to form into line under the stern, while his own canoe was paddled to the starboard side. When abreast of the gangway, notwithstanding the great speed with which it was shooting ahead, it was instantly stopped by a skillful back dip of the paddles."

Kamehameha climbed the side of the ship and, taking Captain Vancouver's hand, inquired if he were sincerely his friend, and if the king of Great Britain were also friendly to the Islands. When assured of the friendly feeling of both Vancouver and King George of England, Kamehameha saluted the Captain by touching noses in the true Hawaiian manner.

Kamehameha wore his famous feather golden cloak. Vancouver described it as the most elegant cloak he had ever seen, composed of bright yellow feathers and reaching from his shoulders to the ground. Kamehameha also wore a handsome helmet, and made altogether a very "magnificent appearance."

The King brought valuable gifts to Captain Vancouver. He first presented him with four helmets of "beautiful fabrication." He then ordered the canoes alongside. Each of these contained nine of the largest-sized swine. There followed a fleet of smaller canoes, loaded with fine vegetables and fruit. All of this produce was placed on the decks of the vessel. Kamehameha also gave the captain a large number of mats, pieces of tapa cloth, and other articles of Hawaiian manufacture. Vancouver could not take care of all of these things, and

Kamehameha had them stored on shore until the captain should call for them.

The friendship which developed between Captain Vancouver and Kamehameha was, without question, one of the greatest influences towards civilization in the King's experience. Kamehameha listened with keenest attention to everything said to him. He was alert to any idea that would increase his own knowledge, especially regarding methods of war. He begged Vancouver for guns and ammunition, but they were refused. The captain told him that they were tabooed by King George. This settled the matter for Kamehameha. He had the greatest reverence and admiration for the British King. But when Captain Vancouver attempted to interfere in Kamehameha's private life, he met opposition. At one time Captain Vancouver was much concerned when he learned there was a misunderstanding between Kamehameha and his queen over Kaahumanu's supposed flirtation with the handsome chief, Kaiana. The captain decided to speak to Kamehameha about it, thinking he might bring about a reconciliation. Kamehameha expressed his thanks and said that he would always be happy to receive Vancouver's advice on state affairs, or on any public matter, especially about peace or war; but his domestic happiness, he said, he considered to be totally out of Vancouver's province.

However, a little later, when Kamehameha had had time to think things over, he did plot an intrigue with Captain Vancouver. Kaahumanu had gone home to her father, and Kamehameha wanted her back again. So a plan was made by the Captain and the King that Kaahumanu and her retinue should be invited on board the ship for a pleasant call. While they were there, Kamehameha was unexpectedly to arrive and the meeting between him and the Queen would appear to be accidental. In this way Vancouver brought the two together in such a manner as to cast no reflection upon the King's independence or prestige. Kamehameha arrived aboard ship at the appointed time and, seemingly preoccupied with paying his respects, he turned to leave. As if by accident, his glance fell upon Kaahumanu but momentarily as he reached the door. There was an eon of frozen silence as the King and his queen regarded each other. Then Vancouver, silently taking Kaahumanu's hand and placing it in Kamehameha's, broke the spell. Suddenly weeping and laughing, King and Queen embraced each other in a burst of endearments. Only one shadow hung darkly over the reconciliation — when Kaahumanu begged Vancouver to ask Kamehameha to promise not to beat her.

It is to be assumed that, on this delicate point, Vancouver heeded an earlier royal decree and declared the matter out of his province.

Meantime, Vancouver was greatly alarmed over the depletion of the population of the Islands through continued warfare. He constantly talked peace to Kamehameha and to the chiefs of all of the islands, not only for the sake of the Hawaiian people themselves, but in the interest of trade between Hawaii and foreign countries. To this end, before he left for England, he urged Kamehameha to declare himself and the people of the island of Hawaii as subjects of the British crown. This Kamehameha refused to do unless Vancouver would agree to leave one of his ships at the island to help him in defending himself and his people from attacks by their enemies.

Vancouver did not leave a vessel for the King, but before he went away he did have his men outfit one of Kamehameha's largest canoes with canvas sails, and he gave him a Union Jack and a pennant. He arranged for the building of a vessel named the *Britannia,* the keel of which was laid before he sailed. He also promised Kamehameha that a man-of-war, equipped with brass cannons and filled with European supplies, would be sent to him by the British government.

It is claimed that Vancouver did, finally, persuade Kamehameha to make a "cession" of the island of Hawaii to Great Britain, but historians say there is no record that England at that time took any official action concerning the matter, and that if such a plan had been made it probably amounted only to a protectorate. The Hawaiian people declared that Kamehameha never intended to give the island away.

In all of Vancouver's writings of his experiences in Hawaii, he tells of the fine cooperation which was given him by Kamehameha, while at the same time keeping his own independence and control. Dr. Ralph S. Kuykendall, eminent Hawaiian historian, says of Kamehameha that, in his dealings with white men, he was "never their servant but always their master."

Captain Vancouver was anxious to build an observatory near a *heiau.* Kamehameha allowed the observatory to be built, but with the distinct understanding that Vancouver's men were in no way to disturb the observance of the taboo or to enter the sacred precincts of the temple. He also insisted that no man should be allowed to wander about the country. He said he had enemies and they might make trouble; that if anyone wished to travel in the district he must first ask his, Kamehameha's, permission and that he, the king, would then provide proper guidance and protection.

The writings of an early explorer to the Islands tell of visiting, in company with John Elliott, who had at times acted as surgeon to Kamehameha, the spot where Captain Cook lost his life. While there he picked up a stone to carry away as a souvenir. John Elliott then told the King that he had visited this place with Kamehameha and that he, too, had picked up a stone for the same purpose. Kamehameha asked him why he was keeping the stone, and when he told him he planned to send it to England in memory of Captain Cook, the King snatched the stone from his hand, saying, "Your sending that would only revive the recollection of the unhappy event. People, after reconciliation, should not open old sores."

Vancouver lost no opportunity to give Kamehameha an understanding of what civilization would do for the Islands. He advised him regarding the people who were arriving. He told him not to permit any man whom he could not trust to remain. He once said that only John Young and Isaac Davis should be allowed to stay. He told Kamehameha that most of the foreigners who had already settled in the Islands were men of "very bad character, evil-hearted, desiring to secure lands but not the right persons to live thereon."

Captain Vancouver died in England not long after his return to that country. The plans which he may have made for further assistance to Kamehameha and his people were not carried out. When he left the Islands, Kamehameha, Kaahumanu, John Young and Isaac Davis followed his ship out to sea, no doubt feeling that their best friend had gone.

The dial of the next few years tells of Kamehameha's advancing power. The "black tapa" covered the body of the old King Kahekili, who died in 1794 at his home in Waikiki. At the time of his death, he was in control of the islands of Maui, Oahu, Molokai, and Lanai, and through his brother, Kaeo, of Kauai and the small island of Niihau. His son, Kalanikupule, was the reigning chief of the island of Oahu.

Kamehameha was looking forward to including all of these islands in the great empire of which he dreamed. But he had a long road of conquest to travel before reaching his goal.

Following the death of Kahekili, Kaeo decided to make a visit to his old home on Kauai. He sailed from Maui by way of Oahu, taking his army with him. When he reached Oahu he stopped at Waimanalo. Disputes, partly over inheritance, arose between him and Kalanikupule, which resulted in war. The Oahu king was in a desperate situation. At this juncture, three foreign ships arrived. Two of these vessels, the *Jackal* and the *Prince Lee Boo*, were English ships under the command of Captain William Brown. The third vessel, the *Lady Washington,* was an American ship with Captain John Hendrick in command. These vessels were not strangers in the Islands; they were trading vessels and had made rather frequent visits to Hawaii. (It was Captain Brown who was given credit for discovering the harbor of Honolulu. The tender to one of his ships was the first vessel to enter Honolulu harbor.)

Kalanikupule appealed to Captain Brown for assistance. The Captain decided to help him. The two mates of the *Jackal* and the *Prince Lee Boo* also volunteered to fight for the king of Oahu. This was a successful move, and Kaeo was killed. Captain Brown fired a salute to celebrate the victory. Unfortunately, the guns were loaded with shot which pierced the side of the American ship, the *Lady Washington,* killing Captain Hendrick and several of his crew. The *Lady Washington* immediately set sail for China.

Kalanikupule decided that if he could get control of the two English ships he might be able to attack and conquer Kamehameha on the island of Hawaii. A cunning plot was made and, as a result, both the *Jackal* and the *Prince Lee Boo* were captured by the Hawaiians. Brown and Gordon lost their lives and the surviving members of the crews were taken prisoners.

Kalanikupule planned an immediate attack on the island of Hawaii. The crews of the *Jackal* and the *Prince Lee Boo* were ordered to get the ships ready for sea. This was done. The King and Queen and their retinue then went on board and took possession of their new vessels.

The two mates of the English ships decided that they, with their crews, would try to retake the vessels. This was a daring venture, but they succeeded. The natives were either killed or driven from the ships, with the exception of Kalanikupule and his queen and their personal attendants. Near dawn, the ships were put out to sea. While still off shore, the King and Queen were placed in a canoe which would carry them home. The ships sailed on to the island of Hawaii, where the two mates secured supplies. They left a letter for John Young and Isaac Davis, telling them of the situation on Oahu, and sailed at once for Canton.

FULFILLMENT

Chapter III

> "I have made my Islands an asylum for all nations."
> —KAMEHAMEHA

THIS WAS KAMEHAMEHA'S great opportunity. His war canoes, built of beautiful koa wood, were seventy feet long and more than three feet deep, and each canoe carried seventy men. His fleet was sufficient to carry all of his warriors. It was with such equipment that he sailed to accomplish the greatest feat of his career. The campaign was carefully planned. He went first to Maui and then to Molokai, successfully taking those islands.

When Kamehameha reached Oahu, he learned that one of his *alii*, the handsome and proud Kaiana, king of Kauai, who perhaps had aspirations of his own for Kamehameha's Hawaiian Kingdom, had deserted him, taking his men with him and joining the forces of Kalanikupule. This was the first time one of his chiefs had so acted and it was a staggering blow to Kamehameha. Nevertheless, he pushed on and met the enemy in what proved to be the greatest victory of his career—the Battle of Nuuanu. The year was 1795.

The Oahu king and Kaiana, with their warriors, took their stand on the steep slopes of the mountains bordering Nuuanu Valley. They had built up fortifications of earth and stone behind which they faced the enemy. Kamehameha and his army, after a brief encampment at Waialae Bay, moved forward and took stations below them. John Young manned the cannon and, it is claimed, his first salvos reduced the defenders' fortresses to rubble and, moreover, killed the faithless Kaiana. The Oahu warriors, most of them never having heard the roar of a gun, were terrified. They broke their ranks and fled in confusion up the valley.

Now, the valley of Nuuanu is a narrow, verdant corridor that rises gently from the level of the sea to a tiny gorge that is edged by a sheer *pali* (cliff) towering 1,186 feet above the ground below it. Toward the gorge in a disorganized, hapless scramble fled the armies of Kalanikupule and Kaiana, this route being their only path of escape from Kamehameha's advancing forces. Kamehameha, holding his war god before him and shouting to his men, "Forward, my children, till you drink of the bitter waters!", moved closer and closer to the *pali*. A few of the Oahu men were able to escape over the steep ridges of the gorge, but the rest—and the main body of the vanquished army—were hurled screaming and twisting over the cliff to be dashed to death on the rocks below.

The battle over, peace and tranquility returned to Nuuanu Valley. It is said that, at the close of the bloody day, Kamehameha stood at the edge of the *pali,* gazing at the quiet land and waters stretching before and below him, saying, "How beautiful! On yonder hills I see a double rainbow. It is the sign of a lasting peace."

It was the custom, following a great battle, to hold a *hookupu* in honor of the victorious chief. A *hookupu* is a time set aside for the presentation of gifts to a high chief, and such a celebration in honor of a king was called a Royal *Hookupu.* The following tale is told:

The great day of the "Royal *Hookupu*" was set. From the mountains and from the sea the people came, bringing their gifts to Kamehameha. His friends, and those of his enemies who had survived the Battle of Nuuanu, laid their offerings at his feet. The *pali* peaks were dark above their heads, and deep shadows filled the greenness of the valley. The rainbows, of which Kamehameha had spoken, arched the sky, dipping into wells of golden light on the sunlit, azure sea—a promise of better things.

Even wars do not prevent romance, and so it proved in Kamehameha's time. Preceding the Battle of Nuuanu, while Kamehameha, at his Waialae Bay encampment, was making plans for his first attack upon the Oahu king, one of his young officers, a well known warrior, fell in love at first sight with a pretty girl at Waikiki. It was a complicated matter, for she was the daughter of an Oahu chief. Night after night, lingering near Leilehua's home, officer Hakuole played his *ukeke* (a reed flute) in serenade, but Leilehua made no response. Some of her friends, however, told him that Leilehua was really much interested but that she was afraid to let him know. He was Kamehameha's man.

Then came the battle, and Hakuole had to go to war. When the battle was over and the *hookupu* was held, Hakuole accompanied Kamehameha as one of his personal guards. Among the many people crowding forward, came an old man leading a very young girl by the hand, she pulling backward, away from him. When they reached the King, the man pushed the girl ahead of him and presented her, his daughter, Leilehua, as his offering to Kamehameha.

Leilehua stood alone, terrified and ashamed, then fell upon her knees and covered her face with her hands. She had never looked more beau-

tiful. She was dressed in yellow tapa, which was designed in a striking
zig-zag pattern in shining black. About her head she wore a *lei* of yellow
feathers and upon her wrists were bracelets of lovely shells. About her
neck was the ivory *Niho Palaoa,* suspended by the mystic three-hundred
strands of human hair. This alone would have indicated her high rank.
This child was an *Ehu,* a Hawaiian blonde. Her eyes were soft brown,
and her hair was tinged with gold and hung to her knees, completely
covering her shoulders. Her father hoped to gain favor with the new
ruler through the gift of his daughter. He waited.

Hakuole was amazed. Not considering what such a move might mean
to him, he stepped out before the people and, leaning over little Leilehua, he lifted her up, and taking her hand he led her away. There was
a murmur through the crowd. The girl belonged to Kamehameha. What
would he do?

At first the King was irritated that Hakuole, his personal attendant,
should show such disrespect to him, but in a few moments, somehow
comprehending the situation between the two young people, he called
Hakuole back. As the young warrior groveled before him, Kamehameha
said, "It seems that you are tired of being a soldier." Hakuole bowed
still lower, shaking his head in denial of such an insult. "And you prefer
the society of women to that of your comrades in arms?" The King then
spoke to another warrior and said, "Bring the tribute girl here."

Leilehua was led before Kamehameha. Hakuole lifted his head with
courage. Kamehameha turned to him, saying, "Listen to me! This is
your punishment; you are suspended from your official rank for thirteen
moons. Take this girl and retire to her father's estates, which I give to
her children forever."

Kamehameha was now the "conqueror." But he was not yet to be
called "Kamehameha the Great." Years of a changing world and of
adjustment within his own mind must be lived before that title could
be placed above his head.

He must have done some hard thinking during the early days of
reconstruction following the Battle of Nuuanu. His victories and his
authority were unquestioned, but in their wake walked many chiefs
who were still his bitter enemies. This he well understood. At times he
may have felt very much alone, but his name—Kamehameha (lonely
one)—may have been to him a prophecy. He was now the great *Alii,*
the highest chief.

In taking over the control of the island of Oahu, Kamehameha made
no immediate changes in the old plan of government. The taboo held
its mystic power for the king and for the people, and feudalism was

the rock upon which Kamehameha continued to build his growing empire.

From the time that Kamehameha had been chosen by the great Kona chiefs to be their leader, they, with other high ranking men, had formed the council of the king. Upon their judgment and loyalty he felt he could at all times depend, and he seldom made an important decision without their approval. Nevertheless, the final word was his. The law of the ages remained intact. The king was all-powerful. It meant death to any man even to cross the shadow of the king or of his house. Life and death were centered in the king.

As was the custom after a victorious battle, the lands of the kingdom were divided among the chiefs according to their rank and service. But that he might keep a close watch upon the chiefs who were overly ambitious for prestige, Kamehameha gave them lands in detached places, located on different islands, and they were not allowed to live upon their lands but were obliged to follow the court wherever the king might please to travel.

The court of the king was a movable institution. Often as many as a thousand people followed the court. Kamehameha's chief pleasure was fishing, which many times accounted for his moving from one place to another. He sometimes set up his headquarters where living conditions were very uncomfortable for everyone, himself included, that he might be near the good fishing grounds.

As the king could be present on but one island at a time, Kamehameha did plan one new venture. He appointed a governor for each island excepting Kauai. This official represented the king in all matters of concern. The lands were divided into districts, the districts into plantations, small farms and villages, with certain forest and fishing rights attached. The people must build canoes and fish for their living.

To the higher ranking chiefs Kamehameha gave the larger districts, they in turn alloting lands to lesser chiefs. This division continued on down the line until it reached the common laborer who tilled the soil and did the menial work of life for those above him in station. The chiefs received the greater share of the product of the land, but everyone, high and low, was expected to pay an annual tax to the king.

Kamehameha's court was expensive. His navy was demanding more and more revenue, and the increasing expenses must be met through taxation. Tax collectors were appointed by the governor. Taxes consisted of what was raised on the land, fish, fishing lines, dogs, feathers, or whatever the people possessed. District by district, these supplies were delivered to the chiefs and through them were turned over to the governor as tribute for the king.

But with all of Kamehameha's planning, the matter of Kauai was uppermost in his mind. That remained to be settled. All of the islands must be united under his rule. His ambition knew no respite and, the year after the Battle of Nuuanu, Kamehameha attempted an invasion on Kauai.

Now, Kauai is separated from the island of Oahu by a wide, treacherous, and sometimes almost impassable channel. A great storm broke over the sea. Many of Kamehameha's canoes were wrecked and lost, and his army was so disabled that he was obliged to turn back to Oahu; his attempted invasion was a complete failure.

A dozen years went by. In the meantime, trouble had been brewing on the island of Hawaii. Some of the chiefs had started a rebellion and Kamehameha returned to Hawaii to check the disturbance. He remained on Hawaii for several years, enlarging his navy. It is reported that he had as many as eight hundred canoes and a squadron of small schooners which his foreign carpenters had made for him. With a quantity of ammunition, guns, and cannon, Kamehameha felt that his plans for attacking Kauai were complete. He left Hawaii, stopped at Maui for a short time, and then moved his army to Oahu to make the last preparations for war.

On Kauai there had been political changes. The present ruler was King Kaumualii, an *alii* of great personal charm. He was very popular with his subjects and with foreigners, but he feared Kamehameha's greater power. Some of the foreign carpenters in his service built a ship for him in which, if worst came to worst, he and his family might escape to the Orient or to the islands of the southern seas.

After his attempted invasion, Kamehameha did offer to the Kauai king a peaceful settlement if he would acknowledge him as his sovereign and pay to him an annual tribute, but the offer was ignored. Kaumualii was determined to defend his kingdom as long as possible. It was at this time that an awful scourge, possibly cholera, attacked the island of Oahu. Several of Kamehameha's older chiefs and closest friends lost their lives. Kamehameha, himself, was stricken but recovered. This upset the King's plans, and the invasion of Kauai was again postponed.

Many foreign ships were putting in at Honolulu harbor, and an entirely unexpected development in a business way was demanding Kamehameha's closest attention. The Sandwich Islands had suddenly become of intense interest to foreign traders. Sandalwood was the watchword of the hour. The value of sandalwood and of pearls was not known by the Hawaiians until the white man came.

Captain Kendrick, the American commander of the *Lady Washington* is given the credit for discovering sandalwood in Hawaii. While sitting before an open fire, he had detected the sweet odor of the burning wood. Investigation revealed that the Islands were filled with the precious trees, and so began the nefarious trade which wrecked many lives. India, where sandalwood was first known, had for centuries been the only base of supply. The Orient was calling. Both India and China were willing to pay exorbitant prices for sandalwood, and men grew rich from the fragrant forests of Hawaii.

The story of sandalwood in the Hawaiian Islands is a stark and unhappy tale. It was through sandalwood that slavery touched the freedom of the people. The native workers were treated like cattle. Up the mountain trails and down again they toiled, logs of sandalwood strapped to their shoulders by ropes and thongs of hibiscus and coconut. Men started to become deformed through the weight of the wood on their backs. Agriculture was at a standstill, food became scarce, and famine stalked the land. Disease and death marked the trail of sandalwood from mountain to waterfront.

Kamehameha was swept along with the tide. His great desire was to own European and Oriental goods of all sorts. These he acquired in such quantities that he was forced to build storage houses to care for his treasures, for many of which he had no use. The monopoly on sandalwood was his own. He tabooed the oyster beds of Pearl River that he alone might profit from the sale of the pearls. His love for beautiful and shining things tempted him to purchase a looking-glass for which he paid $800.00, and for a brass cannon he spent $1,000.00.

Kamehameha was not blind to the ill-effects the sandalwood trade was having upon his kingdom and his people. When its ravages became clear to his conscience, he stopped the sandalwood destruction and ordered his chiefs, instead, to cultivate their lands again. To set an example for the people, he personally labored at tilling his own lands and planting his crops. It was not until after Kamehameha's death and the sandalwood monopoly was divided among his chiefs, each greedy for a share in the new mine of wealth, that its scourge was felt again in the Islands.

Meantime, Kamehameha's successes in trade had proved so profitable that he determined to go into the shipping trade for himself. From Mr. James Hunnewell, of Charlestown, Massachusetts, he bought the *Bordeau Packet* and sent the ship to the Orient with a cargo of sandalwood. This was the first Hawaiian ship to enter any foreign port, and the venture was a great disappointment. In Canton, the port charges were so heavy and the crew, including the captain, became so dissipated that, when the vessel returned, Kamehameha found he was in debt over $3,000.00. The matter of port charges, however, which included pilotage, storage, and customhouse fees, suggested to Kamehameha that he might raise funds from the same sources, and he shortly established such fees for the Islands.

Kamehameha's astuteness in trade won for him great distinction among the foreign merchants. There are many records of what the white man thought of Kamehameha, but little is known of what he thought about the foreigner. He kept his own counsel, and in all matters and at all times he was master of the situation. Men who knew him best both admired and trusted him. Even in the early days when Kamehameha had had little contact with the outside world, those who saw him were impressed with his mind and judgment. Archibald Menzies, who was with Vancouver in Hawaii, says of Kamehameha: "In our broken conversation with him he possessed a quickness of comprehension which surprised us, and in his behavior he was open, affable and free, which attached us to him." In speaking of Kamehameha's independent thinking, one man records that, while he listened to advice and placed much dependence upon certain high chiefs and upon John Young, the "foreigner," he never allowed any man a position which would in any way jeopardize his own government. Another writer describes Kamehameha's system of government as a wheel. Of the King's cabinet he says: "These men were, in fact, each a check upon the other, but the hub, in which the spokes of the wheel were held in place, was the highest interest of the kingdom which they, the chiefs, had helped to establish." It was upon these men that Kamehameha greatly depended, but his word was the law.

Pages of old log books and journals continue the story of the impression made by Kamehameha upon the men who knew him, and it is these comments which make possible the picture of his personality and character which we have today: "His style and appearance was truly grand and becoming so great a prince. On his head he wore a very rich helmet of red feathers, and he had on a magnificent cloak that reached from his shoulders to his heels, of yellow feather." . . . "He had on an English dress of blue broadcloth for his coat and pantaloons trimmed with red. His waistcoat was red trimmed with fur." . . . "I saw the old man, Kamehameha, one day, in full dress of an English General, which had been sent to him by his late Majesty, George III. But he felt so awkward in the cocked hat, boots, etc., that he quickly got rid of them and in a few hours afterwards we saw him lounging about the village sans coat, sans shirt, sans everything. There was a degree of negligent simplicity which strongly characterized the royal philosopher."

At a later period, men write of Kamehameha's consideration for and his just dealing with men of all classes under his protection: "Kamehameha metes out even-handed justice to all alike. After a quarrel between a native and a Portuguese, the King asked to have the quarrel explained to him. He called witnesses on both sides. He then ordered the native to work four days in the garden of the Portuguese, and he gave the Portuguese a hog." On another occasion, a sailor pointed a loaded pistol at a native and threatened to fire. The King ordered the sailor to be brought before him and heard the case. He took the pistol from the sailor and handed it to an attendant to be placed in the royal armory. He then told the sailor that his only punishment would be the loss of the pistol, but that if he did such a thing again he, the King, would have him put to death.

Many men tell not only of Kamehameha's fairness in judgment of others, but also of the fact that he governed himself as well. One man says of him: "Kamehameha considers himself the last person in his dominions who ought to violate the laws and regulations of the country which he governs."

In Kamehameha's day, ancient customs were accepted laws. The strange and repellent observances at the time of the death of a high chief were carried out to the letter. These funeral rites were described by Archibald Campbell in his *Voyage Round the World, from 1806 to 1812*. Mr. Campbell writes:

"The public mourning that took place was of so extraordinary a nature that had I not been an eye witness I could not have given credit to it. The natives cut off their hair and went about completely naked. Many of them, particularly the women, disfigured themselves by knocking out their teeth and branding their faces with red hot stones and the small end of calabashes which they held burning to their faces till a circular mark was produced; whilst at the same time a general, I believe I may say universal public prostitution of women took place, the queens and widows of the deceased alone exempt. When the captain of a brig which lay in the harbor remonstrated with the King upon this disgraceful scene, he answered that such was the law and he could not prevent it."

Archibald Campbell was a weaver, and the captain of the ship which brought him to the Islands told Kamehameha that Campbell could not only make sails for him but also could make the cloth from which the sails were made. This interested the King very much; he needed sails. Under Campbell's direction he had a loom made for him and the King used often to sit on Campbell's doorstep to watch him work and to talk with him. He would show the sail cloth to the captains and men who arrived, telling them, with great pride, that his Islands had produced it.

Campbell writes, in speaking of the King: "Although a conqueror, he is extremely popular with his subjects. I never knew of his taking any undue advantage; on the contrary, he is distinguished for upright and honorable conduct in all his transactions."

When Campbell decided to return to England, Kamehameha was loath to see him go. Campbell says: "He desired me to give his compliments to King George. I told him that though born in his dominions, I had never seen King George, and that even in the city where he lived there were thousands who had never seen him. He expressed much surprise at this and asked if he did not go about among his people to learn their wants, as he did. I answered that he did not do it himself but that he had men do it for him. Kamehameha shook his head at this and said that other people could never do it as well as he could himself. Kamehameha sent a letter and a cape to the King by Captain Spence, saying he was sorry he was so far away and could not help him in his wars." After the coming of Vancouver, Kamehameha had placed the utmost confidence in England's King and in England's friendship for, and protection of, the Sandwich Islands.

As ship after ship from foreign countries came and sailed again out beyond the Island's reefs, Kamehameha became not only intelligent regarding the outside world of men and affairs, but also alert as to what their coming meant to him. The Islands were still a busy market for sandalwood and for many other commodities. The foreign traders were much alarmed for fear there would be war between Kamehameha and the Kauai King. While they admired Kaumualii and appreciated his friendliness, they realized that, should the Islands be torn with rebellion as they had been in the past, their own business interests would materially suffer. As Vancouver had repeatedly done, they talked with both kings, urging them for their own sakes to be friends.

It was not until 1810 that the Kauai matter was settled. Kamehameha said again that he would be satisfied if Kaumualii would acknowledge him as the ruler of all the islands and pay to him an annual tribute. After much pressure from foreign friends, and fully realizing that he could not successfully meet Kamehameha in battle, he finally agreed to Kamehameha's proposition. But Kamehameha also insisted that Kaumualii come in person to Oahu and offer submission to him. Recalling the fate of Keoua Kuahuula, the Kauai king was not inclined to make the trip. An American trader, Captain Winship, after talking with Kaumualii, offered to leave his mate on Kauai as an assurance of good faith if the King would go with him to Oahu as Kamehameha had requested. So the two kings, Kamehameha and Kaumualii, met "face to face." It was agreed that Kauai should become a tributary kingdom, but that Kaumualii should continue to rule that island while acknowledging Kamehameha as his sovereign.

The chiefs were not all pleased with this arrangement. A secret plan was made to kill Kaumualii while he was on Oahu. Isaac Davis, learning of the plot, warned Kaumualii. Not waiting to attend the feast which was planned in his honor, the King slipped away and sailed for Kauai. It is said that the poison which was designed for Kaumualii was given to Isaac Davis. Whether this is true or not, the faithful Isaac Davis suddenly died. He was buried in Honolulu. On his tombstone was placed the inscription,

"The remains of
Isaac Davis
who died on this island
April, 1810
Aged 52 years"

Isaac Davis had been one of Kamehameha's closest friends and advisers. His death was a great shock to Kamehameha and cast a dark shadow over the satisfaction which the King must have felt with the settlement of the Kauai matter and the fact that he could continue his plans for the further development of the entire group of islands under his own direction. Kamehameha's great ambition was to promote an increasing trade between Hawaii and outside powers, and to do so on the basis of friendliness and exchange.

Looking back to 1804, two ships could have been seen cruising along the island coasts. These ships were unfamiliar in Hawaiian waters. Russia had sent them on a round-the-world voyage, and the vessels hoped to secure supplies in the Sandwich Islands. They were named the *Hope* and the *Neva*. The *Hope* was crowded for time and obliged to hurry on to Japan, but the *Neva* stopped over in Hawaii. She remained five days at Kealakekua Bay. The captain met John Young and, through him, obtained the supplies he needed. Hoping to see Kamehameha, Captain Lisiansky decided to go to Oahu, but learning that a terrible disease was raging on that island, he changed his course and sailed to Kauai and soon left the Islands without having met Kamehameha. Captain Lisiansky said in his report: "I am of the opinion that these Islands will not long remain in their present barbarous state. They have made great advancement towards civilization since the period of their discovery and especially during the reign of the present king."

The Russian American Company, dealers in furs, had long been established in Alaska. It had not been a very satisfactory experiment.

The people were suffering for want of food almost to the point of starvation. Alexander Baranov, the governor of the company, had learned of the possibility of resources in the Hawaiian Islands and, through the traders coming and going, both North and South, Kamehameha had heard of the needs of the Russians in the great Northwest. He sent word to Baranov that he would be glad to send one ship every year with swine, salt, sweet potatoes, and other articles of food if, in exchange, the governor would let him have sea otter at a reasonable price. But Baranov had other plans. In 1810 the *Neva* returned to the Islands for a cargo of salt. It was on this vessel that the aforementioned Archibald Campbell arrived in Hawaii.

Four years went by, at the end of which time Governor Baranov sent still another ship to the Islands for supplies. The Captain was cheerfully supplied with what he wanted at Honolulu and he sailed for home, but on the Kauai coast his vessel was driven ashore and wrecked by a storm. The Captain gave the wrecked ship to the king of Kauai in appreciation for his having assisted in saving the cargo; this, too, he left in the care of the King and took the first opportunity to return to New Archangel.

Whether Baranov was laying definite plans for a Russian settlement in Hawaii, and, perhaps, hoping to secure the control of one of the islands, is not known, but developments point to this direction. In 1815, a German doctor, George Anton Scheffer, arrived on the American ship *Isabella,* having been sent to the Islands by Baranov. He introduced himself as a botanist wishing to study the interesting plant life in Hawaii. Kamehameha was at once interested in the doctor's scientific work. He built for him a fine grass house set in a grove of breadfruit trees, where the doctor could work in quietude as he pursued his studies. This intercourse between Kamehameha and the doctor was, at all times, friendly and understanding, or so it seemed to the King. He was especially grateful to Scheffer for having cured him of a miserable cold, and for having successfully treated Queen Kaahumanu of an illness. So, Kamehameha was greatly surprised when three more Russian ships stopped at Hawaii and the doctor decided to leave. He sailed on one of the vessels for the island of Kauai and there took up his residence.

Disloyal to the friendship which Kamehameha had given him, Scheffer gradually prejudiced the Kauai king against Kamehameha, telling him that the Russians were his best friends and would help him to get back his independence. He also suggested to King Kaumualii that, with the assistance of the Russians, the King might also get control of the island of Oahu. He persuaded Kaumualii to sign a written statement placing himself and his people under the protection of the Russian Emperor. Scheffer was responsible for the Russian's building a fort, which may still be seen today at Waimea on Kauai, and over the fort he raised the Russian flag.

Through the influence of Dr. Scheffer, Kaumualii gave the Russian American Company the right to export sandalwood from Kauai, and also to erect buildings and establish plantations on that island. The doctor then turned his attention to Oahu. He built a blockhouse or fort on the waterfront at Honolulu, at the foot of what is now Fort Street.

While in Honolulu, the Russians invaded a *heiau* during a sacred taboo and did much damage. Word of this reached Kamehameha on Hawaii. He at once sent several chiefs to Oahu with orders to expel the Russians from the island. They were forced to leave, but threatened to return with a Russian man-of-war and to conquer the Islands.

Dr. Scheffer went back to Kauai and tried to regain a foothold there. But Kaumualii had become convinced that Scheffer was not so much his friend as an imposter, and ordered him and his associates to leave the island. They at first refused to go, but pressure was used and they were forced to leave. The doctor escaped to Oahu and from there he secured passage on a vessel to the Orient. He eventually reached St. Petersburg, and it is said that he gave a veiled report of what had happened in the Sandwich Islands.

From evidence available it is believed that the Russian Government had not at any time authorized Governor Baranov to lay plans to establish a base in Hawaii with the idea of eventually getting control of the Islands. The attitude of the Russian government is emphasized by the coming of the *Rurik* to Hawaii. This small ship had been sent out to discover, if possible, the "long sought passage around the American continent from the Pacific to the Atlantic." The captain of this vessel was Otto von Kotzebue, who became a valued acquaintance of Kamehameha. Before leaving Russia, Captain Kotzebue requested that the *Rurik* be equipped with guns, and he flew the Russian war flag as a protection in case of unexpected trouble in far seas. When he reached Hawaii, these guns aroused the fear of the Hawaiians. The Russians had returned, and, fearing trouble, Kamehameha stationed 400 soldiers along the coast ready for any emergency.

With Captain Kotzebue were several important men, among them Adelbert von Chamisso, the naturalist, and Louis Choris, the Russian artist, to whom history is indebted for a rare portrait of Kamehameha I. Another voyager was John Elliot, who had been in the Islands before and had acted as surgeon to the King. Elliot, evidently, had prepared the Russian visitors for their reception in the Islands. As they approached Hawaii, the young men were much impressed with the beauty of the landscape, and Chamisso tells that, from out at sea, they could discern the European built houses of John Young towering above the grass shacks of the native people.

When Kamehameha learned that the *Rurik* was a friendly ship, he invited the captain and his friends to come ashore. A small boat was first put over with Chamisso, Choris, and the ship's doctor, who preceded Captain Kotzebue in landing. It is Chamisso who describes his impression: the view from the village set among palm trees, the lava flow, and the great cone of Mataroi (Mauna Loa) beyond. "On the shore countless people were under arms. The old King, in front of whose house we landed, was sitting on a raised terrace surrounded by his wives, dressed in native costume, the red *malo* (girdle) and the black tapa (the wide, beautifully folded cape of bark cloth). The only things he had borrowed from Europeans were shoes and a light straw hat. In front of the King, on a lower level, sat all of his subordinates with uncovered shoulders.

"The old gentleman gladly welcomed his old doctor, though without overflowing signs of pleasure, and allowed him to explain the friendly purpose of our expedition." The party then waited for Captain Kotzebue to arrive. While they were waiting, Chamisso asked to be allowed to do a little botanizing, and Choris, the artist, stayed behind in order to draw the King's picture. Chamisso started out on his botanizing trip. He tells later of having met a chief on the way.

"A chief, coming toward us, whom we could not fail to recognize as such, because of his bearing and almost gigantic build, brandished his spear in our direction, playfully, as we met on the path, laughing the while, and then shook my hand with the friendly greeting, 'Aloha.' The chief said, 'We thought we were to fight and now you come as good friends.' Our guide yelled and danced like a jointed doll. Such is the way of these people; they are happy as children and one soon becomes like them when living amongst them. Here in these Islands laughter had no spirit of malice. Each laughs at the other, king or subject, without prejudice because of difference in rank."

Kotzebue also describes his reception by Kamehameha:

"I now stood beside the famous Kamehameha, whose deportment and unrestrained relations inspired me with the greatest confidence." The Captain tells that when he and his men landed, Kamehameha, accompanied by his first warriors, met him at the landing place and shook him heartily by the hand. He then took the Captain and his friends to his thatched palace "which after the fashion of the country consisted of one single room. We were offered some pretty European chairs and a mahogany table was set before us. Although the King had several houses built in European style he prefers this simple habitation, not wishing to infringe upon the manner of the country; everything he considers useful he imitates and endeavors to make the people adopt it; stone palaces he considers superfluous, the thatched houses being more comfortable, and he wished to increase the happiness and not the wants of his subjects."

Captain Kotzebue further explains: "The King having poured out for us some very good wine, and having himself drunk to our health, I acquainted him with my intention of supplying myself here with water and food. A dexterous, and tolerably well informed young man, named Cook, was the only white person in attendance on the King and spoke the language of the country with perfect ease. Kamehameha directed him to speak as follows:

" 'I am informed that you are the commander of a man-of-war, on a voyage similar to that of Cook and Vancouver, and, consequently have nothing to do with trade; it is therefore my intention not to enter into any with you, but to supply you gratuitously with everything my Islands produce. This matter is now settled and requires, therefore, no more mentioning. But I beg you will tell me whether it is the wish of your Emperor that his subjects should inconvenience me in my old age? Since Kamehameha has been king of these islands, no European has had reason to complain of any injury done him here. I have made my Islands an asylum for all nations; and honestly supplied every ship that wanted provisions. Sometime ago, Russians from the American colony of Sitka came here; they are a nation with whom I never had any connection before; they were well received and supplied with all necessities, but they have basely required me, having treated my subjects on the island of Oahu with great hostility, and threatened to conquer the Islands with men-of-war. Yet, as long as Kamehameha reigns, that will not take place! A Russian physician, named Scheffer, who came here a few months ago, pretended he was sent by the Emperor Alexander to botanize on my Islands; now I had heard the good fame of the Emperor, and was particularly pleased with his bravery; I not only permitted Mr. Scheffer to botanize, but also promised him every assistance, granted him a piece of land, with peasants, that might insure him against any want of provisions; in short, I tried to make his abode as pleasant to him as possible, and refused him no demand. But what was the consequence of my hospitality? Even in Hawaii he repaid my kindness with ingratitude, which I bore with patience; after this he went by his own will, from one island to another, settling at last upon the fruitful island of Oahu, where he proved himself my worst enemy, by destroying the *marai* or sanctuary, and stirring up against me, on the island of Kauai, King Kaumualii, who had submitted years ago to my government.' "

Kamehameha, being assured that the Russian Emperor knew nothing of the situation and had no intention of conquering the Islands, was greatly pleased, and drank to the health of the Emperor. Captain Kotzebue comments that the interpreter, Cook, could not always translate Kamehameha's words, "which being peculiar to the Hawaiian language, and so witty, it frequently set his ministers laughing."

After this audience with Kamehameha, he invited the party with him to call upon his queens, and also upon the Crown Prince, Liholiho, at his own palace. From there they went to the temple. At the entrance, Kamehameha stopped to embrace one of the statues, saying to Captain Kotzebue, "These are our gods which I worship; whether I do right or wrong in thus worshiping them, I know not, but I follow my religion which cannot be bad since it teaches me to do no wrong." At another time, in speaking of his religion, Kamehameha made the statement, "These shall be my gods for they have power, and by them I have become possessed of this government and through them I come to my throne."

Dinner followed the visit to the temple. The King commented: "I have seen how the Russians eat, now you may satisfy your curiosity by seeing how Kamehameha eats." The manner of eating may have surprised the men from Russia, but Kotzebue explains that Kamehameha followed the usual Hawaiian customs "with dignity," and said: "This is the custom of my country and I will not deviate from it."

"After having drunk the health of each of us in English fashion, he called upon us to drink the health of our Emperor; this being done, one of the ministers handed me a feather tippet, made with great skill, and which was formerly worn by the King himself, on solemn occasions, the King telling me at the same time, through Cook, although he speaks English pretty well himself, 'I have heard that your monarch is a great hero; I love him for it, because I am one myself. I send him this tippet as a proof of my affection.' "

Kamehameha then told the Captain that on the island of Oahu he could get whatever he needed for his ship in the way of provisions. In return for the King's hospitality, and wishing to assure him of the goodwill of the Russian government, Captain Kotzebue presented Kamehameha with two metal eight pound mortars with the name "Rurik" cut into their carriages, including grenades and powder. He also gave him apples from California, which he and the chiefs enjoyed, preserving the seeds to see if they would grow in Hawaii.

The artist, Louis Choris, did paint the portrait of Kamehameha, but he had some trouble in persuading the King to allow him to "put him on paper." The artist first made sketches of several of the chiefs. The King was much interested in these pictures, but he would not allow his own picture to be made until he was told that the Russian Emperor would be greatly pleased to have his portrait.

When Kamehameha finally appeared for the sitting, instead of being in his native costume as the artist had expected, he was dressed as a sailor. He wore blue trousers, a red waistcoat, a clean white shirt, and a necktie of yellow silk. Choris begged him to change his dress, but he refused absolutely and insisted on being painted as he was.

Captain Kotzebue, who was present at the sitting, writes: "To my astonishment Choris succeeded in taking a very good likeness of him, though Kamehameha, in order to embarrass him, did not sit still a moment, and made all kinds of faces, in spite of my entreaties." (Mr. John F. G. Stokes, an authority on the life of Kamehameha I, explains that Kamehameha probably made faces, not to disturb the artist, but because of his fear of magic and his superstition regarding his having his picture taken.)

Kamehameha was greatly pleased when, the following year after Choris had painted his picture, the *Rurik*, with his old friends, returned. Captain Kotzebue stopped at Kailua, but found that Kamehameha had gone fishing. He soon returned, however, and, not waiting to dress, he came up to the Captain in his *malo* and shook hands most heartily. One of his ministers dragged a couple of "bonitos" behind him, and the King said, ordering one of the fish to be laid at the Captain's feet, "This fish I hooked myself, and beg you to accept it as a testimony of my friendship."

In his old age Kamehameha was to receive still another ship from the far-off land of Russia. Only a few months after the *Rurik* left the islands, Captain Golovnin, with his vessel, the *Kamchatka,* visited Hawaii. The Captain says in his log: "Kamehameha is already very old; he considers himself to be seventy-nine years of age. It is probable that his exact age is unknown even to himself . . . However, he is alert, strong and active; he is temperate and sober; he never takes strong drinks and eats very moderately. In him one sees a most amazing mixture of childish deeds and of ripe judgment and actions that would not disgrace even a European ruler."

The Russians came no more, but Spanish pirates stopped to call, bringing with them unexpected interest and excitement. This was in the early part of the year 1818. The pirate ship, the *Victory,* was, strangely, under the command of an Englishman, Captain Turner. The crew of the vessel were a questionable lot. They came ashore with plenty of both gold and silver, and they showed around crucifixes, cups, and sacred ornaments, taken somewhere from Roman Catholic churches.

Kamehameha may have been growing old, but he had lost none of his keenness for trade. He decided to purchase the *Victory*. He renamed it the *Liholiho* in honor of his son, and planned to send the vessel with a cargo of sandalwood to China. But one bright morning a Spanish man-of-war cast anchor in Kealakekua Bay and proceeded to seize the *Victory*, the commander explaining to Kamehameha that the crew of the ship were pirates. They had stolen the vessel, the *Santa Rosa,* and changed the name, then sailed along the coast of Chili, ravaged a town, and stripped the churches of their sacred ornaments.

When Kamehameha heard this report he at once rounded up the pirates and turned them over to justice. Most of the church ornaments were found and, eventually, at the King's request, were returned to the churches from which they came.

Among the early foreigners who gave assistance and advice to Kamehameha, and with whom he formed a warm and genial friendship, was John Palmer Parker from Massachusetts. It has been said that Kamehameha had the keenness of a Yankee; this may have accounted for his liking of young John Parker. He found him a man of ability. He trusted him with important matters, placing him shortly in care of all his canoes, large and small. He sent him to carry a cargo of sandalwood to China and, through the advancing sandalwood trade, Kamehameha depended upon the New Englander for advice and counsel. In 1815, John Parker settled in Waimea on the island of Hawaii, setting up his home on lands allotted to him by Kamehameha. The King placed in Parker's trust all of the wild cattle on Mauna Kea. His job was to shoot them, prepare their hides and salt their carcasses for trade with the foreign vessels touching the Islands. Through later years of careful breeding and astute business acumen, Parker's lands became what is today the great Parker Ranch, the second largest ranch under the U.S. flag.

Sometime before Kamehameha's death he announced, in open council of the chiefs and of the people, that his son, Liholiho, would inherit the kingdom. And to the young prince, Kekuaokalani, who Kamehameha knew would be as loyal to his ancient heritage as he, himself, had been, he left the keeping of the war god. Remembering Waipio, it was thus that Kamehameha set his house in order.

It was in the early springtime, on the eighth day of May in 1819, that Kamehameha died. His son, as well as Kaahumanu, John Young, and the chiefs who had served him to the last in loyalty and devotion, all were with him. One of the chiefs spoke to the King: "Here we all are, your son, Liholiho, and your foreigner; impart to us your dying charge that Liholiho and Kaahumanu may hear." Then Kamehameha inquired: "What do you say?" The chief repeated, "Your counsel for us." He then said, "Move on in my good way and . . ." He could proceed no further.

To the snowcapped peaks of Mauna Loa, through the valleys and the plains of old Hawaii, the word went forth: "Kamehameha, the king, is dead!"

Kamehameha, the son of the stars of heaven, the high chief, the great warrior, the staunch friend, the supreme actor of old Hawaii was dead. The entire group of islands was thrown into confusion as old customs held their sway. The wailing of the people in their fear and in their madness struck terror to the soul. But in the secret silence of the night, as Kamehameha had requested, in some deep cavern of the rocks along the Kona shore, his bones were laid to rest. And no man has ever told just where that cavern lies.

THREE FRIENDS

Part Two

JOHN YOUNG--GENTLEMAN

Chapter IV

> *"If honesty is the best policy,*
> *gratitude for past favors should*
> *never be obliterated from the mind."*
>
> —JOHN YOUNG

IN THE NUUANU VALLEY home of the late Queen Emma, wife of King Kamehameha IV, hangs a portrait of her mother, Fannie. The portrait would not be there today, and Hawaii would have been deprived of one of the most beloved rulers of the Kamehameha dynasty in the person of Queen Emma herself, had not a lonely and terrified English sailor, many years before, been abandoned by his ship on the alien shores of Hawaii.

To stand on the shore of an island in the vast Pacific Ocean — an island supposed to be inhabited by savages — and to see the ship in which you came, and in which you expected to sail, weigh anchor and put out to sea leaving you behind, could be a distressing experience. So it was to John Young, the English sailor, in 1790.

While the personality and character of John Young stand out in high relief from the pages of Hawaiian history, very little is known about his life before he came to the Hawaiian Islands. The logs of ships and recorded voyages of sea captains tell little of the life of the common sailor. John Young has often been referred to as "an ignorant seaman." He was not ignorant, although, like many men of his time who walked the higher roads of society, he was unlettered. He was a gentleman— "a well-bred man of fine feeling."

Captain Vancouver in his *Voyages* says that John Young was born in Liverpool. An old letter tells that John Young had two brothers, Peter and James, who were pilots in Liverpool. Reared in a family of seafaring men, John was versed in the lore of the sea, and it may be assumed that he had the love of adventure in his heart from the time he was born. His childhood being where and what it was, little could he have imagined that he would one day be the personal friend and adviser of the King of the Sandwich Islands so many thousand miles away from England.

It is the story of the years he lived in the Sandwich Islands that this chapter tells, using the simple words he would have used in the telling, for he was plain and direct in his speech.

To begin with, near the close of the American Revolutionary War there were two ships—the *Eleanora,* an American snow square-rigged vessel, under the command of Captain Simon Metcalf, a fur trader, and the *Fair American,* a small schooner which the Captain had purchased to act as a tender to the larger vessel.

He placed five or six men on the schooner as crew, and his young son, a boy of eighteen or twenty, he put in command. Captain Metcalf, in carrying on his fur trade, voyaged between the northwest coast of America and the Orient. In making his passage one way or the other he sometimes stopped over at the Sandwich Islands for supplies. He made the arrangement with his son that, should the two ships become separated at sea, they were to meet at Kealakekua Bay in Hawaii. The boat first reaching the Bay was to wait there for the other vessel. John Young was the boatswain on the *Eleanora.*

On the way to Hawaii, Captain Metcalf stopped at the island of Maui. One night a small boat, in which a sailor was sleeping, was stolen from the stern of the ship. When the Captain learned about this, he demanded that the man and the boat be returned at once. He was told that the boat had been broken to pieces for its nails and that the man had been killed. He then offered a reward for the return of the bones of the dead seaman and for what was left of the boat. (Since this was not the Captain's first visit to the Islands, he probably knew of the Hawaiian custom of preserving the bones of the dead.)

In the meantime, the natives had been permitted to continue their trading with the men on the vessel. Three days later, the bones of the dead sailor and the stem and stern posts of the small boat were brought to the ship. The Hawaiians, believing the Captain was entirely satisfied, asked when he would give them the reward. He replied that they should have it at once. He then ordered the guns of the ship to be loaded with musket balls and nails, and having tabooed one side of the vessel in order to get all of the Hawaiians with their canoes on the starboard side next to the shore, the ports were hauled up and the guns fired amongst the canoes. Nearly one hundred natives were killed and many wounded. After taking this revenge, the Captain sailed for the island of Hawaii. Reaching Kealakekua Bay ahead of the schooner, Captain Metcalf waited there for his son.

It was during this time that John Young went ashore. Different reasons have been given as to why he did go ashore. But the only story about the first nights he spent on Hawaii, quoted from John Young himself, is told by Captain Charles Barnard in the *Narrative* which appears in the book of his travels.

Captain Barnard was an American sea captain who, during the War of 1812, became a castaway on the Falkland Islands. He was finally rescued and joined his old friend, Captain Samuel Bailey, in making a world voyage. Captain Bailey was commander of the vessel *Milwood* of New York. On his way to the Orient, he stopped at the Sandwich Islands hoping to pick up a cargo of sandalwood for the China trade.

The two captains made a call on Kamehameha. The following day the call was returned by the King and his retinue. During the call, Captain Bailey approached the subject of sandalwood. Kamehameha told him that he left all such business matters with Mr. Young. John Young soon visited the ship and the deal for the wood was concluded, at which time Captain Barnard made his acquaintance. John Young, himself, always superintended the weighing and loading of the sandalwood, and, since the wood came down from the mountains in small lots, there were periods of waiting. Captain Barnard took this opportunity to ask John Young about his experience and as to how long he had been in the Islands.

John Young told of his coming with the *Eleanora* early in the year 1790. He said he was tired of being on the ship and had obtained permission to go ashore. He took a musket with him, thinking that he might get a few birds. He then went hunting. It was late in the afternoon when he returned, expecting to go aboard the ship which was anchored some distance out. To his consternation the small boat, in which he had come ashore, was gone. Looking about, he saw that the native canoes were all hauled high on the beach. The grass houses were closed and not a person was to be seen. He waited some time, thinking a boat would surely come for him, but no boat came.

When night set in he was still pacing the beach. In his story to Captain Barnard, he said: "I felt a strange fear creeping over me. All was as gloomy as death." He decided to knock at one of the closed houses. He knocked, but there was no reply. He said that his own knock startled him, so great was the silence. He was almost afraid to knock a second time, not knowing what he would encounter. But realizing that he might be in greater danger outside, alone in the darkness, he ventured to knock again and, much to his relief, the door was opened and he was invited in.

The people in the house seemed friendly. They offered him something to eat. But the expression on their faces and their strange manner told him that something dreadful had happened or was about to happen. Since he did not understand the Hawaiian language, he did not know what they were saying. He was given a place to sleep, but he was so worried that he could not close his eyes. He later said the shadows that night were as specters, and he was afraid for his life.

As soon as it began to get light, he crept from the hut and hurried to the beach hoping for a boat, but no boat came. The canoes, which he dared not touch, were still high and dry on shore. He returned to the hut. There was great concern on every countenance. The narrative does not tell, but John Young probably wondered if the people had not heard of what had taken place on Maui. They knew that he had come from the ship, which they could see standing off shore.

John Young may also have known of another incident: when Captain Metcalf had ordered a high chief to be flogged with knotted ropes, the chief had declared that he would take his revenge upon the first white man who came his way. So, it was not without reason that John Young was afraid.

All day the natives remained in their closed houses. The second night was a repetition of the first, filled with apprehension and fear. Morning found John Young again on the beach looking for a boat. Then suddenly he saw that the ship was moving. All the forenoon, like a preying vulture oblivious to her nestlings, she stood in and out of the bay. In telling of this to Captain Barnard, John Young said: "Who can describe my feelings when I saw the ship wear off and rig out her sail booms? This almost overpowered me. I imagined the hour of death had arrived."

But, after the sailing of the ship, the people came out of their houses and went about their own affairs. That day John Young met a native who was able to make him understand that there was another white man not far away. The Hawaiian took John Young to Kealakekua where, much to his surprise, he found Isaac Davis, who had been the mate of the *Fair American*. Davis told of the taking of the schooner by the Hawaiians and of the massacre of the crew. Although Isaac Davis had been badly injured by both clubs and daggers, he was able to give an account of what had happened. He told John Young that the schooner had arrived at Kawaihae five days before. It was evening when they anchored, and, thinking it would be safer to spend the night where they were, they decided to meet the *Eleanora* the following day. The natives came on board seemingly much pleased. But Isaac said he did not like the appearance of things, and had advised young Metcalf not to allow the people on the ship that night. But the chiefs had brought presents to the Captain and he was in the very act of receiving them when an attack was made upon the crew. In the skirmish that followed, all the white men were murdered and thrown overboard, including Captain Metcalf's son.

Isaac Davis, himself, managed to jump from the stern of the boat into a canoe. There was a native in the canoe who at once attacked Davis with a paddle, beating him until he believed him dead, and leaving him in the bottom of the boat. Davis was later rescued by another native and taken ashore.

When Kamehameha learned of the taking of the schooner, he feared retaliation. So, when Captain Metcalf stood off shore, Kamehameha placed a taboo with the penalty of death upon the sailing of any canoe. He hoped, by so doing, to keep Metcalf ignorant of the theft of the *Fair American*. This taboo accounts for the closed houses. John Young, knowing nothing of the system of the taboo, was unaware of the situation. When Kamehameha met John Young and Isaac Davis, he took them home with him to his own houses, showing them the greatest kindness. Isaac Davis' wounds were given careful attention. He was blind for several months, but eventually recovered his sight.

It has been said many times that John Young and Isaac Davis were prisoners on Hawaii. They were not prisoners, although a careful watch was kept that they did not leave the Islands. The captain of an incoming ship, learning that the two Englishmen were stranded on Hawaii, sent a letter ashore offering them passage. The chief, Kaiana, who was especially jealous of the friendship of Kamehameha for the two men, volunteered to take them out to the vessel in his own canoe. But Kamehameha, knowing the secret desire of the chief, perhaps to destroy them, persuaded them not to go. It was with this background that John Young and Isaac Davis began their lives in the Sandwich Islands.

There are no foreigners in the recorded history of Hawaii who did more for the upbuilding of the Hawaiian people than did John Young and Isaac Davis. It seems remarkable that two sailors, stranded among a people whom they knew to be at least semi-barbarous, were able to hold their own integrity, never deviating from a strictly moral code in their own lives. They have been called the first missionaries. They were not missionaries, of course, but they certainly prepared the way for the work of missionaries. Men from Botany Bay, and others who slipped in from ships of the night, left no such good influence as they.

The friendship which developed between Kamehameha and the two men was another astounding thing. It was not alone the fact that Kamehameha had learned the value of the help which foreigners could give him (for there were several white men in the Islands when John Young arrived) that prompted his unusual interest in Young and Davis. With his keen insight, Kamehameha must have soon recognized in these two sailors men whom he could trust. He not only took them into the inner circle of his court and made them his friends, but wherever he went, either for business or for pleasure, they were expected to accompany him. To this friendship, John Young and Isaac Davis responded, refusing to leave the Islands when Vancouver offered to take them back to England.

Only once had Davis and Young attempted to leave Hawaii, and the reason they gave for wishing to go away does much to reveal a facet of the character of John Young. It is claimed that Young is the only man who ever dared to stand up to Kamehameha and express an opinion, when in so doing his life must have been endangered. The King asked why he and Davis wished to leave when he was doing everything he could to please them. In a few emphatic words, John Young told Kamehameha the truth. He said that while he and Davis appreciated all that had been done for them, they dared not trust the King because he was so frequently under the influence of liquor, and that, when he was intoxicated, he was no longer master of himself. The King was impressed, and, through the continued influence of John Young, he became a temperate man. Later, Kamehameha actually offered the two men a chance to leave, but they chose to remain in the Islands, saying that they were both under great obligations to the King. Young added, "If honesty is the best policy, gratitude for past favors should never be obliterated from the mind." The two men followed Kamehameha into battle after battle, watching for every opportunity to do him personal service and to protect his life. It is said that Vancouver gave John Young rockets and hand-grenades to be used only in protection of the King.

It was the spirit in which they accepted the situation—two sailors fast turning into capable warriors—which won them high praise. John Young, himself, told the following story. He said that it was customary in an engagement, when Kamehameha was well on the way to winning the battle, the enemy yelling as they came nearer, for the King to push upon them so rapidly that it was impossible to keep up with him. At such times a chief would take John Young on his shoulders, and another strong chief would carry Isaac Davis on his, and they would be rushed to the front where they would fire, reload, and fire again.

The Hawaiian warriors did their fighting in the open. They knew nothing of ambush or strategy in war until the white man came and brought with him his firearms. The old warriors depended upon hand to hand fighting with spears, javelins, slingshots, and clubs, along with the fierce yelling of both sides, and the influence of the images of the war gods which were always present. There is no doubt that Young and Davis very often saved the day for Kamehameha. Other white men were in the ranks of the King, but they left no special records behind them.

Meantime, the jealousy of the King's friendship for John Young had steadily increased, not only among the chiefs, but also within the priesthood. It was finally decided to get rid of the "foreigner," as Young was called by the people. Kamehameha understood this. He warned Young that a *kahuna* was threatening his life; that he had already built his prayer hut at the edge of the woods and was preparing to "pray him to death." John Young replied that he would follow the *kahuna's* example. He, too, went to the woods and built a small grass hut exactly like that which the *kahuna* had made, and very near to it. He then spread abroad the word that he, John Young, would "pray the *kahuna* to death." So strong was this superstition in the minds of the Hawaiians that, much to Young's amazement, the *kahuna* became terrified and reportedly died from fear, as he had expected Young to do.

As official pilot for Kamehameha, John Young had great responsibility in bringing ships to safe anchorage in the reef-torn waters of the bay and out again to the open roads of the sea. There is a graphic account of how John Young saved the *Jefferson*. In the log of the ship, the captain writes: "Moderate fine weather the fore part of the night. At midnight we were about five or six miles from shore. I then went off the deck and Mr. Boules took charge of the watch, but being negligent in keeping a lookout and himself getting asleep while standing in for the land, about three a.m. he ran on a dangerous reef of rocks about a mile from shore which instantly aroused all hands on deck where we found ourselves surrounded in every direction by rocks and breakers and the ship heaving with such violence as threatened her immediate dissolution. It was judged best to get our anchor out (as the ship appeared fast). We accordingly cleared the pinnace and got in the stream anchor and cable, the ship rolling and thumping excessively hard. It seemed impossible that she could survive the shock or get off. Three natives who were on board (as were Messrs. Young and Davis) were sent ashore to bring canoes to our assistance."

Evidently, as was the custom, John Young and Isaac Davis, with the three natives, had gone out to meet the ship and spent the night on board. The Hawaiians, after swimming ashore, returned with the canoes and, under the direction of John Young, the ship was released, and Young and Davis returned to the shore. John Young later told the captain that for two days they could not see the ship from the beach, so high was the surf. He also said that he, himself, after the ship had left, went over the track that the ship had made upon the rocks, which were "ploughed through and broken in an astonishing manner," and that the natives were diving in all parts of the reef picking up nails and spikes.

As time passed, the influence of John Young steadily increased. It was not only the captains of ships who depended on him and recognized the authority invested in him by the King. The people of the Islands, both native and foreign, well understood the place he held in Kamehameha's scheme of government. Few written records are to be found concerning John Young. A paragraph here and there in the logs of ships does tell of business transacted with him by the captains of the vessels. It is unfortunate that all of John Young's private papers were destroyed in a flood which swept away the house in which they were stored. And, strange as it may seem, there are no living descendants of John Young. But descendants are not needed to tell the story of the high standing and great esteem in which John Young was held and still is held in the minds of the people of Hawaii. He was called *Olohana* by the Hawaiians. *Olohana*—the call of the boatswain—"All hands!"

John Young entered into every phase of the life of the people: instructing, directing, controlling the native workers and advising not only the King, but other men as well. He kept men busy. But while he was a strict taskmaster, he was also a leader, setting for himself the same high standards of practice and workmanship that he demanded of others.

For many years John Young practically controlled the commercial life of the Islands. Old voyagers tell how he and Isaac Davis gradually built up the understanding of the Hawaiian people regarding the value of their products. Ships could no longer get supplies such as salt, water, potatoes, etc., in exchange for a few nails or a scrap of iron. Water had to be carried in calabashes from the mountains, a distance of several miles. One captain tells that, previously, a moderate sized nail would purchase for his entire ship's company excellent pork for the day.

In speaking of the great changes in both government and trade which followed Kamehameha's victories, Captain Turnbull, who made rather frequent voyages to Hawaii, gives much credit to John Young. He says in his records: "The first civilized methods of rule emanated from the house of Young." The "House of Young!" The very phrase tells the story of the position which John Young had achieved. He was given the high rank of *Kapu* chief, which placed him on an equal footing with the highest chiefs of the Hawaiian Kingdom. He was "Chief Young," the adviser of the King.

It was in the early years of John Young's life in the Islands that he made his first marriage. His wife, a Hawaiian, while not of high rank, was of sterling character. There were two sons born to this marriage, Robert and James. The boys were both sent to America to be educated. Robert joined the U. S. Navy and fought in the War of 1812. He was captured by the British and sent to Bermuda. Nothing definite was ever heard from him again. James returned to Hawaii and became a prominent member of the new government, at different times being appointed governor of the islands of Kauai and Maui. Mrs. Young died during an epidemic which swept the Islands, and lies buried at Waimea, Hawaii.

In the Archives building in Honolulu is preserved the diary of John Young. On the cover is written in plain rounded figures the date, 1801. The diary has been called a log book. It is certainly not a log book; it was not written at sea nor does it give the log of any ship, although John Young's experience as a sailor is seen throughout the pages. Between the lines one can read the story of the years as John Young lived them in his mind. While keeping his accounts, scanning the ocean for incoming sails, watching the ships far out to sea, wondering from whence they came and whither they were bound, he was, it would seem, sometimes homesick.

"Sunday—thick and foggy with small rains and the winds from the N.W. and heavy surf."

"Clear, light winds from N.W. but no surf on the reef. No fish." No fish was an important item; fishing was the main industry of the people. An added item tells that John Young was sending his canoes to Maui, since there was no fishing at home. By this time John Young had a business of his own. He manufactured canoes.

"Moderate and cloudy. The first time this month of March that we have had the wind from the natural quarter."

"This twenty-four hours blowing very hard from the N.E. but perfectly clear. Saw two ships to the norard of Tohay Bay island. Still blowing hard from the N.E. Saw another large ship. By the way of their maneuvering I take them to be whalers."

"The ships still in sight cruising to the south of Tohay Bay. April 1. Moderate and clear. The three ships still in sight. Though I haven't heard what they are, take them to be whalers by their cruising in a line at regular distances from each other."

"Nets catch twenty flying fish."

"Saw a large ship standing to the south. But it was a long ways off."

"To rents—5 tapas." (Pieces of fine cloth pounded from the bark of the mulberry tree.)

"Ten feathers." Feathers, too, were of great value. These were prepared in bunches of approximately seventy-five feathers, so the item, ten feathers, indicated that there were ten bunches of feathers in one payment. These were probably the choice feathers used in making cloaks and helmets for the King and for the chiefs. John Young explains,

"Want to build a canoe for the King and get a feathered cloak made for him." He also tells of receiving forty bundles of potatoes and some coconut lines from Kona. Coconut lines were necessary to the fishing business.

"April 4—This day I heard there was a Russian ship at Kona but did not learn what they were about or where bound."

"At eleven o'clock at night there was a heavy earthquake. Though we often have them here, this last was truly alarming." There are several references in the diary to earthquakes, but they seem to have done little damage.

"Small bundles of taro." (This is the plant from which *poi,* the staple food of the Hawaiians, is made.) "No tapas—no dogs." (*Poi* dogs— dogs raised and fattened with *poi*—were considered a great delicacy by the Hawaiian people of those days.)

"No feathers. No paws." (The original *pa-u* was a woman's skirt, a garment that reached from the waist to the knees. A strip of tapa, five yards long, was wrapped about the body and held in place at the waist- line by a fold. Across the shoulder was thrown a scarf-like piece of tapa called the *kiheki.*)

There are a few pen sketches in John Young's diary which were evi- dently drawn in idle moments—a very good drawing of a horse standing under a tree, and a house with two windows and a door. Memories of other lands may have prompted these pictures, since there were no horses and no houses with windows and chimneys in the Islands at the time he made these particular entries.

It has been pointed out that John Young was not a missionary, but he nevertheless did some thinking about religion. His family back- ground possibly had a religious trend, since his parents named their sons John, Peter and James. He took time one Sunday to copy into his diary the prayer of St. Chrysostom.

The little diary reflects but a portion of some of the more quiet hours of John Young's life in Hawaii—hours when he listened to the wind, when he watched the flashing surf as it turned white the long dark reef, when the distant mountain peaks may have seemed to shut him in. He may have grown weary of the bright blue sea, and, as he watched the strange ships sailing by on the edge of the horizon, he may have longed for darker oceans and the friends of other days:

> "He lives every longing
> Who dwells by the sea."

About 1805, Kamehameha sent for his niece, the daughter of his fa- vorite brother, and she became the second wife of John Young. This marriage brought John Young increased recognition and prestige. The

Hawaiian people themselves were pleased. John Young was now a member of the royal family. He had cast his lot with Kamehameha. The King appointed him governor of the island of Hawaii, and life took on a new meaning.

It was at Kawaihae on the island of Hawaii that John Young established his home. A community grew up around him which he called "The Young Settlement," and which was often a refuge for the missionary, the scientist, and the traveler.

Four children were born to John Young's second marriage—Fannie, Grace, John Jr., and Jane. To Fannie, when she had grown up and married, was born a daughter, Emma. Emma, granddaughter of John Young, when she herself grew up, became one of the most beloved queens in the Kamehameha dynasty.

The home life of the Youngs was conducted on a European basis. Writers tell that Mrs. Young always dressed in Oriental silks, and that her dresses were made in foreign style. The daughters were given the most careful training. They, as well as John Young's granddaughter, Emma, attended the school for young chiefs which was conducted by the missionaries. At the time of the death of Kamehameha, when all restrictions were abolished for several days and the community was seething with the strange debauchery of an uncivilized people, John Young protected his family from even seeing what was taking place. One of the children incidentally remarked that, as a matter of course, they would attend the funeral rites of the King. Their father immediately replied, "If any of my children do attend, they will never again cross the threshold of my house." He nailed up every avenue to his dwelling and sat with his native wife and with his children without the light of the sun during those days of riot.

Mrs. Lucy Thurston, in her story of her life as a missionary in Hawaii, in speaking of John Young, says: "He had long been a rare example in that degenerate age, of building a hedge about his family and standing in the gap thereof. When occasion offered, he spoke with energy and decision, giving no uncertain sound, well understood by his children and by strangers. By marriage, by deeds and by counsel, he had justly risen to the eminence of a peer with the chiefs of the nation. Saxon blood flowed in his veins. He was Mr. Young, the noble grandfather of our most noble Queen Emma."

It was a great grief to John Young when his old friend, Isaac Davis, died after having been poisoned by jealous chiefs in 1810. He at once took Isaac Davis' children into his home and brought them up with his own sons and daughters. His son, James, married a daughter of Isaac Davis. In John Young's will, he left his property to be divided between his own children and the children of Isaac Davis. At the end of the will, John Young speaks of his friends, the Hawaiians: "May that great Being who rules the nations of the earth continue you in peace and happiness with each other and all mankind and happiness in the world to come."

In a speech delivered by His Excellency, J. H. Kapena, Minister of Foreign Relations, on the occasion of the laying of the cornerstone of the Royal Palace, Honolulu, in 1879, His Excellency says:

"Here in the premises of *Pokukaina* was erected the tomb of the departed chiefs and at the entrance of that sacred place was placed the body of John Young, one of Kamehameha's intimate friends. In order that the spot may not be forgotten where a tomb once stood, King Kalakaua has caused a mound to be raised there, crowned with ferns and flowers in memory of those who slept beneath it. Doubtless the memory is yet green of that never to be forgotten night when the remains of the departed chiefs were removed to the Royal Mausoleum in Nuuanu Valley. Perhaps the world had never witnessed a procession more weird and solemn than that which conveyed the bodies of the chiefs through the streets, accompanied on each side by thousands of people until the mausoleum was reached, the entire scene and procession lighted by large *kukui* torches, while the surrounding darkness brought in striking relief the coffins on their biers. Truly we cannot forget the weirdness, the solemnity and the affecting scene afforded by that strange midnight procession."

At the Royal Mausoleum, on the flat, gray stone which covers his grave, is the following inscription:

"Beneath this stone
are deposited the remains of
John Young
(of Lancashire, England)
the friend and companion in arms of
KAMEHAMEHA
who departed this life
December 17th, 1835,
in the 93rd year of his age
and the 46th of his residence on the
SANDWICH ISLANDS"

One can hear the softly dropping waters of Kapena Falls in the near background. The dark mountains which edge Nuuanu Valley and the old trees above the grave stand guard. Close by is the little stone chapel, and just beyond are the Royal Tombs of the kings of old Hawaii. In this sacred spot sleeps John Young, the sailor lad from Liverpool.

OBOOKIAH

Chapter V

> *"By religion, then, I understand a propitiation or conciliation of powers superior to man which are believed to direct and control the course of nature and of human life."*
> —THE GOLDEN BOUGH

AT THIS POINT we turn our attention briefly from the kings and chiefs of old Hawaii and focus it upon a frail Hawaiian youth who, at the age of 26, died in the bleak New England winter of 1818, but who, for all his fragility and tender years, probably did as much, by quite different means, to change the tide of Hawaiian history as did the robust, long-lived warrior, Kamehameha I, himself. This is the story of Obookiah, the young Hawaiian boy whose religious zeal in New England was largely responsible for the coming of the first Christian missionaries to Hawaii.

New York harbor was filled with silent ships. Five hundred sailing vessels were crowded together, their sails unbended, their tall masts reaching skyward in mute mockery as the vessels rode at their moorings, their bottoms rotting in the water where they lay. Merchants and captains wore grave faces, and sailors restlessly lounged along the wharves and in the taverns. Trade was at a standstill. Little business was transacted and that behind closed doors. Young Robert Fulton was having trouble raising money to further the building of his steamboat. No man felt secure. It was a strange, new world for free America, and such a crisis had been brought about by wars in Europe. Following the Napoleonic regime, international complications resulted in the passing of the Embargo Act of 1807, which closed all American ports to foreign commerce. No American ship was permitted to sail to any foreign country.

It was during this period that Obookiah and his friend, Thomas Hopoo left the Sandwich Islands with Captain Brintnall, commander of the sailing vessel *Triumph,* voyaging by way of China and around the Cape of Good Hope, reaching New York on August 5, 1809.

Captain Brintnall, no doubt, received a hearty welcome in New York because the *Triumph* was, probably, one of the first ships from far seas to enter the harbor after the embargo had been lifted. Since business matters in the shipping trade were still precarious, Captain Brintnall, after a brief stay in New York, discharged his crew and left for his home in New Haven, Connecticut, taking Obookiah and Thomas with him.

Obookiah was born about 1792 at Ninole, Kau, on the island of Hawaii. His Hawaiian name was *Opukahaia,* which in itself sheds an interesting light not only on the Hawaiian practice of naming children to commemorate important events, but also on its ancient medical practices. *Opukahaia* was born at the time that a chieftess of his family gave birth to a child by Caesarean section. The chieftess died, but her child lived, and, in memory of the occasion, *Opukahaia* was given his Hawaiian name, which means, literally, "stomach cut open." His Hawaiian name was pronounced and spelled "Obookiah" by his American friends; he was also given the name of Henry, and it is as Henry Obookiah that he is best known.

Obookiah tells that his parents ranked as common people, although his mother was by some family connection related to the King. When Obookiah was ten or twelve years old, his parents were both killed "in a war, made before the old King died, to see who should be greatest among them." As was the custom following a war, the victorious party ravaged the country, destroying life and property. An alarm was given to the village where Obookiah's father lived. He took his wife and his two children with him and fled to the mountains and hid in a cave. The family remained in the cave for several days, but thirst finally compelled them to seek water. They found a neighboring spring, but at the spring they were surprised by warriors from the enemy's camp. The father, thinking he was the one in immediate danger, ran to hiding, but the cries of his wife and children were so terrifying that he quickly returned to their protection. He and his wife were both killed. Obookiah, carrying his baby brother on his back, tried to get away. A spear was thrown at them and the baby was killed. It was evidently believed that Obookiah might be made useful. He was taken to the home of the very man who had killed his parents. Obookiah tells that the man and his wife were both kind to him and gave him a good home, but he was lonely and unhappy. He did not like to live with the man who had killed his father and mother and his brother. He was determined to look for some of his relatives. After several months he found his uncle, who was a high priest among the people, and it was finally decided that he would stay with his uncle, who would train him for the priesthood.

Obookiah lived with his uncle for several years while studying to be a priest. He was obliged to commit to memory long ceremonial prayers said in the *heiau.* These ceremonies often continued from sunrise to sunset, and again the whole night through. (This *heiau* is at Napoopoo, where the monument to Captain Cook now stands. It is the same *heiau* in which Captain Cook received the worship of the Hawaiian people, who believed he was their returned god, Lono.)

But the enemies of Obookiah's family were still on the alert. One day he and his aunt were taken prisoners. Obookiah heard that his aunt and perhaps he, himself, were to be killed. He watched for a way to escape. Seeing a hole in the side of the cellar of the house where he was confined, he managed to creep through the opening and hide outside. It was not long before he saw the men bring his aunt from the house and take her to a high precipice, over which she was thrown to her death. Obookiah followed them, thinking he would throw himself over the *pali,* but one of the chiefs found him and he was taken back.

Obookiah writes: "While I was with my uncle, I began to think about leaving that country. I did not care where I shall go to. I thought to myself that if I should get away and go to some other country, probably I might find some comfort, more than to live there without father and mother. I thought it would be better for me to go than to stay. About this time there was a ship come from New York. Captain Brintnall the master of the ship. As soon as it got into the harbor, in the very place where I lived, I thought of no more than to take the best chance that I had, and if the captain have no objection, to take me as one of his own servants and to obey his word. As soon as the ship anchored I went on board. The Captain soon enquired whose boy I was, yet I knew not what he says to me for I could not speak the English language. But there was a young man who could speak the English language, and told the Captain that I was the minister's nephew."

Captain Brintnall invited Obookiah to spend the night on the ship and return home in the morning. He also asked him to have supper with him, at which occasion Obookiah met another Hawaiian boy, Thomas Hopoo, who was to become his best friend. The name "Thomas" had been given Hopoo by the supercargo of the ship. The Captain talked with the two boys and asked if they would like to go to America. Obookiah writes, "This man was very agreeable and his kindness much delighted my heart, as if I was his own son and he was my own father."

The next morning the Captain told Obookiah to go home and talk with his uncle and get his permission to leave. His uncle, greatly angered by the request, shut him in a room, refusing to give his permission for the trip. His grandmother came and talked with him and asked him why he wanted to leave his own people. She left the room crying and said that he was a foolish boy. The Hawaiian houses of the day were grass huts, and Obookiah again found an opening through which he could escape imprisonment. He went back to the ship and hid himself aboard. When his uncle found that he had gone from the house, he took a canoe and paddled out to the vessel. There was a Hawaiian man on the ship who found Obookiah and took him back to his uncle's house. It was finally settled, however, that he should be allowed to go with the Captain. Obookiah explains, "My uncle would not let me go unless I pay him a hog for his god (for I was taken under his care to be made for a minister)." So it was that Obookiah came to leave the Hawaiian Islands.

Captain Brintnall was engaged in the seal trade. Leaving Hawaii with Obookiah and Thomas as members of the crew, he returned to the northwest coast of America where he had left twenty to thirty men on the Seal Islands to look after his business. Obookiah tells: "Among those men I found a very desirable young man by the name of Russel Hubbard, a son of Gen. Hubbard of New Haven. This Mr. Hubbard was very kind to me and taught me the letters in the English spelling book."

The Captain remained at Seal Islands for six months, then sailed to China to dispose of his furs. Obookiah relates some of his and Thomas' experiences on the long voyage to America. "On the way towards China," he writes, "my poor friend Thomas fell overboard. He was so careless; not knowing what he was about, he went outside of the ship and drew salt water to wash plates with (for he was a cabin's boy). When the ship rolled he got in the water. The Captain called all hands upon the deck, and ordered to have all sails pull down in order to let about. While we were working upon our sails, my friend Thomas was out of sight. While he was in the water he pulled off all his clothes in order to be lighter. We turned our ship and went back after him. We found him almost dead. He was in the water two and one-half hours. O how glad I was to see him for he was already gone.

"We took our direct course from hence as it was before. Soon we landed at an island belonging to that part of China, and in the evening after the sundown we anchored. On the next morning we fired one of our cannon for a pilot. When we had fired once or twice there was another ship of war, belonging to the British, which stood about four or five miles apart from us. As soon as they heard our cannon they sent one of their brigs. We were then taken by it for awhile. They took our Captain and he went on board the men of war's ship. He was there for a number of days. After this the Englishmen agreed to let us go. We therefore leave that place called Mocow or Mockow (Macao) and directed our course to the city of Canton. We were there until we sold out all our sealskins and loaded our ship with other sort of goods; such as tea, cinnamon, nankeens and silk &c."

It would be interesting to know the experience of the two Hawaiian boys in the city of Canton, but Obookiah's journal speaks only of their continued voyage from China to America.

"At the Cape of Good Hope or before it, our sailors on board the ship began to terrify at us . . . They said that there was a man named Neptune who lived in that place and his abiding place was in the sea. In the evening the sailors begun to act. One of them took an old great coat and put on him, and with a speaking trumpet in his hand, and his head covered with a sheepskin; and he went forward of the ship and making a great noise. About this time friend Thomas and myself were on the quarter-deck, hearing some of them telling about Neptune's coming with an iron canoe, and iron paddle. Thomas questioned whether the iron canoe will not sink down in the water. 'No,' said some of them, 'he will make it light for he is a God.' While we were talking the first we heard the sound of trumpet as follows: 'Ship hail! from whence came you?' The Captain immediately giving an answer in this manner: 'From Canton.' 'Have you got my boys?' added the old Neptune. 'Yes,' answered the Captain. 'How many boys have you?' added the old Neptune. 'Two,' said the Captain (that is myself and friend Thomas). As soon as we both heard the Captain say 'two' we were both scared almost to death, and wished we were home. The old Neptune wished to see us; but we dare not come near at it. He continued calling to us to come to him, or else he would take both of us to be as his servants. We therefore went up immediately and shook our hands with him in a friendly manner. I thought that he was quite an old age; by seeing his long beard and his head covered with gray hairs; for his head was covered with a sheepskin. After our conversation with him he wished for a drink. So that I went and filled two pails full of salt water (as the sailors told us) and I set them before him. Then he took his speaking trumpet and put it in my mouth for funnel, in order to make me drink that salt water which I brought. But while he stooped down to reach the pail of water, I took hold of the speaking trumpet and held it on one side of my cheek so that I may not drink a drop of salt water; did not anybody know it for it was dark. But friend Thomas he was so full of scare, he took down a great deal of salt water. On the next morning he was taken sick and puked from morning until the evening.

"About this time our provision was almost out. We had no bread, meat and water; only when the cook put in our tea. We were looking out for a vessel for a long time. In a few days we come close to a schooner going to the West Indies sailed from Boston. We fired at her in order to stop her. So did she. We got from them as much provision as we wished, and this lasted until we got to New York. We landed at New York in the year 1809."

New York must have held many thrills for the two boys, but Obookiah tells only that he and Thomas went to the theatre. "One evening two gentlemen called on board the ship to see us. After our conversation with them, they wished us to go into a play-house and show the curiosity. We then went with them into the play-house and saw a great number of people as I ever saw before. We stayed during the forepart of the evening, then went on board the ship. The next morning the same two gentlemen called again and invited us to come to their house that forenoon. So we both went. I thought while in the house of these two gentlemen how strange to see females eat with men."

No doubt home ties and customs were constantly in mind as Obookiah and Thomas saw the strange manners of people in America. But in a few days, following the visit to the theatre, the boys left with the Captain for New Haven. This was in August. The early fall coloring of the New England forests had scarcely begun and the countryside between New Haven and New York was not as picturesque as it would have been later on. The boys may have compared it with the beauty of the Hawaiian landscape and perhaps felt a little homesick for the Islands. But Captain Brintnall was their friend and they were going home with him.

Captain Brintnall was well known in New Haven. The *Connecticut Herald* for August 8, 1809, gives the following statement: "The ship *Triumph,* Brintnall, belonging to this port, has arrived at New York, in 5 months from Canton. The *Triumph* sailed from New Haven the 9th of January, 1807, on a sealing voyage to the Pacific Ocean and China, and it is with pleasure that we can inform the friends of the numerous crew that they have all returned in health except Mr. Mix (one of the owners) whose death was sometime since announced." Maritime records also say, in speaking of the vessel *Zepher:* "She was commanded by that veteran navigator, Caleb Brintnall, who made more voyages to the Pacific than any other New Haven shipmaster of his day."

The Captain took Obookiah to his own home, where the youth lived as a member of the Brintnall family; a neighboring home was found for Thomas. The Brintnall family were, evidently, "church-going folks." Obookiah tells of attending many meetings on the Sabbath, but finding it difficult to understand the minister, since he knew so little of the English language. The Captain, himself, was a religious man. The New Haven Genealogical Magazine contains the statement, "Caleb Brintnall was baptized April 4, 1774." He was, probably, a Congregationalist.

For more than a century New Haven had been the center of religious and educational matters in Connecticut. Captain Brintnall and his Hawaiian wards had landed in 1809 when Connecticut and all New England were again stirred by an intense religious revival—the Revival of 1805, which brought back into the fold many dissenters and many new converts. Among the converts was a group of earnest young men from Yale, Harvard, Williams, and Dartmouth colleges. There had already been established a theological seminary at Andover for the training of young men who desired to enter the ministry, and it was through a small number of these college students that one of the most momentous movements of the century was begun in America in the interest of foreign missions.

The story of the Haystack Band holds the inspiration which accounts for the movement, and for the special interest, later, in the two Hawaiian boys, Obookiah and Thomas, transforming their lives and the life of the people of the Sandwich Islands.

Samuel J. Mills, Jr., who was to become a close friend of Obookiah, was the leading spirit of the group of students at Williams College who were intensely interested in religious matters. Following the revival, these young men held two prayer meetings each week to pray for the evangelization of the world. On Wednesday afternoons they met beneath the willow trees near the college campus, and on Saturday afternoons they gathered under the maples in Sloan's meadow.

"It was a sultry afternoon in August, 1806, that five men met for a prayer meeting beneath the trees in Sloan's meadow. The afternoon was laden with moisture, and the threatening clouds had doubtless detained many who on a fair day would have been present. The five who attended were Samuel J. Mills, Jr., James Richards, Francis Robbins, Harvey Loomis, and Byram Green. The meeting was interrupted by the approaching storm. It began to rain. The thunder rolled with deafening sound, familiar to those who dwelt among the hills. The sharp, quick lightning seemed like snapping whips, driving the men to shelter. They crouched beside a large haystack which stood on the spot now marked by a missionary monument. Here, partially protected from the storm, they discussed the situation in Asia. The work of the East India Company, with which they were all somewhat acquainted, naturally turned their thoughts to the people with whom the company sought trade."

Samuel Mills waxed eloquent in urging the possibility and the need of missionary work in Asia. Mr. Loomis objected, saying that he felt that before a mission could be carried on, the East must first become civilized. The others contended that God would cooperate with all who did their part for "He would that all should be partakers of the salvation of Christ."

"Finally, at Mills' word, 'Come, let us make it a subject of prayer under the haystack,' while the dark clouds were gathering and the clear sky was coming, they all knelt in prayer. When Mills prayed he remembered certain objections raised by Loomis in heated discussion, and with all the intensity of his being he prayed: 'O God, strike down the arm with the red artillery of heaven, that shall be raised against the heralds of the cross.' "

At the close of the meeting, Mills saying, "We can do it if we will," the group joined in singing,

> "Let all the heathen writers join
>   to form a perfect book,
>   Great God, if once compared with thine,
>   How mean their writings look."

The group organized themselves into a band which they called the *Brethren,* but which has come down through the years in missionary lore as *The Haystack.* Mills' words, "We can do it if we will," became the guiding spirit of the Haystack Band, the influence of which was to accomplish great things in the mission fields of the world.

It was·four years later that Captain Brintnall, with Obookiah and Thomas, reached New Haven. As in all college towns, students were about everywhere, and Obookiah and Thomas evidently attracted attention. They were "heathen" boys. For some reason, Thomas had the first opportunity to study English. Obookiah says in his journal, "Friend Thomas went to school to one of the students in the college before I thought of going to school. I heard that a ship was ready to sail from New York within a few days for Hawaii. The Captain was willing that I might take leave of this country and go home if I wish. But this was disagreeable to my mind. I wished to continue in this country a little longer. I staid another week. Saw Mr. E. W. D. who first taught me to read and write."

The meeting with Mr. Edward Dwight changed the world for Obookiah. Edward Dwight was a student at Yale. One day, as he was entering the college, he saw Obookiah sitting crying on the steps. He was dressed in a rough sailor's suit and appeared so unpromising a boy that Mr. Dwight almost passed him by. But when he saw that Obookiah was in tears, he stopped and asked him what the trouble was, and Obookiah replied that he had no one to teach him. Obookiah tells of the meeting: "The first time I saw him, he enquired whether I was one who came over with Thomas (for Thomas was known among many scholars in College). I told him I was one who came over with Thomas. He then

asked me if I wished to learn to read and write. I told him that I was.
He wished me to come to his room that night and begin to learn. So
that I went in the evening and began to read in the spelling book. Mr. D.
wished me to come to his room at any time when it is agreeable to the
Captain with whom I then lived. I went home that night and the next
morning I mentioned all this matter to the Captain. He was pleased
and he wished me to go to school to Mr. D. Thus I continued in school
for several months."

Mr. Dwight writes that when he asked Obookiah if he wished to
learn, his countenance began to brighten. And when it was proposed
that he come to the college for that purpose, he seized it with great
eagerness. "It was not long after he began to study and had obtained
some further knowledge of the English language, that he gave evidence
that the dullness which was thought to be indicated by his countenance,
formed no part of his character. It soon appeared that his eyes were open
to everything that passed around him, and that he had an unusual
degree of discernment with regard to persons and things of every description that came within his notice. When he began to read in words
of one or two syllables in the spelling book, there were certain sounds
which he found it very difficult to articulate. This was true especially
of syllables that contained the letter R, a letter which occasioned him
more trouble than all others. In pronouncing it, he uniformly gave it
the sound of L. At every different reading an attempt was made to
correct the pronunciation. The language generally used was. "Try,
Obookiah, it is very easy."

Later on, when Obookiah better understood English, Dwight talked
with him about the customs of his own country. Among other things,
Obookiah told of the manner in which his countrymen drank from a
spring when out hunting. They made a cup of their hands by so
clasping them together, adjusting the thumbs and bending the hands,
as to form a vessel which would contain a considerable quantity of
water. Obookiah demonstrated this. "After preparing his hands he was
able from the pliableness of his arms to raise them entirely to his
mouth without turning them at all from their horizontal position."
Dwight tried the experiment himself but found that before he could
get his hands to his mouth, they were so inverted that most of the water
was lost. He tried over and over again until he became discouraged.
Then Obookiah, with a very expressive countenance, said to him, "Try,
Mr. D. It is very easy."

Edwin Dwight also tells of his first conversation with Obookiah
about the religion of his own people. He explained to Mr. Dwight:

"Hawaii gods, they wood, burn; me go home, put 'em in fire, burn 'em up. They no see, no hear, no anything."

The time soon came when Obookiah wished to be more independent. He felt that he had stayed with Captain Brintnall long enough. He talked this over with Mr. Dwight and asked him if it might be possible for him to go somewhere to school and at the same time earn his living. It was arranged for him to live with the family of Dr. Dwight, the president of Yale College. He was happy there and made rapid progress in his studies.

In the meantime, Samuel Mills had returned to Yale. One evening, when calling upon Edwin Dwight, he met Obookiah. Mr. Mills remained in New Haven several months. He became so interested in Obookiah that, when he left, he took him with him to his father's home in Torringford. In writing of his life with the Mills family, Obookiah says: "It seemed to me as my own home. It was. And I have made my home there frequently."

The Rev. Mr. Mills and his son, Samuel's brother, were farmers. While Obookiah continued his studies under their direction, he was also learning many things about farming: cutting wood, pulling flax, mowing, and other important matters concerned with the running of a farm. Mr. Mills, Samuel's father, in a letter to a friend, says there was something very unusual about Obookiah: "His attention to what passed before him and his talent of imitation were singular. He had never mowed a clip until he came to live with me. My son furnished him with a scythe. He stood and looked on to see the use made of it and at once followed to the surprise of everyone who saw him. We furnished him with a sickle. He stood and looked and followed on. It was afterward observed by a person who was in the field that there were not two reapers who excelled him. In these respects and others he was truly a remarkable youth."

So carefully was Obookiah's education continued under the teaching of the Mills family that, in a few months, he was able to read the Testament and to speak English just as readily as he learned to read. He became proficient, in a manner, at writing. He wrote his first letter to his friend Thomas, who was still in New Haven; his second letter was to his instructor, Edwin Dwight.

"Mr. E. D. Sir:

I here now, this place, Torringford. I glad see you very much. I laugh Tom Hopoo—He say 'Obookiah write me that? Me no write.' I want you tell Tom, Mr. S. Mills say if we be good boys we shall have friends. One morning you know I come into your room in college and you tell me—read—you say, what C.A.P. spell. Then I say, pig. I spell four syllables now and I say what is the chief end of man. I like you much. I like your brother and your friend Mr. Dean. I wear this great coat you gave me to meeting every Sunday. I wish you write me a letter and tell me what Tom do.

This from

Henry Obookiah."

At this time Samuel Mills was a student at Andover and he decided that Obookiah should go there with him. Samuel Mills evidently wished for Obookiah the more intensive religious instruction of the divinity school, looking forward to the possibility of his becoming a missionary. Obookiah tells of his experience at Andover. He says in his journal that he enjoyed his association with the students. "I spent a little time with some of them, and in going from one room to another to recite to them, for I was taken under their care. Whenever I got a lesson I had a right to go to any room in college to recite." One can scarcely picture Obookiah among the Andover men, going from room to room as it pleased him. The spirit of the Haystack Band was, evidently, responsible for this freedom, and Obookiah's personality won him many warm friends.

The Andover experiment did not prove to be what Samuel Mills most desired for Obookiah. He finally told him that he thought it would be well for him to go where he could better improve his time. He said he would try to find someone who would support him while he was in school, and Obookiah was taken to Bradford Academy. In telling of his life at Bradford, Obookiah says: "The people where I boarded at the house of Dea. H., were a most pious family. But while I was here in school I lost all, and became very ignorant of religion by being among some unserious company."

A letter written in these years by Mr. Joshua Coffin and preserved by Dr. George Allen, a distinguished clergyman of Massachusetts, gives Obookiah's story of the death of Captain Cook. This letter was published for the first time in *The Friend* in Honolulu, in March, 1875. It is here quoted from that paper:

"Dear Sir:

In the summer of 1811 I attended the Academy at Bradford, and was a boarder in the family of Deacon Jno. Haseltine, whose family consisted of himself, his wife, son, and three daughters, Abigale, Mary, Ann (afterwards Mrs. Judson) and several boarders among whom was that very interesting native of Hawaii, Obookiah. He gave me at different times a particular account of his life, adventures &c. He gave me a particular account of the death of Captain Cook and the causes which led it. Said he,

" 'Captain Cook he came to Hawaii on a ship and he had a great many sailors. One day a sailor tie a boat to the shore with a rope. Then the sailor came and say Hawaii steal the boat and they *didn't*; the wind and the wave they carry him away. The sailor get mad, Hawaii men get mad, wouldn't give sailor no hog, no coconut, no banana, no wood. Then sailor go ashore and find no wood and so he get old wooden god and take on board the ship and burn in caboose. The King of Hawaii he mad and Captain Cook he mad too.'

" 'Why was the king mad?'

" 'You see,' said Obookiah, 'Hawaii men take a log and make a great wood god, look just like a man, and when they have a new king, they kill men and hang them up right before the wood god.'

" 'But,' said I, 'Did they think the wood god knew anything?'

" 'O, no,' said he, 'when they get the wood god all made and put up, then the spirit come and live in the wood and when the wood get old they make a new wood god and spirit go out of the old wood god and live in the new one. The Hawaii men get mad because the sailor burned up old wood god' (deeming it, I suppose, a sort of sacrilege). 'Then,' said Obookiah, 'the sailor began to fire bullets at Hawaii men and Hawaii men hold up blankets, then boards. Then Captain Cook heard the noise and came running down to see what was the matter. Then one man say, "You kill Capt. Cook but he 'fraid.' Then a man say "I will," and he came behind him and kill him with a spear.'

" 'Well,' said I, 'what did they do with Captain Cook?'

" 'They cut him in pieces and carried him up into the mountains and burnt him.'

" 'Why,' I said, 'did they burn him?' 'O,' said he, 'they fraid his soul live and go back to King George and tell him how Hawaii men kill Capt. Cook, and then King George send men and kill Hawaii men and so they burnt up body and soul together.'

" 'How,' said I, 'do you know all these things?' 'O, my grandfather tell my father and my father tell me.'

"I have thus hastily given you a very brief outline of a part of many very interesting conversations which I had at various times with this very interesting young man. He was a great favorite with all the family. He had so much frankness, honesty, and sympathy that no one could be offended with him. I am constrained to say that I was one of these persons whom he mentions in his life as 'unserious.' With one or two exceptions the students were not professors of religion. He afterwards, as you well know, became a devout Christian, as did Thomas Hopoo, who came to America in the same ship with him. Please execuse the chirography of this hurried letter and oblige,

Yours truly,

Joshua Coffin."

During vacation at Bradford, Obookiah returned to Andover. His health was not very good and he decided to get work on a farm so that he might be in the open air. He found work about five miles from Andover and spent the summer there. His stay at Bradford seems to have entirely upset his religious life. One day he said to a friend, with whom he lived at Andover, that there was a time when he "wanted to get religion into his head more than into his heart."

The friend with whom he formerly lived at Andover tells that Obookiah was very inquisitive; he would never be satisfied until he saw the whole of a subject. "This was peculiarly observable during an eclipse of the sun, concerning which he asked many troublesome questions; and also in regard to many kinds of business, particularly the mode of levying, collecting and appropriating taxes. He was seen one morning very early with a rule measuring the college buildings and fences. He was asked why he did it. He smiled and said, 'So that I shall know how to build when I go back to Hawaii.' When he heard a word that he did not understand he would ask, 'How you spell? How you spell?' When I told him he never forgot."

Samuel Mills and his family kept close touch with Obookiah. They, with others, felt that he held great promise as a missionary to his own people. His growing knowledge of the scriptures was a surprise to all who knew him. He studied the Bible day and night, and his conversation was constantly filled with quotations from the Bible in application to daily life. When he did not fully understand the meaning of a passage he would insist upon a more explicit interpretation. In talking with one of his friends one day he asked, "What our Saviour mean when he say: 'In my father's house are many mansions—I go prepare a place for you.' What he mean—I go prepare a place?"

While Obookiah was receiving his first education in English and new experiences were deepening his understanding, the prayer meeting under the haystack was bearing fruit. Samuel Mills and the Brethren were determined to push forward their plan to go as missionaries to foreign lands. They decided to appeal to the powers within the church, asking for advice and assistance, even to the financing of their project.

The history of the *American Board of Commissioners for Foreign Missions* relates that the elders of the church were greatly moved by the appeal of four Academy students who appeared at the annual meeting of the committee at Bradford. The discussion following was long and heated, but a favorable decision was finally made, which, eventually, led to the organization, in 1810, of the American Board.

When it was decided that the American Board should send missionaries abroad, Obookiah could not understand why his friends did not leave immediately for Hawaii. He took one of them aside for a private talk. He pleaded earnestly that he go with him to Hawaii to preach the gospel. When the response was not what Obookiah had hoped for, he said, "You 'fraid? You know our Saviour say 'He that will save his life shall lose it, and he that will lose his life for my sake, same shall save it' " At another time, one of the older clergymen asked him why he was so anxious to return to Hawaii. He replied, "To preach the gospel to my countrymen." The minister then asked him what he would say to them about their wooden gods, and he answered, "Nothing." "But," said the clergyman, "suppose your countrymen should tell you that preaching Jesus Christ was blaspheming their gods, and should put you to death?" To this Obookiah replied with emphasis, "If that be the will of God, *I am ready, I am ready.*"

But changes were coming into Obookiah's life. In 1814 a special committee of men was appointed by the American Board to plan and supervise Obookiah's further training as a missionary. The Board felt that a school for heathen youths should be opened without delay if the funds could be obtained. The education of the American Indian, who had always been classed as heathen, formed the background of missionary educational work in New England for many years. Dartmouth College owed its inception to one American Indian who was converted to Christianity in the Whitefield Revival of 1740. This history was no doubt an encouragement to the men who decided to open a school.

A revival was started at Amherst, and Obookiah was called upon to assist at these meetings. In writing of Obookiah at this time, a friend says in a letter: "Obookiah had now attained the full stature of nearly six feet and he presented a singularly impressive, dignified, graceful and attractive presence. His handsome olive complexion and piercing eye, his fine command of English and an affectionate disposition, keen mind and common sense won friends everywhere." It was said at Amherst that Obookiah's personal interest was so great and his speaking was so interesting, that much was accomplished in breaking down the old prejudice that the heathen were not capable of receiving instruction and education. This was the result which had been hoped for from Obookiah's presence at the revival. Interest and money came from all sides, and plans for the school were carried out.

The American Board first opened the Foreign Mission School at South Farms, Litchfield, Connecticut, but it was later permanently settled at Cornwall, Connecticut, that being chosen because of "the fine location, healthful climate, and the sound moral and Christian influence that pervade that community."

Both Obookiah and Thomas entered the school at South Farms and later continued their studies at the Cornwall School. Obookiah was a natural leader, able to influence the students. The group of Hawaiian boys, who, like Thomas and himself, had reached New England on different sailing vessels, found a great friend in Obookiah. He became their adviser under all circumstances, and, when he made a decision, they accepted it as final. He often talked with the boys about their futures, impressing upon them the value of time, encouraging them to persevere in their studies.

One clergyman who knew Obookiah at Amherst said he had never known anyone who placed so high a value on time. "What others would call leisure hours were working hours for Obookiah. When alone he delighted in his literary studies; when in company improvement was his object. If conversation was not immediately interesting to him he would take his pocket Testament and read."

While Obookiah constantly talked of returning to Hawaii, he kept up his close application to his studies. His inventive mind and his ambition led him into intricate lines of education. Learning something of the grammatical construction of the English language, he determined to make at least a beginning of a system of grammar for his native tongue.

While he was still living at Goshen and before he attended the school, he made his first attempt in translation. He tells about this in his diary: "A part of the time I was trying to translate a few verses of the Scriptures into my own language; in making a kind of spelling book; taking the English alphabet and giving different names and sounds (for his language was not a written language) I spent some time in making a kind of spelling book, dictionary, grammar, &c."

Obookiah later translated the entire book of Genesis and several of the psalms into Hawaiian. A footnote in the little book tells that, while he received some assistance from his teachers in the school and from friends, the manuscripts were all in his own handwriting and must have cost him many months of constant labor. A comment was made at the time: "These manuscripts, though now imperfect, will afford much aid to future Translators and missionaries." And so it has been.

The study of Latin was a joy to Obookiah, and he even ventured into the first book of Euclid's Elements of Geometry. The Hebrew language, however, was his greatest interest, since it so resembled his own. He was delighted when he succeeded in translating Hebrew into Hawaiian.

Obookiah was making every preparation to return to Hawaii, and he hoped that Samuel Mills would go with him. It was a bitter disappointment to him when he learned that Mr. Mills had decided to go to Africa. Samuel Mills, too, was greatly troubled. He said to one of his Brethren, Mr. Gordon Hall: "What does this mean, brother Hall? Do you understand it? Shall he be sent back unsupported? Shall we not rather consider the Southern Islands the proper place for the establishment of a mission?"

The Hawaiian people were born with a heritage of sensitiveness; alert to inner voices, they sometimes seem to almost touch the unknown world. For Obookiah, the Scriptures had a great appeal. The beauty of the language and the art of the great writers inspired his mind, while the spirit of the gospel message enthralled him and set his soul ablaze. All else paled before its power.

From time to time Obookiah made traveling tours throughout New England. He was a traveling evangelist. As he spoke, he experienced a feeling of satisfaction, looking back to the day he sat on the college steps weeping for his ignorance and that of his people. He was now addressing large audiences and he may have been speaking in New Haven. The ministers from the churches were all his friends. One clergyman, in writing of Obookiah, says: "His name was as well known among the churches as that of any prominent minister of the gospel."

The record of Obookiah's work has come down through the years in different parts of the country. A student of a western college who spent his vacation as a colporteur in Indiana writes of meeting an old lady to whom he gave a tract. She told him that she had tracts which were given to her in Connecticut by Henry Obookiah of the Sandwich Islands, more than forty years before, when he was distributing good books. She said that she had brought them west with her in the early days and had often loaned them to her neighbors.

Obookiah continued to distribute good books, but although he was eagerly looking forward to his return to the Islands, he was never again to see the beautiful shores of Hawaii. The bells of the New Year of 1818 had scarcely ceased their ringing when Obookiah was stricken with typhus fever. He was living in the home of the Rev. Timothy Stone, at Cornwall. Mrs. Stone became his nurse as well as his constant friend.

She had help from several of the Hawaiian boys who were in the school, all of whom were devoted to Obookiah.

It was mid-winter in New England. The long, cold days and nights were filled with wonder for those who watched Obookiah's life slowly slipping away. His firm, unfailing faith was amazing even to his closest friends. One of the Hawaiian boys asked him if he was not afraid to die, and he replied emphatically: *"I am not!"* He wanted the Hawaiian boys with him every moment, and was satisfied only when he was told that they were eating or resting. The day before he died he asked that they be called. When they came, he talked with them about their lives, their education, and their futures until he was exhausted. The chilled silence of the New England room was broken only by the muted sobbing of Obookiah's countrymen. A little later, Obookiah lifted his hands and cried out: "Oh, how I want to see Hawaii, but I think I never shall." As the end drew near, he was quiet and composed. He shook hands with each of his friends, and, in their native tongue, he said his last farewell: *"Aloha o'e"* (my love with you).

Within a few months after Obookiah's death, fourteen young men and women volunteered to go as missionaries to the Islands which he had loved. Monuments in New England and Christian churches in Hawaii today honor the memory of Henry Obookiah, the Hawaiian boy who wanted, above all else, to bring to the shores of his homeland the tenets of Christian goodness and grace.

THE SPANIARD

Chapter VI

> *"This day I planted seeds. . . ."*
> —DON FRANCISCO
> DE PAULA MARIN

MUCH OF THE WAVE of foreign influence that engulfed the Hawaiian Islands after their re-discovery by the White Man brought with it grief and tragedy for the Hawaiian people and a gradual loss of many of their lands to the foreigners themselves. We leave to inglorious anonymity those strangers who introduced to Hawaii such alien commodities as firearms and venereal disease, who took for themselves of the richness of the Islands and their inhabitants and offered nothing good or constructive in return. Instead, we point here to a man who, during his forty-odd years' residence, enriched the Islands more than himself, leaving behind him a heritage of unsurpassed beauty and an assurance of what the future might hold of accomplishment and prosperity for the people of Hawaii. His name was Don Francisco de Paula Marin, or, as he was called in the affectionate Hawaiian equivalent, *Manini*.

In 1837 appeared the following unusual notice:

An Editorial
The Sandwich Island Gazette
Obituary
Died
On October 30th, at twelve o'clock,
Don Francisco de Paula Marin.

"We 'come to bury Caesar.' The life of Don Marin, whatever inconsistencies may have chanced to mark its course, has been signalized, if we may credit the testimony of those who knew him best, by examples of industry and by acts of real benefit towards the un-enlightened children of nature. However severe, perchance, be the censure of some who have survived the decease of Don Marin, (we speak now to prevent unnecessary animadversion), it must always have been acknowledged that his industrious perseverance has given the Sandwich Islands many advantages—advantages which if the opinion of those influential men had supported would have afforded to the present population of this land a decided superiority over the actual condition."

S. D. Mackintosh

In 1850, the Royal Agricultural Society was in session. The Minister of Foreign Relations, Mr. Robert C. Wyllie, addressed the assembly.

He gave a careful and comprehensive review of the development of agriculture in the Sandwich Islands from the time of Kamehameha the Great. Passing through early years, he lingered to give emphasis to the work of Don Francisco de Paula Marin, the Spaniard. "From the brief accounts of the life and work of Francisco de Paula Marin, from 1809 to 1820, few of you will doubt that most of the present wealth of these Islands is owing to seeds, roots and plants introduced by this one man. In my opinion it may be fairly questioned if there ever existed in these Islands, or exists at the present time, any man to whom the Hawaiian people are so generally indebted."

Whatever the shadows may have been which marred the life of Don Marin, they have long since, numerous though they may be, been pushed beyond the horizon by the brilliance of his accomplishments. Marin gave to Hawaii the first real understanding of the soil and the possibilities which it held. The great plantations of sugar cane, the tall smokestacks of the sugar mills, the vast number of acres of fragrant pineapples which sweep over Hawaiian valleys, plains, and mountain sides, bringing wealth yet uncounted, are monuments to the knowledge and persever-ance of the young Spaniard who cast his lot with Kamehameha and the Hawaiian people more than a century ago.

Don Marin possessed the "growing hand." In the reports of the Royal Hawaiian Agricultural Society one may read: "He successfully raised oranges, figs, grapes, roses, pineapples, beans, melons, turnips, tobacco, coffee, wheat, barley, cloves, tomatoes, saffron, and cherries. He made butter, cigars, coconut oil, candles, hay and wine. Most of his experiments in growing plants were begun and developed before 1820. He acted as ship's carpenter and he was also a mason, setting an example of thrift and work to the people about him."

It is believed that Don Marin came to the Islands sometime between 1791 and 1794. Mr. Wyllie speaks of his having arrived on the sailing vessel, the *Princess Real,* but no official record marked his coming. There are, however, two stories regarding his arrival which seem to verify each other and are probably true. Aldelbert von Chamisso, the German naturalist who accompanied Captain von Kotzebue, commander of the *Rurick* in the years 1815-1818, came to know Don Marin well. Chamisso says in his journal: "Marin was still very young when at a port on the Spanish-American coast, I believe it was San Francisco, he was sent to a ship with fruit and vegetables. The sailors enticed the boy to drink and he fell asleep. They concealed him. When he awoke he was on the high seas." The second story comes from a sea captain, one Captain Spalding of the *Dolphin.* He says that Don Marin's own account of his coming to the Islands was as follows: "He was invited on board a vessel that visited the California coast. While on the ship, in the evening, he fell asleep and when he awoke he found himself at sea and the vessel running on a fair wind to the Sandwich Islands. All his entreaties to be returned to land were in vain, and he finally arrived off Hawaii." So, evidently, Don Francisco de Paula Marin was shanghaied.

Captain Spalding tells a little more about Marin. He says that he wandered from island to island looking for work. He finally met Kamehameha and followed the fortunes of the great warrior. With Kamehameha he found, not only employment, but friendship as well. If Don Marin followed the fortunes of Kamehameha, he may have been one of the sixteen foreigners who were in the King's service when Kamehameha fought and won the great Battle of Nuuanu. These were stirring times. Marin was young, and, with his warm Spanish temperament, he doubtless responded to the excitement of the time. Chamisso also writes in his journal: "Marin was always helpful when I looked him up, quickly grasping the point I was arriving at. He taught me most of what I know regarding the Islands. During our first conversation something he said interested me very much. It was an account of the latest news regarding Napoleon. He, Marin said, 'would have "fitted" in our Spanish Americas.' I had yet never heard such a statement from a Spaniard."

Francisco de Paula Marin was born in Jerez, Andalusia. The old Spanish city has been famous for centuries for its fine sherry wine. The English word, sherris, is the exact sixteenth century pronunciation of Jerez, and from the name of the city came the name of the wine. Jerez is sixteen miles from Cadiz and only seven miles from the Atlantic coast. Jerez, with its atmosphere of the sea, is still an important and strategic city, and its interesting history, even in his youth, did much to color the background of the life of Don Marin.

There was beauty in Jerez when Marin was a boy. The warmth and color of the old Moorish walls, mellowed by time, which enclosed the city streets; the great cathedral of San Miguel, standing for the faith and the strength of the people; the ancient Moorish castle, every line softened by the years; and the old Town Hall, where matters of state were discussed and settled—these were the landmarks of his youth. One sees Francisco Marin climbing the cathedral steps to attend the morning mass. He was a Romanist by birth and education. The Catholic faith was that in which he believed and which he practiced throughout his life. When the services were over, he wandered through the vineyards, for it was at Jerez that he learned his first lessons in agriculture and in making wine.

The story is told that Don Marin came to California with an expedition from Spain under Don Bodega y Quadra, a man who became well known in the great Northwest. Doubtless Marin knew something of the history of the early Spanish explorers and believed that the entire Pacific Ocean belonged to Spain. When he reached San Francisco, he may have felt somewhat at home. It was Spanish-America, and he was surrounded by his own countrymen.

Spain holds a marked place in maritime history. In the early centuries, through discoveries in the New World, she claimed the exclusive right to the use of the Pacific Ocean. But with the development of the fur trade along the Northwest coast of America, both English and American ships carried their cargoes over the Pacific. This, Spain claimed, was illegal, but she was helpless to prevent it. The Spanish colonial governors received orders to capture, if possible, all poachers which should put into their harbors. The Commandant at San Francisco was ordered "by force or fraud" to seize the *Columbia,* the first ship to carry the American flag around Cape Horn. At an earlier period, in 1789, two Spanish ships were sent to Nootka Sound, and several English fur traders were seized, among them the *Princess Royal.* The *Princess Royal* once visited the Sandwich Islands under the flag of Spain. About the time that Don Marin came to the Islands, the final treaty was made by which Spain acknowledged "an equal right for English subjects with Spaniards to carry on all branches of commerce in Pacific waters." But while the Spaniards in the early centuries preceded all other nations in exploration and discovery, they did little colonizing. No Spanish settlement was ever made in the Sandwich Islands. Spanish ships came and went, but the Spaniards did not settle in Hawaii, and, as far as his countrymen were concerned, Don Marin was very much alone.

In a pile of rubbish in the cellar of the residence of a former premier of Hawaii was found the dilapidated journal of Don Marin. A translation of the old journal is now preserved in the Public Archives of Hawaii. It was written in Spanish and was translated into English by Mr. Robert C. Wyllie so that the important history which it contained might be made available. The first entry is dated November 14, 1799. Mr. Wyllie points out that there is reason to believe that several volumes were lost. As far as is known, the original journals which were found were destroyed after Mr. Wyllie's death.

A journal or a diary is not only a record but an interpretation. Lives once lived live again in the pages of history. As Don Marin set down his words in beautiful Spanish script, he may have felt that such recording might be of importance to those who would follow him. So it was and is. The lost pages of the journal, if they existed, would surely have told Marin's experience in his association with Kamehameha in his last great wars, and of his own adjustment to circumstances. Notwithstanding Kamehameha's continued friendship and increasing intimacy and his own understanding and personal liking for the people, Marin was not blind to his possibly precarious situation. He was still the foreigner and a Spaniard. He may have been inwardly apprehensive when he wrote in his journal: "A female chief dies and a woman and a boy were killed to be buried with her." This, it is said, was the last human sacrifice to be made in the Hawaiian Islands, for old customs were passing.

Accompanied by Marin, travelling from island to island, Kamehameha was impressed with Marin's interest in agriculture, and allotted land to him for his experiments. It was in Honolulu that Marin made and developed his first planting. Gilbert Farquhar Matthewson, Esq., in his *Narrative of a Visit to Brazil, Chile, Peru and the Sandwich Islands,* tells how greatly impressed he was with Marin's gardens and his success in growing plants. He says: "He spoke much in favor of the soil and assured me that if the natives, by any means, could be forced to regular habits of industry they might turn the whole country into a garden."

Deciding that he would spend his life in the Islands, Don Marin married into the Hawaiian group, as did John Young. His wife was a woman of standing among her people, but she did not live many years. She left him several children. Marin later married a high chieftess, and together they raised his large family of sons and daughters, descendants of whom are living in Honolulu today. Travellers tell of seeing the Marin home, a two-story adobe house, from the harbor. It was located near the Nuuanu stream in what is now the Vineyard and School street section of the city, and Marin's vineyards covered acres of that part of Honolulu, the land of which had been allotted to him by the King. He also ran a boarding house for transient white men.

So the Marin family was well established in Hawaii and Don Marin found himself becoming an increasingly important personage in Kamehameha's kingdom. But the years brought misfortune as well as joy. Marin writes in his journal:

"This day died my daughter, Francisca, who was baptized at 2 P.M."

Two days later he adds: "This day I buried my daughter, Francisca, in my land within the fence."

Many entries in his journal say, simply: "This day I beat my wife." Since Don Marin was an honorable gentleman, it follows that he was merely adhering to the Hawaiian custom of the day.

Civilization was progressing, and Kamehameha was interested in progress. Kalanimoku, dependable and strong, was the prime minister.

Boki, handsome, ambitious and outstanding, was the governor of Oahu, and Kaahumanu, the young queen, held the center of the political and social stage. These, with many other high chiefs, including Liholiho, the son and heir of Kamehameha, constituted the court. They accepted Don Marin because he was helpful and entertaining and because he had come from the outside world. Amazed at his knowledge, they believed in his powers.

When the people learned that Don Marin understood the use of herbs in the healing of the sick—herbs which old Hawaii had never known—they listened to his advice and appreciated his willingness to help them. He became to them Manini, "the man who knew." There were continuous epidemics of fatal diseases, and Marin's journal tells that many people died. But Marin himself was saving lives.

The people of the court, including Kamehameha, received from Marin all sorts of personal service. Marin recorded, "Made two pairs of trousers for the King." He tells also of making trousers for Kalanimoku, and that together they went to cut wood. One day Marin called upon Kamehameha and the minister, taking with him valuable presents: a great coat made of fine cloth and a cigar case of tortoise shell. At another time he presented Kamehameha with two bars of iron. This was an important gift. Iron was precious. He also gave the King a saw, a gimlet, and two panes of glass. No doubt Marin had opportunity to accumulate these things in his trading with the captains of the ships which stopped over in Honolulu. He tells of having breakfast with Kamehameha and of boiling potatoes for him. The King previously had helped himself to Marin's own great coat. This he returned at the breakfast. Marin wrote, too, of building a stone house for the King. Kamehameha may have been interested in having a stone house, although he said that he much preferred the cooler and more comfortable grass houses.

Kaahumanu, while imperious in manner, was friendly to Marin. She sent some fine birds to him from the island of Maui and two hundred and fifty coconuts from her estate at Waikiki. The nuts were probably meant for coconut oil. Kaahumanu liked nice things. Marin painted a chest for her and he gave her several pieces of silk of different colors. Marin went fishing with Kaahumanu and the King, and tells that Kaahumanu gave him forty fathoms of rope. These were days of great fishing. Marin describes a "fishing feast" when 50,000 fish were caught in the nets and ten thousand people attended the party. Life was not prosaic in Honolulu in the early eighteen hundreds.

Many opportunities were turned Marin's way by Kamehameha and the chiefs. Following the King's example, he soon learned to traffic in sandalwood and pearls. For Marin, it was a fascinating experience to lay the foundation of a fortune with shining pearls and "perfumed wood" either for himself or for the King. While the products belonged to Kamehameha, he may have shared his good fortune with Manini.

"A native brought some pearls for scissors, a looking glass and a pipe.

"20 pearls	Bought 20 pearls and to receive
" 6 pearls	10 more
"10 pearls	Bought 14 pearls.
"14 pearls	
" 2 pearls - for a knife."	

On February 16, 1812, he wrote: "Today the steamer *Maiope* left for Maui and Hawaii and the Minister gave me the estate called Oau, on Jamacua on Veji." (The estate of Au, Hamakua, Hawaii.) Other lands were also given to Marin. He was constantly studying the different types of soil and the use to which they might be developed. He knew and taught that the soil was the hope of the Islands. Among Marin's occupations for a year he listed:

"Planted coffee, cotton, made lime, planted cloves, salted pork, made pickles, planted tomatoes, turnips, pepper, and chiles, sowed wheat and barley and made castor oil, soap, molasses, syrup of lemon juice, planted saffron, cherries, and made shirts. Planting sugar. Making extensive purchases from vessels for the King, planting vines for the King, selling vegetables for the King, making nails." At another time Marin wrote of making 33 gallons of wine, 5 flasks of brandy and a barrel of beer. He walked in his vineyard and found that many branches of grapes had been carried off. He dug a ditch for the vineyard.

Through the years, Don Marin was always conscious of the needs of the people. He began raising small animals, especially goats and rabbits. For this purpose he was given Mokuumeume, the "Isle of Strife," now known as Ford Island, located in the center of Pearl Harbor. On February 9th, 1818, Marin wrote, "This day, Kalanimoku gave me the sea of the island of little goats." He also tells that, when he arrived at the island to take possession, the people killed a small hog and he took possession of the sea. By this he meant that his friends gave Marin a *luau* (feast) in his honor. He recorded in his journal: "This day I castrated 35 little goats and a man came to prevent me from taking the sea of the island, and I sent a man to the minister who said that it is time." So, according to Hawaiian custom, Marin held the right of the sea which bordered his land.

The War of 1812 between England and America interfered with trade in the Pacific, but ships sailing around Cape Horn stopped at the

Islands on their way to Canton. Among these vessels was the merchant ship *Albatross* under the command of Captain Nathan Winship, of Boston. The ship spent considerable time in Honolulu. Captain Winship became well acquainted with the chiefs and with the people. While the *Albatross* was in port, Marin wrote:

"July 4th, 1812. The ship kept the 4th of July today. A grand feast."

Kamehameha and Marin, accompanied by the queens and several of the chiefs, including Kalanimoku, visited the ship. The King remained on board all day. He was given three salutes. The same day Marin recorded: "On board the *Albatross* they made three christians, the daughter of Captain Guynap, Maria Kalanimoku, and my daughter Maria Marin." The Christian religion was beginning to take root in the Sandwich Islands.

In 1812 an opportunity came to Don Marin to make a voyage to California. A ship from New York was in port. There were passengers and Marin was invited to join them. They were going to the Columbia River country. But, for some reason, Kamehameha objected to Marin's leaving at that time. Three years later Marin did make the voyage to New Archangel and return, and it is believed that he later made several voyages not only to California, but also to the Orient. Many business men were traveling back and forth, stopping at the Islands, and there is every reason to think that Don Marin may have been one of them. Old correspondence so indicates.

The Sandwich Islands were in touch with the outside world. News traveled over the seas in those days of maritime adventure. Don Marin wrote in his journal on October 14th, 1812, that word had been received that Bonaparte was a prisoner of the Russians. While this was not true, the news brought the excitement of world interest. "At 2 P.M. came a schooner from Boston, Captain Brown. I do not know the name of the schooner. It brought the news of peace with all the world." A feast was given in honor of the Emperor of Russia.

But Honolulu was not so peaceful. Many white men of questionable character were constantly making trouble. Manini tells of the repairing of muskets and of the accumulation of ammunition. Pirates were caught in the woods and punished on board the ships. Sailors were deserting. Kamehameha had gone into residence at his old home in Kailua on the island of Hawaii. From there he had sent word that all of the white people not holding land under the King were to be sent away. A ship was in readiness to take them. This edict was not, finally, put into execution. Kamehameha, evidently, changed his mind.

Don Marin acted as an interpreter for Kamehameha on the island of Oahu, as did John Young on the island of Hawaii. To do this he must have found the languages of the men of the sea a strange medley, but through constant application and continued practice he did acquire considerable efficiency as a linguist. In a letter to a friend in California he wrote, "Please pardon the mistakes which this letter may contain as I have so many languages mixed."

Don Marin was a very hospitable person. Travelers speak of his house as being the meeting place for the captains of the ships while in port, and that Mr. Marin often served tea instead of wine to his guests. Marin had been told by Kamehameha to harbor no white men in his house, but when a negro, who has escaped from the ship *Liberty,* asked for his protection and a lodging, Manini took him in. At the same time, he "signed the cross to the entry."

Don Marin was a deeply religious man at heart, retaining the ideals of his boyhood in old Spain. His journal, year by year, gives the reality of his Christian faith. In the latter part of his life he made a copy in his journal of the Lord's Prayer. It is written in alternating lines of Spanish and Hawaiian . . .

"Our Father who art in heaven, hallowed be thy name. Thy will be done on earth as in heaven. Give us today our daily bread, Lord, and forgive us our debts as we forgive our debtors. And let us not fall into temptation, but deliver us from all evil. Amen.

"For my sin, for my great sin, and for so much, I pray to the always blessed Virgin Mary, to Saint Peter and to Saint Paul, and to all the saints, and to the Father, for I sinned gravely in thought, word and deed.

"I believe in God, the Father Almighty, creator of heaven and earth. I believe in Jesus Christ, his only son, so that we may be worthy to obtain the precious promises of our Lord, Jesus Christ. By the sign of the holy cross, from our enemies deliver us, Lord our God."

Definite changes in the life of the Islands were imminent. Trade with foreign ships steadily increased. The whaling industry was on the way. Men of responsibility were looking anxiously to the future. Kalanimoku placed Marin in command of the *Bordeaux Packet* which Manini called the *Craymoco* (Kalanimoku). Kamehameha purchased the *Albatross,* and put Marin in charge of re-equipping the vessel. These ships, and others owned by the King and the chiefs, plied between the different islands and also made longer voyages in the interest of the sandalwood trade. A captaincy was granted to Marin by Captain Bouchard of the war frigate *Argentina.* At a later date, Captain Bouchard granted Don Marin a commission which reads, "Captain in the Armies Patriotic of the provinces of the Rio de La Plata." This commission authorized Marin to take charge of any prize ships that were brought to the Islands. So, Marin was becoming a man of the sea as well as an agriculturist.

These new honors, with their added responsibility, may have also given Manini greater opportunity in his chosen field. The people were learning the value of the soil. Sometime the land would surely come into its own. He would plant and build until all the world would hear and know. The Sandwich Islands would stand supreme in production of the soil!

"This day they brought me the first orange, though I planted the seed eight years ago."

Kamehameha remained at Kailua. He was tired. His strenuous life was telling on his health. The important chiefs were with him. Kalanimoku assumed the greater responsibilities in matters of State. In January, Governor Boki had married the princess Liliha. They were with the King. Marin continued his work on Oahu, caring for many details of the King's business.

It was springtime. While to the average person the changes of the seasons in Hawaii are but slightly marked, to Manini, every morning and evening as they blended through the years, seem to have brought to him a deepening understanding of the mystic quality of the world around him. He wrote in the journal:

"It was cloudy in the morning with squalls of small rain, and fog from the North. At half past seven in the morning the tide fell five feet in five minutes; in the same time it again flowed and it again fell about 3 or 3½ feet, and in 5 or 6 minutes it flowed again, and so on nine times it fell and flowed from 4 to 5 feet, and at 6 it was falling and flowing but very regularly until sunset.

"April 13th, 1819.

"This day the sea while ebbing, ebbed more quickly, but in flowing in five minutes after ebbing it rose two feet, and again in the same time it rose higher than before and from half past three in the afternoon it was falling and flowing till 6 when it began to ebb."

To the Hawaiians this "extraordinary tide" foreboded ill. The people became depressed and apprehensive. On April 15th, word was received on Oahu of the serious sickness of Kamehameha. Manini took time to leave a note in his journal:

"April 16th,

"This day the Bordeaux Packet proceeding from Veji (Hawaii) came seeking me to cure the King." Marin sailed immediately for Kailua. He found Kamehameha very sick. Days passed and, while everything possible was done for him, the King continued to fail. As a last

resort, Manini prepared a stimulant hoping to relieve acute suffering.
He, himself, carried the calabash into the King. Kamehameha grasped
the bowl, but when the odor of the liquor reached him, he was angry
and dashed the contents into Manini's face. Marin crawled from his
presence, knowing his life was in danger. He said, "If he do so to me
again I will resent it." He knew and respected Kamehameha's habit of
temperance, acquired in his later life, but he and the King had been
close friends for twenty-five years, and Kamehameha's refusal to accept
from him the help he might give was a great shock. Nevertheless, Manini opened his journal and wrote the words:

"May 8th, 1819.

"This day the King, Kamehameha died, at three o'clock in the
morning, aged 60 years and six months. People are coming from all
parts of the island to weep for the King."

* * * * *

Unfamiliar lights were appearing along the shores of old Hawaii,
lights from ships that were strangers in Hawaiian waters. The whalers
had arrived. To Don Marin, the steadily increasing interest in the
Islands by men from foreign countries emphasized more strongly the
pattern of his own future. Young Liholiho was now the King. What
that might portend was uncertain. Though kings might come and kings
might go, the soil would still remain, and to the soil he had given his life.

The months following the death of Kamehameha were filled with
new undertakings. Manini, in constant cooperation with Governor Boki,
was given the care of much important business. His opinion and his
judgment were relied upon. He was a man of large affairs. On November 30th, 1819, he wrote:

"The governor gave an entertainment with forty seats and covers.
He fired 50 guns during the toasts and the American ship the same.
He gave me the rank of Captain and passed me two epaulettes. The
toasts were Kamehameha 1st and 2nd, and the President of America
and the King of England, and the dinner ended at sunset."

The Russian Consul visited Honolulu on his way to Manila, and a
ship from Calcutta arrived bringing copper. There were two Spaniards
on board the Calcutta vessel. Marin speaks of one of them, Don Herrea,
as having purchased 100 pounds of sugar, twenty barrels of beef at
$30.00 a barrel, and fifty pounds of coffee. Such details constantly
crowded Manini's time.

Through the years Don Marin had kept in touch with his friends in
America. Old letters, written in Spanish, explain how he was able to
continue his planting. He constantly appealed to his friends to send him
seeds and plants. Among his closest acquaintances were the padres of

the California missions. Through their interest and the cooperation of
the captains of the ships that came to the Islands, seeds and plants
reached Hawaii, not only from California but also from Mexico, Peru,
and the old world. One friend asked Manini to send him some sweet
potatoes, as there were none in California. He sent Marin "Mattock
hoes to work the earth," commenting, "All the missions are using them."
Another friend wrote, "I am glad you have grapes that give raisins like
those in the promised land."

From San Diego, Marin received young peach trees. His friend
explained in his letter, "I fear they will not do well in a warm land for
they like coolness. Keep them in the box until the month of February
and then transplant them." This man also shipped a box of olive trees.
After explaining about the trees, he continued, "The Commando General
is in the Capitol at Monterey at present, with the deputation holding sessions, with whom I shall speak on the first occasion regarding
his proposing you to the High Government of Mexico for the Consul
or agent of this Republic." At another time this same friend sent Marin
a second lot of peach trees. He also included the seeds of a medicinal
herb from Peru, regarding which he comments, "I presume you also
know its great value, principally to reduce fevers, dropsy and kidney
stones, and that it should be taken very close together and if only two
or three times a month, at three separate times." The letter asks Marin
for coconuts.

In time Marin was able to return many compliments from his own
gardens, but he still asked his friends for more and more assistance in
his planting. He wrote, "I shall greatly appreciate it if you will do me
the favor of sending me olive branches to plant here, also laurel or rue,
rosemary, henna, endives and one or two plants of mint and what they
might be worth the Captain will pay you. I enclose for you in this letter,
seed of the egg plant of which I think there is none on the coast, also
a good trinket for Luella; and if there should be anything in these
Islands you desire let me know with all confidence for it will be a great
pleasure for me, and don't fail to write me when you have occasion, and
may you command this your true friend and servant who esteems you
and kisses your hand.

"Francisco de Paula Marin

"Island of Oahu
"Port of Honolulu."

In a few simple words Don Marin recorded on April 14th, 1820,
one of the most important events in Hawaiian history. "This day
anchored a brig of medium size called the *Thaddeus*, Captain Blanchard,
bringing missionaries to these Islands."

When the missionaries arrived in Honolulu, Marin received them very cordially and offered his assistance in helping them get settled. He had grass houses built for them and did everything he could to make them comfortable. There was probably no one in Honolulu who better understood what missionaries might accomplish in the Islands. In his journal Manini recorded: "This day the missionary ladies and gents came to visit me." "This day I planted seeds given me by the missionaries." "There was church service in the house of the missionaries." A few days later he added, "Mr. Chaplin, the surgeon of the mission, and Mr. Bingham, came to see me, and I sent some honey to the mission family." A new era had opened for the Islands.

Liholiho, the King, arrived in Honolulu. With Don Marin he called upon the missionaries. They also visited the Russian ship which was in port. The King asked Manini why the foreigners carried guns when they came on shore. Marin said it was for self protection and not to do injury.

Kaahumanu gave a fine dinner in honor of the King, and the missionaries served a tea. Don Marin tells of these social events and of his attending them. He also received the following invitation:

> "His Majesty's compliments to
> Mr. Marin. Requests his company
> to dine at 3 o'clock tomorrow.
> Tuesday, May 15th
> 1821."

Marin tells that he spent the entire day with Liholiho and that they rode horseback to Waikiki, and that the King gave him land in Kaneohe.

Days, weeks, months went by. The community of Honolulu was stirred and troubled by new experiences. Marin, in his journal, made many brief notes which indicate the feeling of the people. He wrote that the missionaries were trying to establish new laws and were meeting opposition from the chiefs. Times were changing, but Don Marin, while assisting and advising on all sides, continued his careful watch of agricultural interests.

"Grapes grown in Lahaina"
"White Men steal lemons."

Marin had been in the Islands twenty-nine years. There were times when he felt homesick and depressed. He was a strange man, alternately loved and tolerated by those who knew him. There were times when even the great Kamehameha couldn't suffer his company; there were others when he gratefully sought it. He ardently promoted the Catholic mission in Hawaii, but lacked the strength of character to support them when they were touched by persecution. Although he seemingly cooperated with them, he disliked the Protestant missionaries and, in turn, was disliked by them. He expressed his discouragement in a very personal letter to an old friend in California. After first asking for more seeds and more plants, he continued: "Also I shall appreciate it if you will let me know if some ranch can be bought as I shall do it in order to return to the coast to die among my own people, and if I shouldn't go, my sons will go that they might be baptized and live with people of reason." Marin was anxious to have his children baptized in the Catholic faith. But neither Manini nor his sons went to the mainland to live. They had adopted Hawaii as their home.

Throughout the years Don Marin had, perhaps unconsciously, absorbed something of the inner spirit of old Hawaii. In many ways the traditional life of the Polynesians was reflected in his own. The scientist, Peter Corney, in his *Early Northern Pacific Voyages,* tells the following tale relative to Marin which relates back to Ford Island.

"In my tour with Mr. Manning (Manini) we visited the ruin of a large stone house which had formerly belonged to a great chief. It had a double fence of human bones round it; these bones were bones of enemies killed in the wars before the Islands were visited by Europeans. The bones of the great chief are said to be still in the house. The natives are afraid to go near it, preferring to go round five or six miles to passing it.

"Mr. Manning also had an island in Pearl River, as before stated, which we also visited. It is about two miles in circumference, having a large cave in the center. It is covered with goats, hogs, and rabbits. Only one family resides there, a man, his wife and three children, all belonging to Mr. M. One evening the man gave us an account of a singular affair. He was one night awakened by some person calling him by name and telling him to attend to what he said. He looked up and was much terrified on beholding the pale form of the late king, Paleioholani, before him who told him as he valued his life so must he perform what he enjoined, which was to go to the cave where he would find his bones with the bones of several great chiefs. He was to take them from there to a place of safety, out of reach of a chief, Tereacoo, who would come next day to search the island for the bones of the king and chiefs to make points for their arrows to shoot rats with. (They think there is a charm in human bones.)

"The next day, according to prediction, the chief came and searched the island. The man told him that the island belonged to a white man of whom Kamehameha was very fond. He ought not to come there to search for bones when there were many on the main island. The chief took no notice but searched and took several bundles of bones with him, though not those of the king and chiefs. On the ensuing night the deceased king and many chiefs appeared to the man and thanked him for what he had done, assuring him that the white man would protect him and some day he would be a great man.

"Mr. Manning was as superstitious as the natives and declared he had heard instances of a similar nature. Shortly after we went to the sleeping house. Mr. Manning went out to walk about. In a few moments he returned in a terrible fright and perspiration. Seeing him look so wild I asked him what was the matter. When he got more composed he told me very seriously that he was walking by the prickly pear tree when he saw chief Tereacoo, who had died about a month since, walking before him attended by a number of people dressed in the white cloth of the country. I laughed heartily at this relation and tried to persuade him that it was all imagination but he persisted in having seen the spirits. The next morning I went around the island which seemed as though it had been kept for a burial place, for I saw hundreds of bundles of human bones wrapped carefully in cloth and laid in the crevices of the rocks. Mr. Manning had the king's bones actually conveyed to his own house where he still keeps them."

Peter Corney, and other scientists, have left their personal comments regarding the personality and character of Don Marin. He may have believed in the supernatural, a belief perhaps acquired in early childhood, and living in Hawaii may have increased or emphasized this trait of character. But Marin's mind was scientific in interest and to his knowledge men of note bowed their heads.

Meyen, in his *Voyage Round the World,* says of Don Marin: "He is a man of ordinary education but of noble sentiments, whose name will ever rank foremost in the history of the Sandwich Islands. Marin has introduced the most useful plants from all parts of the globe into the Sandwich Islands, the cultivation of which may hereafter be a source of great wealth to others. The possessions of Marin are in the most beautiful order and might serve as model farms for the whole country. It is true that Marin has acquired great wealth in the Sandwich Islands but he has done it in a manner which will be to the advantage of the posterity of the present generation."

Don Francisco de Paula Marin died at high noon. It seems a fitting hour for such a man to step forward into the shining day, when the turquoise waters of the ocean are turning to amethyst and jade and the softly foaming surf and the spindrift spray are flashing in the sunlight. There were no monastery bells to ring for him, but the verdant valleys, the orchards, and the fruit-laden fields of the Islands, where Manini spent so many years, are his monument.

THE GOLDEN CLOAK

Part Three

LIHOLIHO

Chapter VII

"The gods are a lie!"

ENGLAND, FRANCE, Russia and America were emblazoned on the mind of Liholiho, the young sovereign of the Sandwich Islands. He knew the importance which his father had given, with increasing concern, to the rapidly developing interest of these countries in the Islands, which marked a less difficult passage to the Orient. The strong hope had been, and still was, the declared friendship of the English king. But the future was far from assured. In Liholiho's thinking was the possibility that he might go to England and meet the King "face to face," and to talk matters over with him.

Liholiho — like the Kamehamehas, exceptionally tall — was only twenty-two when the golden cloak was placed about his shoulders. Born in 1796, he had lived much of his life on the island of Hawaii. Although he was carefully trained for the kingship he would one day be expected to assume, his father was very indulgent with him. Liholiho enjoyed to the limit his freedom, living the life of a *bon vivant*. It has been said that he was able to down a bottle of spirits at a draft. His nature being one of open friendliness and joviality, he was, for the most part, immensely popular with his future subjects. But during the funeral rites for his father, he had been sent to another district so that he, as heir to the kingdom, might not be contaminated by the license of the people in their madness and abandon. Days passed. Liholiho remained away until the time came for him to be officially proclaimed the ruler of the people, for him to be called Kamehameha II.

Following the death of Kamehameha I, both political and religious interests took on a new meaning. Kaahumanu, the young queen of Kamehameha, and Queen Keopuolani, the mother of Liholiho, had made up their minds that the old law of the taboo must go. While Kamehameha lived, nothing could be done about it. Liholiho was young, and did not like restriction. The two queens felt confident that they might persuade him to break for all times the taboo, which was degrading to all women, including themselves. Kaahumanu no longer believed in the ancient law or the gods for which it stood. She also knew there was unrest among the people.

The taboo was not only the religion of the people but the backbone of the government as well—the very essence of control. Under this

law, wielded by the priesthood, which included the authority of the
king, he being a high priest, the lives of the people were jeopardized
night and day. One of the important aspects of the taboo was centered
in the eating customs of the people. Women were not allowed to eat in
company with men even of their own families. The food for both men
and women was cooked in separate ovens. Women were not allowed
to eat bananas, coconuts, pork, or sweet potatoes, and the finest fish
were reserved for men alone. The law applied to all women, regardless
of rank. Many Hawaiian women, before civilization reached the Islands,
held important places in community life, but the old law was held
strictly above their heads. Death was the penalty for a broken taboo.

The installation of Liholiho was a gorgeous spectacle, replete with
pomp and circumstance. The old *heiau,* set beneath the softly waving
coconut palms and overlooking Hawaii's clear, blue sea, seemed especially sacred that morning. The beach along the shore was crowded
with people wanting to see and hear all that took place. Kaahumanu
and the high chiefs, all in ceremonial dress, were gathered in a group
facing the crowd. They waited for the Prince. He came slowly from
the temple, impressively noble in his bearing, wearing the golden cloak
which his father had worn before him. Several chiefs in feather mantles
and fine helmets, carrying magnificent *kahilis,* emblems of his rank,
attended him. As Liholiho neared the assembled chiefs, Kaahumanu
stepped forward to meet him. There was profound silence as she began
to speak.

"Hear me, O divine one, for I make known to you the will of your
father. Behold these chiefs, and these men of your father, and these
guns, and this your land, but you and I will share the realm together."
This was a tense moment. Liholiho, the Prince and sportsman, was now
the King, the second Kamehameha.

Kamehameha I had created a new office in the government of Hawaii
—that of *kuhina-nui* (premier). Although, ceremonially, the King was
the highest officer of the state, the *kuhina-nui* was ordinarily more
active than the King in the routine administration of the government.
To Kaahumanu he gave this power. She was to share equally with
Liholiho the responsibility of the kingdom, with the high chiefs acting
as councilors. Kamehameha had great confidence in his young queen.
She had superior judgment and keen insight. She knew his thoughts
and his ambition to establish a great dynasty of the Kamehameha family. Kamehameha, evidently, believed that his son, Liholiho, with the
assistance of the chiefs and especially with the wise counsel of Kaahumanu and that of Kalanimoku, his close friend and prime minister,
would take his high honors with credit. To give him added strength

and to insure permanency of procedure, he had created the office of *kuhina-nui.*

After Liholiho's installation, both Kaahumanu and his mother urged him to break the taboo. Remembering his father's counsel to "be loyal to the gods and all would go well with him," he refused. The law had been that of his father and of the Polynesian kings for untold centuries. It is believed that several of the chiefs and, perhaps, the high priest had secretly discussed the possibility of discarding the old law and had decided that the time had not yet come for so drastic a move. It might promote rebellion. There were, also, other matters of state which demanded immediate attention. The sandalwood trade for one thing. Was the King to continue to reap the great returns as Kamehameha had once done?

Liholiho left Kailua and returned to Kawaihae, where he was making his headquarters. While there he received the chiefs in council and the matter of the sandalwood was adjusted. A message from Kaahumanu advised him to come back to Kailua, and told him that she would no longer accept and worship his god. In the face of this defiance, he stood, at the age of 22, between two fires: loyalty to his father and the traditions of his people, and his own inner desire for new experiences in a changing world.

Tolstoy, in his deep analysis of world affairs and human relations in *War and Peace,* tells that, in 1820, the ferment that had long brewed brought swift and great changes in different parts of the world. People thought as they had never thought before. Governments tottered and fell. Who can say that this strange and far-reaching psychological force, if such it was, invaded not only countries but touched as well the islands of the seas?

Kamehameha died in May, 1819, and during the following August a French ship of war, *l'Uranie,* visited the Islands. Captain Louis de Freycinet was accompanied on this voyage by a group of scientists and explorers. The captain in his records tells of their visit on Hawaii. From John Young he learned of the unsettled condition of the government. Mr. Young explained that there were chiefs who were enemies to the King. Secret antagonism was increasing, led by Kekuaokalani, cousin of Liholiho, to whom Kamehameha had committed his war god. John Young said that this young chief "talked of nothing less than overthrowing the royal power and of slaughtering all the Europeans established in the Sandwich Islands. No act of hostility had yet taken place, but war was feared, although the young King and his friends were making every effort to avert it." John Young asked Captain Freycinet to offer his protection to Liholiho, which the Captain said he would do.

A few days later Captain Freycinet and John Young had a conference with the King. The Captain said to Liholiho: "I am not ignorant of the alliance which exists between the King of the Sandwich Islands and the King of Great Britain; the latter being also the friend and ally of France, I declare that the ship which I command and those that shall come hereafter to the Sandwich Islands under the same flag will always be disposed to give you the assistance calculated to maintain the tranquility of your state and the force of your authority." The Captain also told Liholiho that he had heard of the evil designs of the chiefs and that if he thought that his declaration could have any useful influence over them he would authorize him to make it known to them.

Liholiho called a council of the chiefs. Kekuaokalani was not present. The Captain spoke of the disastrous effects of civil war and of the great good which comes through civilization and peace. At the close of his address, Kaahumanu told of the report that was being circulated that the French officer had demanded a cession of the Islands to France, and that a cession had actually been made. Captain Freycinet denounced the report. He said that he could not be a party to any such transaction even if Liholiho, himself, had expressed a wish to make his country a dependency of France.

While Captain Freycinet and his ship were in port at Kawaihae, John Young and Kalanimoku made the Captain a call on board the l'Uranie. The chaplain of the ship, Abbe de Quelen, in his clerical dress, attracted the attention of Kalanimoku. He asked about him. John Young told him that he was a priest of France and of the true God. Kalanimoku then said that he had, for some time, desired to become a Christian and that he would like to be baptized by the French priest. Plans were made for the ceremony the day following the meeting of the captain with the chiefs. Liholiho asked that he might be present. The captain sent his pinnace for the King and his party. Captain Freycinet, in his records, gives a description of the party. He tells that Liholiho wore a blue gold-trimmed uniform of the hussars with thick, colonel's epaulets. One of his officers carried his sword and another his *kahili*. He was saluted with eleven guns. The quarterdeck was decorated with flags. The King's favorite queen, Kamamalu, and Kaahumanu were given chairs in front of the altar which had been erected on the deck. The Abbe performed the sacred ceremony of Christian baptism and Kalanimoku, during the entire proceeding, "showed a deep emotion." He received the name of Louis, after Captain Freycinet, who acted as his godfather.

The visit of the French captain gave Liholiho courage. When he again returned to Kailua he had, evidently, decided to ally himself with Keopuolani, Kaahumanu and Kalanimoku, who favored the new regime.

When he reached Kailua he ordered a great feast. The tables were laid separately for men and women as usual. Several foreigners were invited to sit at the King's table, among them John Parker of Waimea and John Young, the great friends of Kamehameha. Liholiho asked John Young to do the carving and he walked around each table, seemingly to see that everyone was cared for, when, suddenly, to the utter amazement of those who were not in his confidence, he took a vacant seat at the table where the women were seated and sat down to eat with them. To those who did not understand what was happening, his action was incredible. They were horror stricken and expected the King would be struck dead and all of his people with him. But when nothing occurred a great murmur arose. . . . "The taboo is broken! The taboo is broken!" Someone called aloud: "The gods are a lie!"

Soon after the feast was over, Liholiho gave an order that all of the temples should be burned and the images destroyed. The high priest lighted the first torch, he having been in sympathy with the plan for a long time. Criers were sent to the different islands to announce the great news: that the old law was abolished and the people were set free. The excitement, intense and unexpected, was like the ringing of a fire-bell in a quiet country town.

The taboo system was too ancient and too deeply rooted to be abolished without a struggle. Civil war followed led by Kekuaokalani, who lost his life in the battle. The young chief had broadcast that Liholiho was disloyal to Kamehameha and to the faith of the fathers. Kalanimoku and Kaahumanu led the royal forces to victory. A great reaction set in. The common people and many of the opposing leaders and chiefs became convinced that they had been deceived by the priests and that the gods which they had been taught to worship were worthless. They now made more thorough work of destroying their images and sacred enclosures, with a few reservations, such as the *Hale a Keawe* at Honaunau. All public worship and sacrifice ceased, the priesthood, as an organized body, was dissolved, and as Jarves says, "Hawaii presented to the world the strange spectacle of a nation without a religion." But many individuals and families secretly kept the little wooden gods.

It was around this time that the first company of missionaries arrived from New England. Several Hawaiian boys, among them George Kaumualii, the son of the king of the island of Kauai, came with them. The boys had all been at the Cornwall school with Obookiah and were his closest friends. They acted as interpreters for the missionaries in their first interviews with the Hawaiian people.

The coming of the missionary ship caused a great stir. The *Thaddeus* was not a merchant ship. Liholiho was not sure that he should allow the strangers to remain. He feared the English government might not like their coming, since they were Americans. But when John Young assured him that there was no trouble between England and America, and that the English king would approve of the desire of the missionaries to be helpful to the people, he consented to talk things over.

The royal family were invited to dine on board the *Thaddeus*. The missionaries received them cordially and the King was seated at the head of the table. This was the first time that the Islanders had ever seen white women. The missionaries sang for them. George Kaumualii accompanied the psalm singing with a bass-viol, which was both amazing and delightful to the Hawaiians. Altogether, the first missionary party was considered a great success.

The next day a committee of both men and women from the *Thaddeus* called upon the King. They talked with him and with the chiefs about what they hoped to do if they were allowed to stay. But Liholiho said that he would give no decision until Kaahumanu returned from her fishing trip and he had an opportunity to consult with her about the matter.

With an interpreter present, the missionary leaders met Kaahumanu in conference with the King. Liholiho asked that Kaahumanu be told what had been said to him of the reasons for their coming to the Islands and of the useful things which they would teach. After a long discussion, the missionaries were told that they would be allowed to perform an experiment for one year, and if by the end of that time the King felt it was unwise for them to stay longer, they would go elsewhere or return to America. They carefully explained that they had no desire to interfere in any way with the policies or government of the kingdom. They also asked if part of their company might remain at Kailua and the rest of the party go to Honolulu on the island of Oahu, which, from what they had heard, would be one of the most important points at which to begin their work of education. The King replied: "White men all prefer Oahu. I think the Americans would like to have that island." And so it was that the American mission was established in the Sandwich Islands.

Liholiho soon became the staunch friend of the new teachers. He was looking forward, and their coming marked, so it appeared to him, a step ahead. Old diaries tell fascinating tales of Liholiho's interest in learning to read and to write his name. When he first saw his own name in writing, he said that it did not look like him or any other man. But he proved to be a good pupil and in a short time he was able to write a letter in English. One of his instructors tells that he often sat for hours at a time in study, so anxious was he to learn the new language.

There are several portraits of Liholiho. Like his father, he evidently enjoyed having his picture painted. He loved beautiful things and his great ambition was to dress and be like men from other lands. One of the missionaries writes of him: "There is nothing particularly striking about his countenance, but his figure is noble, perhaps more so than that of any chief; his manner polite and easy and his whole deportment that of a gentleman." Again one reads: "Liholiho attended all of the services of the day. He was still sober, and when so, I can readily believe what is said of him to be true—that he is one of the most interesting characters of the nation. He looked remarkably well and spent half an hour at the mission house before the worship in the chapel began. In his suit of dove colored satin, with white satin waistcoat, silk stockings and pumps, he appeared in both dress and manners the perfect gentleman."

The old diary also says that the chapel was thronged with the chiefs in rich dresses of velvet, damask, silk, satin and crepe. There were a large number of foreigners present, the whole audience making not less than four hundred people, "Gathered to this humble temple, by the sound of the church-going bell, which until within the last three years, these valleys and rocks never heard."

With the many changes which were coming into Liholiho's experience, his plan to go to England remained constantly in his thoughts. He had been greatly pleased when the vessel which had been promised to Kamehameha by Captain Vancouver finally reached the islands and was presented to him. In appreciation he wrote the following letter to King George IV of England:

"Oahu, Sandwich Islands, August 21, 1822

"May it please your Majesty:

"In answer to your Majesty's letter from Governor Macquarrie, I beg to return your Majesty my most grateful thanks for your handsome present of the schooner, *Prince Regent,* which I received at the hands of Mr. J. R. Kent.

"I avail myself of this opportunity of acquainting your Majesty of the death of my father, Kamehameha, who departed this life the eighth of May, 1819, much lamented by his subjects; and, having appointed me his successor. I have enjoyed a happy reign ever since that period. I assure your Majesty it is my sincere wish to be thought as worthy of your attention as my father had the happiness to be during the visits of Captain Vancouver. The whole of these Islands having been left me by my father, I have succeeded to the government of them, and beg leave to place them all under the protection of your most excellent Majesty's wisdom and judgment.

"The former idolatrous system has been abolished in these Islands, and we wish the protestant religion of your Majesty's dominions to be practiced here. I hope your Majesty may deem it fit to answer this as soon as convenient; and your Majesty's counsel and advice will be most thankfully received by your Majesty's most obedient and humble servant,

"Kamehameha II,

"King of the Sandwich Islands

"To George IV., King of England."

The year previous to writing this letter, Liholiho made an unexpected trip to Kauai. His father, Kamehameha, before his death, had given up all thoughts of promoting war with Kaumualii, the king of Kauai, telling him that he should continue the government of that island, while acknowledging Kamehameha as the superior chief. Liholiho, evidently, thought it wise to make sure that he, now the ruling sovereign, stood in the same position as that which his father had held in the matter of the island of Kauai.

When making a business trip to Waialua, riding horseback from Honolulu to look after the cutting of sandalwood on that side of the island, he made a sudden decision to sail at once for Kauai. He had with him Governor Boki, Naihe, one of his wives, and about thirty servants. At Waialua he took a small open sailing vessel and set sail. When away from the island he ordered the men to steer the boat, which was heavily loaded, out into the dangerous channel toward Kauai. This channel is a challenge to the most experienced seamen. The little boat sailed on through the day and through the night, the great waves sweeping across the bow and threatening complete destruction of the light craft. His friends begged the King to turn back, but he refused. He said that if they turned back, he would swim to Kauai.

Just before daylight the small boat, with its important passengers, arrived safely at Waimea. Liholiho and his party were given a very friendly reception by King Kaumualii and his people. A vessel was sent at once to Honolulu to announce the safe arrival of the visitors.

King Kaumualii was very courteous to Liholiho. In the presence of others, among them several foreigners, he said to him "King Liholiho, hear! When your father was alive I acknowledged him as my superior. Since his death I have considered you as his rightful successor, and, according to his appointment, as King. Now I have plenty of muskets and powder and a plenty of men at command . . . these, with the vessels I have bought, the fort, the guns and the island, all are yours to do with as you please. Place what chief you please as governor here."

Liholiho must have been surprised and moved by such a declaration and he respected it. He finally answered Kaumualii, "I did not come

to take away your island. I do not wish to place anyone over it. Keep
your island, and take care of it just as you have done, and do what you
please with your vessels."

Rev. Hiram Bingham, the missionary, who was present, recorded in
his journal, "Thus without bloodshed, the treaty made with the late king
is recognized and ratified with his son and successor, a treaty which
allowed Kaumualii the peaceful possession of the leeward islands, as
tributary king. In this transaction it is difficult to say which of the two
has shown the most sagacity or magnanimity." However, when Liholiho
returned to Oahu he took Kaumualii with him as a prisoner of state.
Liholiho's visit to Kauai indicates a measure of statesmanship. There
were reasons for his apprehension regarding the loyalty of the king of
Kauai. The latter's relations with Russia might be repeated if he had the
opportunity. His son, George, did not like the present situation and he,
too, might make trouble. There had been talk of war between Liholiho
and Kaumualii. Liholiho took a decisive step to counteract these reports.
The visit to Kauai strengthened his position and gave him added power.

The chiefs were disturbed when Liholiho decided to purchase the
fabulous and gaudy yacht, *Cleopatra's Barge,* which had belonged to
Salem's Benjamin Crowninshield. To Liholiho there was romance and
adventure in the very thought of it. The fact that it was valued at fifty
thousand dollars' worth of sandalwood did not lessen its attractiveness.
The King also purchased the missionary ship, the *Thaddeus,* adding
another forty thousand dollars to be paid with the fragrant lumber from
the mountain-sides of his kingdom.

Every year Liholiho held a great celebration in memory of his father.
Old journals give detailed descriptions of these grand affairs, which held
the splendor and color of old Hawaii. The people of all ranks took
a personal and intimate part in the play. One description pictures the
elaborateness with which these celebrations were carried out.

"Kamamalu (Liholiho's half-sister and favorite queen) was the most
conspicuous personage in the ranks. She was seated in a whale boat
placed upon a frame of wickerwork, borne on the shoulders of seventy
men. The boat and the platform, which was thirty feet long by twelve
wide, were overspread by costly broadcloth, relieved by the richest colored and most beautiful tapas. The carriers marched in a solid phalanx,
the outer ranks of which wore a uniform of yellow and scarlet feather
cloaks and superb helmets of the same material. The queen's dress was a
scarlet silk mantle and a feather coronet. An immense Chinese umbrella
richly gilded and decorated with tassels and fringes of the gaudy color,
supported by a chief wearing a helmet, screened her from the sun. Kalanimoku and Naihe stood beside her on either quarter of the boat, both

with malos or girdles of scarlet colored silk, and lofty helmets. Each bore a *kahili,* the staff of royalty; these were nearly thirty feet high, the upper part being arranged to form a columnor plume of scarlet feathers a foot and a half in diameter, and from twelve to fourteen feet long; the handles were surrounded with alternating ivory and tortoise shell rings, beautifully wrought and highly polished. More significant insignia of rank conveying at once the ideas of grandeur, state and beauty, as they towered and gracefully nodded above the multitude, were never devised by barbarians.

"The dresses of the queens dowager (Kaahumanu and Keopuolani) were remarkable for their size and expense. Seventy-two yards of cassimere of double fold, half orange and half scarlet, were wrapped around the figure of one until her arms were sustained by the mass in a horizontal position, while the remainder, forming an extensive train, was supported by a retinue selected for that purpose.

"The richness and variety of the dresses and colors, and the exhibition of the wealth and power of the chiefs, their hereditary symbols of rank, the stately *kahilis,* splendid cloaks and helmets and necklaces of feathers, intermingled with the brilliant hues and deep green of flowers and wreaths, from their native forests, rendered the spectacle at once unique and attractive. The beating of drums and other rude music swelled the wild notes of their songs, and the acclamations of thousands of voices, with the heavy tramp of their feet, broke in upon the deep-toned choruses and thrilling responses. Amid the throng the King, with his suite, excited by the revelry of the week's duration, mounted upon saddle-less horses, rode recklessly about. A body-guard of fifty men, dressed in shabby uniform, followed by a multitude shouting and cheering, endeavored to keep pace with the royal troop."

This was the last celebration of this kind in the Hawaiian Islands. Civilization was moving forward. Old customs were disappearing and the missionary teachers were making headway with their program of education. A Hawaiian alphabet of twelve letters had been made from sound; in 1822 the first printing in the Islands was done—eight pages of the *Hawaiian Primer.* Kalanimoku, the King, and many of the chiefs were awed by the little printing press. To them, it was magic personified. With the approval of Liholiho, classes were formed and the English language was taught to the people. The textbooks were Webster's spelling book, Watt's catechism, and the English *Bible.* The Hawaiian language was eventually put into print and, from then on, the people learned very rapidly to read and to write.

In the meantime, Liholiho, following the death of his mother, Keopuolani, pushed forward his plans to go to England. Kaahumanu and the chiefs, as well as the King, were troubled regarding foreign relations with the Islands. A council was held. The chiefs consulted with the missionary leaders, and it was finally decided that the King should make the voyage to England. Fortunately, the whale ship *L'Aigle* was in port and about to return to England. The captain agreed to take the King and his party with him.

Accompanying Liholiho was his favorite queen, Kamamalu, his high chief and adviser, Kapihe, Governor Boki and his wife, Liliha, James Young, the son of John Young and a close friend of Liholiho, several other members of the court, and a number of servants.

Before leaving, Liholiho, in a council with the chiefs, named his younger brother, Prince Kauikeaouli, as his heir and successor. All governmental matters were to be left with Kaahumanu, the Queen Regent, and the chiefs.

The excitement was intense. Many of the people did not approve of the King's leaving the Islands. They were fearful for his safety. The beach was crowded to see the ship sail and, when the moments drew near for departure, Queen Kamamalu stood before the people and, in a "tender and plaintive strain," she chanted her farewell.

"O skies, O plains, O mountains and oceans,

O guardians and people, kind affection for you all.

Farewell to thee, the soil,

O country, for which my father suffered; alas for thee!"

She then addressed the spirit of Kamehameha, her father, in remembrance of his affection and his charge to follow her husband faithfully.

"We both forsake the object of thy toil.

I go according to thy command;

Never will I disregard thy voice,

I travel with thy dying charge,

Which thou didst address to me."

As the Queen entered the ship and it sailed away from the shore, the wailing and the weeping of the people, the roaring of the cannon from the walls of the fort, gave a last *aloha* to Liholiho and his friends.

Unless the adviser to Liholiho was an older man, the group of the Royal House of Hawaii were all young people. A strange and great experience lay before them—another world unlike their own. *L'Aigle* touched at Rio de Janeiro and Their Majesties were presented to the Emperor of Brazil at a court levee. This was the first time that a ship from the Sandwich Islands had stopped at Rio de Janeiro, and the party was given a royal welcome by the people. At the levee the Emperor presented the King with "a most elegant sword," and Liholiho, in return compliment, gave to the Emperor a handsome feather cloak. When the ship sailed, she received a salute of twenty-one guns, speeding the guests on to England. The Royal House of Hawaii was now a part of the great outside world.

The English newspapers, both in Plymouth and in London, give interesting accounts of the arrival and the visit of the Hawaiian royal party. There was, evidently, considerable interest as to why they had come. One London paper makes the statement: "The King of the Sandwich Islands has come for the purpose of placing his dominions under the protection of England, in consequence of his apprehending hostile intentions on the part of Russia." Another paper says, "The King apprehends danger from the United States due to the recent large influx of Americans, both traders and missionaries." As soon as the English government officials were notified of the arrival of the party from Hawaii, plans were immediately made for their reception and entertainment. The Hon. Frederick Byng (known to his contemporaries, because of his unruly head of hair and of his habit of being seen on numerous occasions walking his dog, as "Poodle Byng") was appointed to sponsor and attend them while they were in England. In London, Liholiho and his retinue were given apartments at the Caledonian, a fashionable hotel overlooking the Thames Embankment at Charing Cross.

Members of the nobility escorted the royal party about the city to see the sights of London. They caused quite a sensation. Their dress and manners were of great interest to everyone. Their headdresses were copied and models were placed in the shop windows. But it was not long before tailors and modistes supplied suitable apparel for London, and the wearers were not so conspicuous. Artists were interested and the finest picture we have today of Liholiho was at that time made in London—the lithograph by John Hayter. Other pictures of the party are also extant. A lewd cartoon printed in a London newspaper on June 16, 1824, was titled "Robing Royalty, a treat for the Sandwichers, at the sign of the Hog in Armor." It depicts the Hawaiians tattooed and barefoot, with feathers in their hair. Liholiho, in feather skirt, is trying on a coat, saying: "Oh how I shall astonish the natives!" Kamamalu, smoking a cigar while a chambermaid tightens the strings of her corset, squeals: "Oh my Belly Pelly!" Boki, holding a wig, says: "Oh Missy Smokey Pokey, dese fine feather."

A grand reception was held in honor of the King and his party at Gloucester Lodge. More than two hundred guests were present to meet them. Among the guests were the Duke of Gloucester, the brother of King George IV, Prince Leopold, the Duke of Wellington, and others.

The Hawaiians especially enjoyed the theatre. The King and Queen occupied the royal box at Covent Garden. Liholiho bowed several times to the audience before taking his seat, and he remained standing when the orchestra played "God Save the King." The play was *Pizarro,* and the Queen was moved to tears during several of the scenes.

At the command of King George, Their Majesties were to be his guests at Drury, but this party was never to take place. Liholiho, Kamamalu, and all of the members of their suite, were stricken with measles. It may have been that the great change from the even climate of Hawaii to the dampness and cold of England was largely responsible in weakening their resistance. While every care was given, King George sending his own private physician to attend the sick ones, the Queen grew steadily worse. Pneumonia developed and in a few days Kamamalu was dead. Her attendants dressed her body and carried it—a flower *lei* in her hair, naked to the waist, barefoot—to the dying Liholiho's rooms. He asked that messages be forwarded to Honolulu as soon as possible, announcing the death of the Queen. He requested that her body be placed in some quiet, country church, that the Christian service be read for her, and that her remains be sent back to his Islands.

The shock of the Queen's death was so great that Liholiho lost his courage, and his strength gradually failed. He rallied, however, and was able to talk with Mr. Byng. The day had been appointed for Liholiho's presentation to King George. When the time came, Liholiho remarked that that was to have been the day when he would have had his long anticipated conference with the King. Governor Boki and Liliha were constantly with him and to them and to Mr. Byng he expressed his wishes.

As days passed, Liholiho realized that he was not going to live. His friends were around him, and, turning to Boki, he said, "This is my death in the time of my youth; great love to my country!"

Adelphi—July 14th, 1824.

The King of the Sandwich Islands departed this life at 4 o'clock this morning. The alarming symptoms of his disorder rapidly increased within the last few days; and he at length sunk under it, without much apparent suffering.

Matthew John Tierney
(Sir M. Tierney, Bart.M.D.)
Henry Holland
(Sir H. Holland, Bart.M.D.)
Hugh Ley
(Dr. Ley)

Old documents give many details of the thoughtful and considerate care which was given by England at the time of the death of the King and Queen. They lay in state at the Caledonian Hotel, surrounded by the emblems of their rank. It was at Saint Martin's in the Field that together they waited for their departure to the Islands. The bodies of the young sovereigns were placed in leaden caskets, enclosed in wood and covered with crimson velvet richly ornamented. Suitable plates with inscriptions in English and in Hawaiian gave rank, birth and death dates of the King and Queen. On the casket of the King was also the following inscription:

> "Died July 14th, 1824.
> In the 28th year of his age.
> May we remember our beloved King
> Iolani."

Iolani was the name Liholiho most loved and by which he was most often called by his friends.

The responsibility for the royal party was placed in the hands of Governor Boki. Eventually, when all the members of the suite of the King were well and plans made for their return to Hawaii, King George received them at Windsor Castle. He addressed Governor Boki, as the leader of the party, James Young acting as interpreter. The King asked Boki, "What was the business on which you and your King came to this country?" Boki then stated, "We have come to confirm the words which Kamehameha I gave in charge to Vancouver. . . . 'Go back and tell King George to watch over me and my whole kingdom. I acknowledge him as my landlord and and myself as tenant, (or him as superior and I inferior). Should the foreigners of any other nation come to take possession of my lands, let him help me.' " When King George heard this he said to Boki, "I have heard these words; I will attend to the evils from without. The evils within your kingdom it is not for me to regard; they are with yourselves. Return and say to the King, to Kaahumanu and to Kalanimoku, I will watch over your country. I will not take possession of it for mine, but will watch over it lest evil should come from others to the kingdom. I therefore will watch over him agreeable to those ancient words."

Before their interview was brought to a close, Boki posed another question before King George IV, the King whose shameless debauchery and treacherous, unfeeling treatment of his friends and relatives had lost him the respect of his nation even before he came to the throne. Boki asked if it were wise to encourage the missionaries who had come to Hawaii. The English monarch replied: "Yes, they are a people to make others good. I always have some of them by me."

A few hours after the death of Liholiho, Secretary Canning had informed King George. He added the following note: "Mr. Canning humbly presumes that Your Majesty will not disapprove of a Ship of War being allowed to carry back the suite of the deceased Chief, with the remains of himself and his wife, to the Sandwich Islands. . . . An Attention perhaps the more advisable as the Government of Russia and of the United States of America have their eyes upon those Islands; which may ere long become a very important Station in the trade between the N. W. coast of America and the China Seas."

The English Government ordered that Lord Byron, cousin of the poet and the commander of the Frigate *Blonde,* escort the bodies of the late King and Queen, with members of their retinue, back to the Islands.

Word of the death of Liholiho and the Queen reached Honolulu by an American whale ship on the ninth of March, and the *Blonde* arrived off Diamond Head on the sixth of the following May. So the people had time to prepare for the sad homecoming of their king.

Early writers tell of the carefully planned arrangements and the impressive funeral service. The long procession of dignitaries, friends, soldiers and sailors, and the great number of native people moved from the shore to the thatched house of Kalanimoku. This had been the Hall of Audience, but for the reception of the remains of the late King and Queen the hall was arched and lined with royal black tapa and used as a temporary resting place for the monarchs.

Kamehameha gave his son the name Liholiho—"glorious and bright." It was he who would carry the burning torch of old Hawaii on into the years. All of this Liholiho understood, and in memory of his father he did the best he knew, under increasing local and foreign pressure, in the interest of his kingdom. He may have seemed unstable, but at heart he was a Kamehameha. The gods of the centuries lay in ashes at his feet. He threw open the dark doors of ignorance and superstition, letting knowledge, education, and Christianity march through.

KAAHUMANU

Chapter VIII

*"Of you and all the good I am
the friend."*

—KAAHUMANU

THE OLD LEGENDARY BELIEF that people are sometimes born with a charmed life is, by many Hawaiians, thought to be true of Kaahumanu. When she was a very young baby, during a great battle on the island of Maui, her mother, Namahana, hid her in a cave for several days. There are many such caves in the Islands, and often overhanging vines completely hide them from view. The vines, trailing down from the precipice, formed a protecting curtain for little Kaahumanu, and the sweet music of the trade winds drowned her cries. In fact, at that point, in the geography of Maui, a strong wind constantly blows against the headland, and the high surf pounding against the rocks drowns all other sounds. So, the baby's hiding place was secure.

It was at Hana, on Maui, that Kaahumanu was born, at the very foot of the old battle hill, Kauiki. At the time of Kaahumanu's birth, battles were raging on every side, as was true most of the time in the different islands. There was war between the kings of Hawaii and the King of Maui. The King of Oahu was fighting the King of Molokai. The kings of Hawaii were fighting each other. Every high chief was battling every other for supremacy in one way or another, and young Kamehameha was winning his way to the top.

Kaahumanu's mother, Namahana, had been the Queen of Maui. After the death of her husband she became the wife of Keeaumoku, the great warrior and high chief, and Kaahumanu was their child. Namahana's brother, Kahekili, who was the King of Maui, was displeased that Namahana had taken Keeaumoku for her husband, and he became Keeaumoku's enemy. Their friendship had been broken. It is told of Kahekili, whose name interpreted means "thunder," that he was both crafty and cruel. To make himself more greatly feared, he had one half of his body tattooed almost black. The people, including Namahana, stood in great fear of him, so she hid her baby in the cave.

Keeaumoku was at war on Hawaii. Greatly worried about his wife and child, he decided to make his escape from the Big Island. Diving from a high cliff into the ocean, he located his canoe and sailed at once for Molokai. There, he was once more surrounded by battle in a war between the King of Oahu and the King of Molokai. He was again successful in making his escape and reached Maui, where Namahana was waiting for him. Fearing the vengeance of Kahekili, he left Maui immediately, taking his wife and baby with him.

Wrapping the baby in the royal white tapa, they placed her on the platform of the canoe, as was the custom in traveling. The platform of the double canoe was designed to provide special seating for people of rank. As they sailed along in the night, steering their canoe by the stars, Keeaumoku and Namahana had much to talk over together. They were in a precarious situation and may have become so engrossed in their conversation that, for the moment, the baby was forgotten. The rapid movement of the boat finally rocked the baby off into the water. Keeaumoku happened to look back and saw what had happened. Quickly, reversing the canoe, he was just in time to save his daughter from drowning. Old Hawaiians, when telling the story today, say, "The gods were watching."

At another time, when the baby was just old enough to toddle along the beach and while she and her mother were resting after fishing, Kaahumanu, attracted by the sparkling surf, ventured too near the edge of the water. To her delight the surf crept over her feet, and then a big wave came rolling in and drew her out to sea. A fisherman saw her and called out, "Keeaumoku's child!" Dashing into the ocean, he swam out to the little figure and brought Kaahumanu back to her mother.

As a close friend of Keeaumoku, Kamehameha had watched Kaahumanu develop from childhood to young womanhood. He not only admired her beauty, but recognized and appreciated her intelligence as well. Although Kamehameha had a number of wives, Kaahumanu was his true love. He married her when she was thirteen years old, and their life together was both passionate and stormy. She was intensely jealous of his attentions to other women. When she was sixteen, believing Kamehameha had deserted her, she determined to end her life. Alone she swam out into the shark-infested waters, thinking the sharks would kill her. She was followed and brought back to shore, wild and angry that her plan had been thwarted. Another story is told of the time that Kamehameha absented himself without explanation. Kaahuman, suspecting that he was having a rendezvous, swam through a large expanse of rough channel and hid herself behind a rock on the beach. Before long, Kamehameha strolled along, accompanied only by his dog. The dog stopped suddenly, sniffed the air, and then dashed straight to the rock behind which Kaahumanu was hiding, yelping and lapping the startled Queen's face in fond recognition. Kamehameha was vastly amused as Kaahumanu emerged, shame-faced, from behind the rock, falling into his arms with a cascade of tears.

It was through her mother that Kaahumanu inherited royal blood rank, but her father, Keeaumoku, in addition to being one of Kamehameha's highest chiefs, was of equal station and counted great names among his ancestors. High though her station was, it was only in the matter of rank that Kaahumanu suffered serious competition from another of Kamehameha's wives. Keopuolani held the highest rank in all Hawaii. So exalted was her rank that, even after their marriage and she had given birth to two sons who were to become the second and third rulers of the Kamehameha dynasty, the King never entered her presence except on his hands and knees. But it was only in this matter of rank that Kaahumanu was somewhat inferior. She remained Kamehameha's favorite. Before her eyes he dangled the finest silks and the costliest baubles that he could cunningly barter from foreign traders. Withal, Keopuolani and Kaahumanu were good friends. Together, after Kamehameha's death, they prevailed upon Liholiho to break the great taboo. And it was Kaahumanu's word, even more than his mother's, that had induced the young King to do so.

Captain Vancouver, in his *Voyage of Discovery*, tells of his interest in Kaahumanu and her family. She, with her father and her mother, were guests aboard the Captain's ship in company with Kamehameha and his friends. Vancouver was greatly impressed with the affection shown between the parents and their daughter, leaving no doubt of their relationship. Speaking of Kaahumanu he says: "She appeared to be about fifteen, and, undoubtedly, did credit to the charm and taste of Kamehameha, being the finest woman we had yet seen on any of the Islands. It was pleasing to observe the kindness and fond attention with which, on all occasions, they seemed to regard each other."

Just how much influence Captain Vancouver may have had over the mind of Kaahumanu is uncertain, but she had for him the greatest admiration and respect. The time is recalled when she begged Vancouver to use his influence on Kamehameha to prevent the latter from beating her. She appreciated Vancouver's friendliness and his advice. She must have often listened to the discussions between Kamehameha and Captain Vancouver concerning the Islands and their people. When she learned that the Captain did not approve of Kamehameha's many wars, she was concerned. Kaahumanu, herself, was a noted warrior, going with Kamehameha into the very heart of battle. It may have been Kamehameha as well as her father who taught her the art of war, for she was said to be not only able, but fearless, in battle. Coming to know

Captain Vancouver, John Young, and Isaac Davis opened to Kaahumanu the realization of the evils of war. Her entire life had been lived in the atmosphere and reality of battle. She knew no other life. It was her birthright, but now it gave her cause for apprehension. While Kamehameha, listening, remained loyal to his inheritance, Kaahumanu may have caught a flash of understanding, a vision, a promise, for the future. So, it was not strange when, many years later and many pounds heavier, returning from her fishing, she agreed with Liholiho to allow the missionaries to remain and try out their ideas of peace on earth, good will toward men.

From the beginning Kaahumanu had been exceedingly reserved, if not openly antagonistic, toward the missionaries. Bingham evokes a vivid picture of Kaahumanu at this time. He says: "At first she scoffed insultingly, receiving mission visits lying on her vast belly as she played cards with her suite, greeting mission ladies with a disdainfully crooked little finger." Although John Young had said that their religion was the same as that of Captain Vancouver, she was disturbed. These men and women were not from England but from America. Kaahumanu may have questioned in her own mind, newly awakened to unexpected thinking, whether the religion of the Americans was the same as that of Captain Freycinet, of the French ship on board which Kalanimoku had been baptized at Kawaihae. Kalanimoku had been given the name of Louis, which was Captain Freycinet's name. Boki, too, had been baptized when the ship reached Honolulu. Boki was given the name of Paul. What did these names signify? The Hawaiian people often exchanged names with friends as a simple gesture of *aloha,* but this was not the same. What had it all to do with religion? Her own name, Kaahumanu, which had been given her by her mother, had a definite meaning— "feather mantle"—indicating her inheritance and the possibilities of her life, but it had nothing to do with the gods. These foreigners with their strange ceremonies troubled her. Kalanimoku, Boki, and even Liholiho, all seemed to accept these strangers and what they said. A feeling of concern had wound its way into her consciousness.

Foreigners were not new to Kaahumanu. When she was a small girl she was among those who watched the British ships sail away after the death of Captain Cook. The old King, Kalaniopuu, found her in the crowd and took her with him, sailing for Kau. She was a royal child, and she lived at his court under his care and protection. There she received her early education. It was through Kamehameha that she came to know John Young and Isaac Davis, as she did Captain Vancouver. These were the friends of her youth. And while Kamehameha lived, Kaahumanu had the opportunity to meet the scientists and the artists who came to the Islands as well as the captains of the ships in which they came. But she knew no foreign women.

The first group of missionaries was not formidable in number. They were men and women of staunch character with a great mission in their hearts. There were two ministers, Rev. Hiram Bingham, who was soon to be considered the spokesman of the party, and Rev. Asa Thurston, a devout preacher of the gospel. These two men, with their wives, were the missionaries, and the rest of the workers were "assistant missionaries." Dr. Thomas Holman was the physician, and Samuel Whitney and Samuel Ruggles were teachers, or schoolmasters. Mr. Elisha Loomis was a printer, and Daniel Chamberlain was a farmer. There were several children and three Hawaiian boys who had been students at the mission school in Cornwall, friends of Obookiah. All told, there were seventeen persons. Kaahumanu agreed with Liholiho and the chiefs that the group certainly did not appear warlike. The missionary ladies, with their queer-looking clothes and peculiar manners, did not appeal to Kaahumanu. While greeting them with courtesy, she kept strictly to the reserve of her rank. She was the Queen. That they must understand. She reasoned that, if they made trouble, they could be sent away. Kalanimoku and Liholiho had welcomed them, visiting their ship. Manini was building houses for them and helping them get settled. She had more important things to attend to.

Following the death of Kamehameha, Kaahumanu's responsibility as *kuhina-nui* was very great. She had accepted it from Kamehameha, and, with the advice and assistance of Kalanimoku and the associated chiefs, she prepared to carry on the government. At the time of Liholiho's installation as king, she personally announced to Liholiho, to the chiefs, and to the assembled people, that at Kamehameha's command she was to share equally with the King in the control of the government, with Kalanimoku as the Prime Minister.

There were no written documents to verify Kaahumanu's statement. For years there arose among the chiefs, influenced by foreigners who desired to direct policies to their own advantage, doubts as to whether Kamehameha had not intended Kalanimoku to be the regent. As time passed, however, Kaahumanu's position and authority became unquestioned. As *kuhina-nui,* Kaahumanu held a high position in the country. During the life of Kamehameha no one but he dared enter her presence uncovered. Imperialistic and dominating though she may have been, the people knew and respected her high rank and obeyed her edicts.

The reins of the government were now in Kaahumanu's hands. With Liholiho, she held the power of life and death. As Liholiho grew to young manhood, he was little interested in government. He took his kingship very lightly. This worried Kaahumanu, but turning to Kala-nimoku, she felt reassured that, together, they could hold Liholiho strictly to account.

The court of Liholiho was composed of thirty-five high ranking chiefs. There were men of outstanding strong character among them. This group of nobles stood in the background of the people. Several of these men were the sons of the great chiefs of Kona who had persuaded Kamehameha to lead them in their wars. Theirs was the blood of old Hawaii. They, with other important chiefs, both men and women, constituted the council of the court. But Kaahumanu was anxious. Un-principled foreigners of many nationalities, irritated by the coming of the missionaries, were making trouble in many small ways. There was an undercurrent of disturbance in the Kingdom. International matters were growing more serious. Liholiho was determined to go to England to ask the protection of the British king. Kaahumanu and Kalanimoku both felt that the situation must be faced immediately, and to this end a conference of the chiefs was called. After a long discussion, it was decided that the King should go to England without delay.

In 1821, on the ninth of October, Kaahumanu had married Kau-mualii, the King of the island of Kauai. Old journals give this story in the light of romance, but the marriage was, pointedly, a diplomatic move, welding the two kingdoms under one rule. Liholiho and the chiefs still feared possible Russian influence on Kauai. To further cement the alliance Kaahumanu later took Kaumualii's son as her consort. Kaahumanu, all her life, had been attracted by handsome men, and the son, at least, fitted into this category. One of the missionaries tells about the wedding of Kaahumanu and King Kaumualii.

It was on the day that the first wooden house, which had been sent from Boston for the mission, was finally set up and completed. The members of the royal family were invited to inspect it. At the close of the visit, Kaahumanu and Kaumualii walked away together. It was a beautiful moonlight evening and the walk across the plains may have so stirred Kaahumanu's emotions that she decided to marry Kaumualii that very night. And so it was arranged. A low platform about eight feet square was made ready. Friends covered the platform with many mats of finest workmanship. Upon the mats Kaahumanu and Kaumua-lii reclined, side by side, and over them was thrown the royal black tapa. This little ceremony was performed in the presence of their in-timate friends, the missionaries, and members of the royal court, so pro-claiming the marriage.

King Kaumualii at this time was not a Christian, but he knew of the acceptance of the Christian faith in the kingdom of Pomare, on the island of Tahiti, as had also Kaahumanu, Kalanimoku and others. In explanation, historians tell that Kaumualii was a very intelligent man, far more advanced in his thinking than were most of his people. The story of his sending his son, George, to America in 1806 that he might receive an education, giving the captain of the vessel in which he sailed money to pay all George's expenses and to place him with those who would give him instruction (which trust the captain betrayed) is enlightening. George was stranded without money or friends. He later enlisted in the United States Navy and served through the War of 1812.

There is preserved a copy of a letter from King Kaumualii, written for him in English by some friend. The letter is dated November 27, 1819, and was written from the island of Kauai. The letter never reached George, since at the time he was on his way home on the *Thaddeus* in company with the missionaries, having for a short while attended the Cornwall school. A quotation from his father's letter is of interest in depicting the character of King Kaumualii. He tells George how anxious he is to see him and urges him to return home. He writes: "I want to see you face to face, that I may know you are alive. I was a little displeased at your opinion concerning my religious ceremonies, and speaking so disdainfully of my wooded idols, but I am at last convinced of my error and have left all my taboos, and have this day renounced my wooded gods and soon intend to make firewood of my churches and idols. I hope you will soon be among us to show us the way we should walk." These were the words written by Kaahumanu's future husband before the coming of the missionaries in 1820. And Kaahumanu's mind was ripe for influence.

Two months after her marriage to Kaumualii, Kaahumanu was taken very sick. The Rev. Hiram Bingham tells about her illness in his journal, *A Residence of Twenty Years in the Sandwich Islands.* He first writes of how "sickness is sometimes a messenger of mercy to the proud and gay lovers of the world." Then he continues, "Never, perhaps, was such an unwelcome messenger of mercy more opportunely sent to a haughty ruler when, in December, 1821, the hard and lofty hearted Kaahumanu was laid low and brought to the borders of the grave."

During her illness Mr. and Mrs. Bingham gave Kaahumanu their constant attention. Little by little they won her confidence and friendship. Fortunately, a Russian ship was in port. Commodore Vascilieeff, learning of the illness of the Queen, sent his two physicians to attend her. Her rapid return to health amazed everyone. The missionaries hoped that, since Kaahumanu had learned that Russia was a Christian country, she would realize what Christianity would do for her people. Mr. Bingham comments: "Who would not covet the privilege of giving the right impulse to the mind and heart of one so high in rank, possessing her mental powers and occupying a position so favorable for exerting influence over a nation." But while Kaahumanu, after her illness, was much more friendly to the missionaries and expressed her appreciation of their kindness, Mr. Bingham records that she was still too proud, too independent, too fond of gaiety, honor, and amusement, to be interested in their teaching.

The little printing press, under the direction of Mr. Loomis, was doing valiant service. A small pamphlet had been printed—a few words, sentences, and the vowel sounds, in both English and Hawaiian—which gave a beginning for study. This was a step forward. Mr. and Mrs. Bingham went to call upon Kaahumanu. They found her, as usual, playing cards surrounded by her favorite women. The Hawaiians had learned to play cards from the men of foreign ships long before they knew the meaning of reading and writing, pen and pencil. Mr. Bingham waited until there was an opening for conversation, then asked Kaahumanu to examine the pamphlet, saying it would talk to her. He finally persuaded her to listen to him as he pronounced the vowel sounds, and to try to repeat them after him, one by one. This to Kaahumanu was like a game; something to try her skill. She succeeded so well that she looked at her friends with superior pride. Almost immediately she grasped that letters would make words which she could speak. It amazed and delighted her. From that time forward, Kaahumanu was a student. She was never again found playing cards; she was too busy learning to read and write.

Kaahumanu soon realized what the new learning might accomplish. It was as an illumination in her mind. This experience changed her entire attitude toward the missionaries. The understanding of why they had come to the Islands changed her hardness to appreciation, and set on fire her ambition. She determined to lead her people to the great open spaces of knowledge where they might learn the way in which they could meet the outside world on an equal footing. This, surely, was that of which Kamehameha had dreamed, about which he had talked to her as long as he lived. She was now in his place, looking forward. The opportunity was hers. The old taboo was broken and no longer cramped her life. The old gods had been set aside, and she was determined to eliminate them from the kingdom. She and Liholiho had opened a door to the future.

The native population was alarmed when Kaahumanu ordered Kamehameha's old poison god to be brought out and publicly burned. When she visited *Hale-o-keawe*, the mausoleum of the Hawaiian kings at Honaunau on the island of Hawaii, she had the bones of many chiefs properly buried or secreted in caves along the ocean shore. Civilization was on its way to the Sandwich Islands.

As Mr. and Mrs. Bingham had hoped, when Kaahumanu had learned to read, her interest in education became the center of her life. Encouraged by the mission, she and Kaumualii organized an education tour. Hundreds of native people joined the caravan, carrying their books and slates with them, studying as they went, traveling on foot the many long miles around the island. The missionary teachers took this opportunity to preach and exhort, teaching the new religion wherever the party stopped on the way.

In Honolulu an examination of those studying English was held, at which Kaahumanu had taken her place as one to be examined. Mr. Bingham records that she wrote, signed, and presented for inspection the following declaration: "I am making myself strong. I declare in the presence of God, that I repent of my sins and believe in God, my Father."

Kaahumanu constantly studied the Bible and often commented upon what she read. At one service she was deeply moved by Mr. Stewart's sermon. He preached from the text, "Thy word is a lamp unto my feet and a light unto my path." Kaahumanu cried with emotion and said, "In former days we were in thick darkness. We wandered there, but now God's word has come and I see the darkness and the light." The chiefs were touched by her words and exclaimed, "*Ikaika loa o Kaahumanu.*" (Very strong, very firm, very decided indeed is Kaahumanu). As time passed the people called the Regent "The new Kaahumanu."

Cooperating with the mission, the Regent ordered that schools should be opened on all of the islands, and that the grass schoolhouses should be well constructed. Many classes were held in the open air when the weather permitted. The pupils were called together by the blowing of the conch shell, sacred to the high-born. Surfboards were sometimes used as desks, but generally the pupils sat on mats of woven *lauhala* spread upon the ground. Kaahumanu had her own private school where the young man who were most proficient under the instruction of the missionaries were prepared to go out as teachers.

There was a constant call for more books. Mr. Bishop, who was stationed on Hawaii, sent word to Mr. Bingham that Kamakau wanted four thousand books to send to Kau, where Chieftess Kapiolani and her husband, Naihe, were sojourning. Governor Kuakini asked for forty thousand books for his and Kaahumanu's people, since they had not one on hand. In a brief time, twenty large schools were equipped on the island of Hawaii. The missionaries' work was progressing with great promise.

Kaahumanu's interest in education knew no bounds. Before Liholiho departed for England, she and Kaumualii visited Kauai. They took with them a retinue of eight hundred people. When Kaahumanu learned there were three hundred pupils waiting to study, she sent a letter to Queen Kamamalu saying, "This is my communication to you. Send some more books down here. I want eight hundred books sent hither."

Just before the royal couple left for England, a new company of missionaries arrived. Kaahumanu received them cordially, saying, "Our hearts are glad you have come, very glad. We are glad you came on taboo day and have been with us in worship. Give our *aloha* to all the new teachers and their women."

The King gave a reception in honor of the new teachers at which the members of the royal family received them. The papers and commission of the missionaries were presented, Liholiho and the chiefs endorsing them with their approval and *aloha*. Kaahumanu was present at the reception. She is described as entering the house with majesty in her step and manner. She wore the native costume. Mr. Bingham tells: "The *pau*, or undergarment, was of purple satin in profuse quantity. It was cast over one arm and shoulder leaving the other exposed, and flowed in its richness far on the ground behind her. Her hair was neatly put up with combs and ornaments by a double coronet of exquisite feathers, the colors bright yellow, crimson and bluish green." At this time Kaahumanu appeared to be between forty and fifty years old, but she still retained much of the beauty for which she was so celebrated.

Among the high ranking chiefs present at the party was Kuakini, Kaahumanu's brother, the governor of the island of Hawaii. Governor Kuakini had chosen the American name of John Adams because of his admiration for John Quincy Adams. He was known as Governor Adams of Hawaii. "Governor Adams was wearing a black silk velvet cloak and pantaloons, with buff waistcoat, white silk stockings, a splendid gold watch with seals with rich ornament." Kalanimoku was dressed in a suit of rich Camlet with a white Marseilles waistcoat and white stockings. Kalanimoku, in his conversation with the missionaries and others present, declared his belief in the true God. He said that, as an officer of the government, he would use all of his influence in favor of Christianity.

Following Liholiho's departure for England, Kaahumanu set about promoting some definite reforms. She declared that restrictions on behavior must be established and changes made in the standard of living for the people. She called the chiefs in council, explained her ideas, and asked their cooperation. The council approved Kaahumanu's plans.

Through the crier, the usual means of publication, an announcement declared a strict observance of the Sabbath, even to prohibiting the building of fires on Sunday. This was especially upsetting to some of the foreign element of the community, creating a bitter resentment towards the missionaries who, it was believed, had set that ball rolling. However, when Kaahumanu visited Lahaina on the island of Maui, then the seat of the government, she took into her own hands a still greater effort in reform. Her conversion to the Christian faith had been complete. She saw life from an entirely different point of view. She came to understand and to feel her own great responsibility to better the conditions under which her people lived. Old customs took on new meaning. With clarified thinking, she prepared and proclaimed what is said to have been the first code of laws for the Islands. These five laws touched the heart of old Hawaii.

"There shall be no murder." This law especially applied to the ancient custom of infanticide.

"There shall be no theft of any description." Prohibiting the custom of helping one's self to the property of his neighbor, as, for instance, walking into his garden and taking his growing vegetables.

"There shall be no boxing or fighting among the people." No drunkenness is also listed in this law.

"There shall be no work or play on the Sabbath, but this day shall be regarded as the sacred day of Jehovah."

"When schools are established all the people shall learn the *palapala*. (To read and write.)"

The important chiefs of the council entered with enthusiasm into the new movement, giving Kaahumanu their support. Small churches had been built on the different islands under the direction of the mission. Kaahumanu had devoted herself to providing such buildings for church services, as well as the use of larger buildings which had been needed for storage and other purposes. The churches soon became far from sufficient. People were thronging to the meetings by the hundreds to listen to the gospel. Governor Adams on Hawaii took his men to the forests to cut trees for a larger church building. The new church measured one hundred eighty feet by seventy-eight feet, and seated four thousand eight hundred people. Kaahumanu was delighted. Education and good government were pushing ahead. But the joy of completing the new church was shadowed by the illness and death of Kaumualii. The good king, at his own request, was buried beside the Queen Mother, Keopuolani, at Lahaina. Kaumualii was not only a great chief, but one of the most cultured gentlemen of old Hawaii.

He left his estate in care of Kaahumanu and Kalanimoku for Liholiho when he should return.

In March, 1825, word was received of the deaths of King Liholiho and Queen Kamamalu in London. The nation was thrown into mourning. The following May, the English ship *Blonde* arrived bringing the remains of the young monarchs encased in their lead coffins. With the *Blonde,* by order of the king of England, came Lord Byron. Like Captain Vancouver, Lord Byron soon won the friendship of Kaahumanu and the chiefs. Following the funeral of the King and Queen, the council of chiefs asked Lord Byron to meet with them in conference. Present were Kaahumanu, Kalanimoku, Boki, Naihe, Kapiolani and others, including the newly appointed English Consul, Mr. Richard Charlton, and representatives from the missionary group. Naihe, the orator, was chairman of the meeting.

Chief Naihe explained that Kaahumanu, as Regent, had been introducing some important changes in governmental matters—the restricting of crime, the establishment of hereditary claims, and the teaching of Christian principles, in which, Naihe emphasized, she was sustained by the higher chiefs. He then explained the necessity of confirming the succession to the throne as had been planned by Liholiho.

It was unanimously agreed that the young Prince Kauikeaouli should be the king. It was also decided that, since the Prince was still a minor, the regency of Kaahumanu should be continued, and that the King should be placed under the guardianship of Kalanimoku and under the instruction of the missionaries in religion, reading, and writing.

Lord Byron was asked his opinion regarding the continuance of the American mission in the Islands. He at once said that he claimed no right to make any decision regarding this, but that he would like to be informed about the object and relation to government of the missionary cause in the Islands. Mr. Bingham spoke regarding this matter. In his *Journal* appears the following statement: "I stated on behalf of the mission that we were not employed by the United States government, and that the instruction of the American Board of Commissioners, to us as Christian missionaries, forbade our interfering with the civil and political affairs of the nation." Eventual history proved some members of the missionary group to be slightly wayward in this respect.

Lord Byron followed with a practical and plain talk to the members of the council regarding the need of better laws. While the chiefs thought he might have brought with him from England a code of laws for the Islands, he told them that the making of laws was a matter for the chiefs to settle. However, before returning to England, he left with the chiefs a few suggestions, written in English, for their consideration. The adoption of the principle of trial by jury in Hawaii is credited to the suggestion of Lord Byron ". . . that no man's life be taken away except by the consent of the King, or the Regent for the time being, and twelve chiefs." This suggestion, when adopted by the chiefs, was a great relief to Kaahumanu, who had many times had been obliged to accept the responsibility for the taking of human life.

While in the Islands, Lord Byron instituted the first surveys of importance: Those of Waikiki Bay and the bay at Hilo. Kaahumanu named the Hilo bay "Byron's Bay" in honor of the Englishman, and it was so called for many years. The Regent was appreciative of what had been accomplished and turned over to the surveyors a two-story house which she had recently purchased in Honolulu from an American prospector. This house, with its balcony overlooking the sea, was to be used as headquarters of the surveying party. When Lord Byron wanted to visit the volcano on Hawaii, Kaahumanu sent two hundred native people to prepare the way for the expedition. A careful survey was made at this time of the district surrounding the volcano.

An interesting episode of Lord Byron's visit was connected with the work of Mr. Dampier, the artist of the expedition. Among other pictures, he painted a portrait of Kaahumanu. Lord Byron comments: "The great queen, Kaahumanu, whose temper is violent, although a person of keen, shrewd understanding, was very indignant that the little king and princess were painted before her, and she is not very well pleased with the frown which she sees reflected in her own portrait. She is, however, very kind to us and unites with our shipmates in showing us every possible attention."

The coming of Lord Byron gave a definite uplift to civilization in Hawaii. The chiefs listened to him with interest and accepted and followed his advice in many matters, the results of which are plainly marked in the history of the development of government in the Islands. The years were filled with important experiences, but they were not easy years for Kaahumanu. She had many enemies among the foreigners who were seeking to expand their own interests. She was called a "usurping old woman."

One trouble was the unexpected arrival of Catholic priests with equipment to set up their worship and instruction in the Islands. This movement had come about through the efforts of the Frenchman, Rives, who had acted as a sort of secretary and valet to Liholiho on his voyage to England. He soon proved himself unsavory and was dismissed from the King's service when they reached England. Leaving the King's party, he went on to France where he passed himself off as a rich and important man in the government of the Sandwich Islands. He succeeded in so impressing the powers of the Roman church that it was decided to send priests to open a mission in the Islands. Rives promised that the priests would be met and that all financial matters would be taken care of when their ship should reach Honolulu. He then left for California and was never heard from again. The little group of priests was stranded without money and with few friends, other than the Spaniard, Don Marin.

A critical situation arose with the coming of the Catholics to Hawaii. The use of images in their worship had, evidently, not been clearly explained to Kaahumanu by her missionary friends. She believed that the images in the little chapel were idols to be worshipped and feared by the people. She said the worship of images had been forbidden and discarded for all time, and that she did not wish such influence to be admitted to the Kingdom. Many Hawaiians, attracted by the new religion with its colorful setting, were accepting the Catholic faith. In her own religious zeal, Kaahumanu remained adamant. Eventually, she provided a vessel and the priests were sent to California to join their associates at San Gabriel Mission.

In later years, a Catholic mission was etablished in the Islands and old misunderstandings were forgotten. In the *History of the Catholic Mission in Hawaii,* written by Father Reginald Yzendoorn, is recorded the following testament by Father Bachelot, the leader of the first group of priests who came to the Islands: "Kaahumanu supports the Calvinists with all her power; she is a woman of much character, a friend of the general good and order." Father Bachelot added that Kaahumanu was under an illusion, but that she meant well.

Education continued under the earnest work of the mission. Kaahumanu, with the young King, Kamehameha III, made a tour through the windward islands teaching the gospel. Kaahumanu left governmental matters in the hands of Boki and his wife, Liliha. Kalanimoku was rapidly failing in health, but he still remained in the background; Kaahumanu trusted that all would be well while she was away. But trouble developed.

Boki and Liliha, close companions of Liholiho on his trip to England, had become ambitious for power. They had been courted by the foreign men who resented Kaahumanu and her restricting laws. These men finally succeeded in so influencing Boki and Liliha that they were led to believe that they might seize the throne. A small army was organized and camped at Waikiki. Friends of the Queen Regent likewise took up arms, and the groundwork for a revolution ensued. Kalanimoku was a sick man, but he went to see Boki, his younger brother, and remonstrated with him. He told Boki he would cast him off forever if he continued in his mad plans. Word was sent to Kaahumanu and she came as quickly as possible. She sent a message to Boki that she was at home if he wished to see her. She exhorted him to come and "dispatch" her if he chose, but without the carnage of war. Kekuanaoa, a high chief and a good friend of Kaahumanu, went boldly to Boki and rebuked him for his ignoble design to put Kaahumanu down by war. "No, No!" Boki replied. "If you wish to kill her," Kekuanaoa continued, "there she is, unattended by armed guards; go and dispatch her, if that is what you want, but do not set the nation in arms to destroy one another in war." Boki replied, *"Aole!"* (Not so). He ordered the plans for revolution to be stopped and peace declared. The character of Kaahumanu had triumphed.

In the meantime, the American Board of Commissioners were alert to the steadily growing work in Hawaii. Among the later missionaries to arrive in the Islands were Dr. and Mrs. Gerrit Judd, who very soon became friends with Kaahumanu. Throughout the remainder of her life, Dr. Judd, with William Richards and Mr. Bingham, were her closest advisers.

The death of Kalanimoku, following a long illness from dropsy, was nevertheless a shock to Kaahumanu. She and Kalanimoku had lived through the great changes which had taken place in the Islands since Kamehameha's death in constant friendship and wise counsel. Kaahumanu was no longer young. Many problems weighed heavily upon her heart. She had lost a mainstay in the death of Kalanimoku, her old and faithful friend. Boki, meanwhile, pressed for debts, jumped at the opportunity to lead an expedition to a "newly discovered" island in the South Pacific that supposedly abounded in sandalwood. His company, composed of the King's brig, *Kamehameha* and the *Becket,* sailed on December 2nd, 1829, stopped briefly at Rotuma, and, to this day, were heard of no more. The belief exists that his deck-hands were careless enough to smoke too close to the ship's powder supply. After Boki had gone on this ill-fated voyage to the South Seas, Liliha had continued as governess of the island of Oahu. Clouds of trouble broke into a storm. Liliha, still urged by her unscrupulous advisers, tried again to usurp the government. The young King was not wise in his choice of associates, and, through the influence of Liliha, he failed many times in his allegiance to Kaahumanu. This, to her, was both trouble and cause for alarm.

In 1832 Kaahumanu returned from her last educational tour. She was failing in health and felt her demise was approaching. She had written to the American Board in Boston: "I and he whom I have brought up (the young King) have indeed carried the word of our Lord through from Hawaii to Kauai; with the love of the heart towards God was our journeying, to proclaim to the people his love and his law and to tell them to observe them."

Kaahumanu invited Dr. and Mrs. Judd to accompany her to her home in Manoa Valley, her favorite residence. It was there, surrounded by her friends and devoted servants, that she spent her last days. It may have been at this time that she made the final arrangement for her affairs. The great and important matter was the succession of the regency. This she passed on to her stepdaughter, the noble Kinau, daughter of Kamehameha I. With all things in order, the Queen quietly awaited the closing of the doors of her long and eventful life.

For many years Kaahumanu's greatest joy had been the study of the scriptures. Mr. Bingham records that she was especially fond of the writings of St. Paul. She commented that Paul had a great many friends, and it pleased her that he called his disciples by name. Shortly before her death, Mr. Bingham rushed through the press copies of the New Testament in Hawaiian. He had a special copy bound for Kaahumanu in red Morocco leather with her name embossed in gold letters on the cover. He carried it to her and placed it in her hands. Slowly turning the leaves, she made sure that it was all there from Matthew to Revelation. Then, wrapping the book in her handkerchiefs, she pressed it to her breast, and folding her hands over it, she fell asleep. Toward evening she awoke and asked for Mr. and Mrs. Bingham. Speaking to them, she said, "I am going where the mansions are ready."

Mrs. Laura Judd, in her fine story of early missionary life in the Islands, tells how hundreds of native people camped within a mile-square of Kaahumanu's home, waiting for the final word of her passing. When the word came, on June 5, 1832, it traveled from camp to camp, and the wailing of the old Polynesia filled the valley. The Queen was dead. Governor Adams, Kaahumanu's brother, called for silence, and, from the open door of the Queen's home, Mr. Bingham committed the stricken nation to the care of God, the Father.

Kaahumanu, born of great warriors and capable in her own right of wielding power intelligently through the reigns of three Hawaiian rulers, carried the nation from the dark days of barbarism to the establishment of a modern and Christian government, verifying the trust which Kamehameha the Great had placed in her keeping.

In reviewing Hawaiian history, Kaahumanu stands today with such women as Catherine of Russia and Victoria of England—honored and

revered. And, in remembrance of this noble queen, one would repeat
with her close and faithful friend, David Malo:

> "Ceasing from the storm the sea grows calm
>   and glassy
>   Life a puff of wind flitting over it
>   So her spirit glides away to the far regions
>   of Kahihi (far away shores).

> "She had gone from us to the courts of Kane,
>   treading royally the red streaked path
>   of the rosy dawn.

> "O center of thought! O center of thought!
>   The voice is the staff that one leans upon.
>   Gone! Gone! Gone!

> "She fled at the first gleam of dawn, at the
>   faint ending of the cut off night.

> > "Our true liege lady was she
> >   and I grieve."

KAPIOLANI

Chapter IX

> "Great, and greater, and greatest
> of women, island heroine Kapio-
> lani."
> —ALFRED LORD TENNYSON

NOT UNIMPORTANT IN the development of the government of the Islands was the formal acceptance of Christianity and Christians by the Hawaiian people themselves. The missionaries survived their "trial period" and plunged into their work with renewed zeal. It was an up-hill task. This was understandable. The Hawaiians had behind them centuries of belief in their own ancient gods; four years of missionary effort, however strong, was insufficient to break the spell. If Christianity was to make its indelible mark upon the Islands, it had to prove itself. The burden of proof fell to the lot of a Hawaiian high chieftess —Kapiolani by name—who clutched it with all the ardor her newly-converted heart and mind could muster.

The ancient Hawaiian religion was polytheistic. It was a religion based primarily on the worship of nature. The ceremonial system was utilized to insure friendly relations between man and his various gods. Since the Islands are by nature volcanic, especial obeisance was made to Pele, goddess of the volcano. She was a demanding deity, and for centuries the Hawaiians stood in awe and fear of her powers over them. Then came Kapiolani.

Kapiolani was born in Kau district on the island of Hawaii, daughter of the high chief Keawemauhili. Kapiolani's father was the highest born and most sacred chief of all Hawaii in the early days of the Kamehameha era. He was King of the districts of Kau and Hilo. His was a strong and magnetic personality, and it would seem that his daughter inherited her father's ability and aggressiveness.

When Kapiolani grew to young womanhood, she became the wife of Naihe, the son of one of the four great councilors of Kamehameha. Naihe was a fine public speaker—the chosen orator of the people—and a powerful chief. Together, in 1821, they accompanied Liholiho on his perilous trip to Kauai to visit King Kaumualii. Naihe and Kapiolani were among the first converts to Christianity. Kapiolani was a close friend of Kaahumanu and worked with her to promote education and further civilization in the Islands. When Lord Byron arrived from England to study the situation in the Islands, and to assist the chiefs in forming laws for the development of the government, it was Naihe who presided at the conference attended by Lord Byron. Kapiolani was also a member of the conference, at which time she pointed out that she and her husband had already passed laws in their districts prohibiting drunkenness, theft, infanticide, and murder.

After becoming Christians, Naihe and Kapiolani built, for the mission at Kaawaloa on Hawaii, a church measuring thirty by sixty feet, to which the native people thronged to hear the gospel. They also built a sugar mill and encouraged the people to plant and raise sugar cane. They moved their home to Kona near Kealakekua and, although they spent several months each year in Honolulu, always kept a careful oversight of their people in the Kau and Hilo districts. While in Honolulu, Kapiolani joined Queen Kamamalu in studying English, and returned to Hawaii to help organize classes and appoint students to teach under the direction of the missionaries.

Kapiolani's conversion to Christianity changed her entire life. Laura Fish Judd, in her book, *Honolulu, Sketches of Life in the Sandwich Islands,* tells the following story: "About the year 1821, as one of the pioneer missionaries was walking on the seashore, he saw, sitting on a rock, a large, finely proportioned woman saturating her dusky skin with the fragrant coconut oil, and basking in the noonday sun like a seal or sea elephant. It is difficult to believe this personage to have been our present ladylike and sensitive Kapiolani." This was one year after the coming of the missionaries, and it was not long afterward that Kapiolani became a Christian.

Dr. Stewart tells how he first met Kapiolani: "She is an exceedingly interesting character, and from having been addicted to the grossest intemperance and dissipation, had become perfectly correct in her habits and is, invariably, serious and dignified in her deportment. I first saw her at the mission house on the morning of our arrival, and I was so forcibly impressed with the neatness of her dress and the propriety of her whole appearance as to be led to enquire who she was and whether she could be a Sandwich Islander. She is deeply interested in the success of the mission and is, herself, an indefatigable scholar; incidentally, she showed us a very handsome writing desk for which she had paid seventy-five dollars."

Kapiolani was an ardent worker in the cause of missions, and, being greatly distressed that the mission at Hilo was not doing as well as had been hoped, determined to do something about it. Because she was so high born, Kapiolani was sacred in the eyes of the people. Her word was law. Through her, the will of the gods was revealed to the people. This was true of all the *alii*, and so the missionaries had first to convert the nobility before they could reach the common people. Within four years' time, the missionaries had made considerable progress with the nobility and, through them, were trying to demonstrate to the commoners the power of Christianity over that of the old gods. Kapiolani's faith and power combined proved to be of immeasurable value.

The district of Hilo was impregnated with the superstition surrounding the volcano located some 30 miles distant. Pele, the goddess, was believed to live in the volcano at Kilauea. The natives feared not only her power, but also that of her priesthood. One of the laws of the goddess concerned the *ohelo* berries which grow near the volcano. The berries were not to be eaten by anyone without first casting some of them into the volcano as an offering to Pele. Death was the penalty for breaking this taboo.

Around the volcano existed an almost extinct race who daily offered sacrifices to Pele. Her priesthood was very powerful and there were women wandering about the country, poisoning the minds of the people against Christianity, who claimed to be priestesses of the goddess and were sometimes believed to be Pele, herself, in disguise. Thus, the people were in constant fear. All of this Kapiolani knew, and, as a Christian, she determined to free her people from this superstition. In December, 1824, she decided to go, herself, to the volcano and to defy the goddess on her own ground. She would tell the people that Pele was a myth and could do them no harm. Her husband and friends opposed her plan and begged her not to undertake such a dangerous experiment, for they feared for her life. She was adamant.

Mr. Ruggles, in charge of the mission at Hilo, was anxious to go with Kapiolani, but he had been without shoes for six months and could not attend her. Mr. Goodrich, his associate, had learned to walk the lava rocks barefoot and said he would accompany Kapiolani in Mr. Ruggles' place. Kapiolani traveled over one hundred miles, mostly on foot, from Kealakekua to Hilo, over a very rough and difficult way.

Jarves, in his history of the Islands, written in the early years of missionary work in Hawaii, records the following facts: "The island of Hawaii affords specimens of at once the grandest, most picturesque, and sternest, of nature's works. Raised from the sea by volcanic action at a date never to be ascertained by man, it has accumulated layer upon layer of lava rock, piled in every shape that so fearful and powerful an agency can give them, until it has shot up mountains more than two and a half miles high. Mauna Kea, on the north, and Mauna Loa, on the south, with the lesser mountain, Hualalai, to the west, divide the island between them. Mauna Kea rises to an elevation of 13,950 feet; Mauna Loa, 13,760 feet. Both are vast in their proportions though differing widely in their natural features.

"Mauna Kea is a succession of craters long extinct which have risen one above another, heaping up stones, ashes, sand, and cinders, long enough quiescent to form soil and clothe its flanks with vegetation. To all appearance it has had much longer respite from internal fires than its neighbor. But judging from the late eruptions, all of Hawaii must be a mere crust raised upon a vast glove of fire.

"Mauna Loa forms an immense dome with a base of 120 miles and a horizon, at the top, of 27 miles. The top area is covered with a gigantic crater through nearly its entire extent. Nothing can exceed the cold sterility of this region, or the fury of the blasts that sweep over it. At long intervals its gigantic crater heaves with internal fires, throwing its boiling lava over its crest and bursting vents for it down its sides, from which it spread it's fiery currents to the plains beneath consuming before it every living thing.

"On the eastern flank of this mountain, some 10,000 feet down at an elevation of 3,970 feet above the sea, is situated that vast pit, six miles in circumference and from 400 feet to 1000 feet deep called Kilauea, the fabled residence of the goddess Pele. No region on the globe affords greater attraction to the lover of volcanic phenomena than this. Stupendous in their scale, always active though varying greatly in intensity, they never fail to impress the traveler with wonder, interest, and fear. Vesuvious sinks into insignificance in comparison. The visitor must not, however, expect to find a huge pit, two miles in diameter, filled to overflowing with liquid lava as the imagination readily suggests at the idea of a crater. Kilauea more frequently presents the appearance of a smoking ruin sunken deep into mother earth, flashing with light and flame, heavy with smoke and stunning with detonations and angry noises. Occasionally, the black crust or mass beneath heaves and is rent asunder; rivers of viscid boiling lava arise spouting blood-red jets far into the air; or they spread into a lake which sends its heavy waves against its sides with the noise and fury of the surf on a precipice-bound shore."

Such a scene Kapiolani faced when she reached the great volcano. A letter, which gives an account of her defiance of Pele, was written by one of Kapiolani's head men, who accompanied her to the volcano. He writes:

"When she was on her way to the volcano she was accosted by a multitude and entreated not to proceed any further, lest in her anger the goddess of the volcano should destroy her. She answered, 'If I am destroyed, then you may all believe in Pele.' When she arrived near the crater, a man whose duty it was to feed the Pele by throwing berries and the like into the volcano came out to meet her and said, 'Don't you go to the volcano.' Kapiolani answered, 'What is the harm?' The man said, 'Because you will die by Pele.' Kapiolani replied, 'I shall not die by your god. That fire was kindled by my God. Repent of your sins!' The man was silent and she went on and descended the crater a distance of several hundred feet and then offered up a prayer to Jehovah. She devoured the berries of the Pele, threw stones into her mouth, and then she prayed to God, and all the district see she is not injured and pronounce the Pele to be powerless."

A letter from Mr. Goodrich also relates what took place at the volcano that morning. He writes: "The next day, December 22nd, after attending family worship and breakfast, Kapiolani and her attendants, about fifty in all, began to descend into the crater. The descent for about 400 feet is quite steep, then for a considerable distance it is gradual. Kapiolani and most of her company descended to the ledge which is from a few feet to a quarter of a mile wide and extends nearly around the crater about 500 feet from the top. Below the ledge is a descent of 300 or 400 feet, more difficult in consequence of so many chasms in the lava which in many places is broken off and fallen down. Kapiolani requested that they all unite in singing, and one of her attendants led in prayer. Afterwards, Kapiolani and others with her descended to the bottom which appeared quite smooth when viewed from the top but it was very rugged and uneven. Upon near approach, they found that thick, sulphurous fumes were constantly ascending from a great many places in the bottom of the crater. In twelve different places the lava was red hot. Three of these were liquid and flowed like water, although with not quite so rapid a current."

The world at large gradually learned the story of Kapiolani and quickened to its dramatic and strange picture of heroism. It evidently made a strong appeal to the mind of Alfred Lord Tennyson who wrote the following poem in her honor:

KAPIOLANI

I

When from the terrors of nature a people have
    fashioned and worshiped a spirit of evil
Blest be the voice of a Teacher who calls to them,
    "Set yourselves free!"

II

Noble the Saxon who hurled at his Idol a valorous
    weapon in olden England!
Great, and greater, and greatest of women, island
    heroine Kapiolani
Climb the mountain, flung the berries and dared
    the Goddess, and freed the people
Of Hawa-i-ee!

III

A people believing that Peele the Goddess would
    wallow in fiery riot and revel
      On Kilauea,
Dance in a fountain of flame with her devils or
    shake with her thunders and shatter her island,
Rolling her anger
Thro' blasted valley and flowing forest in blood-red
    cataracts down to the sea.

IV

Long as the lava light
    Glares from the lava-lake,
    Dazing the starlight;
Long as the silvery vapor in daylight
    Over the mountain
Floats, will the glory of Kapiolani be mingled with
    either on Hawa-i-ee.

V

What said her Priesthood?
    "Woe to this island if ever a woman should
    handle or gather the berries of Peele!
Accursed were she!
And woe to this island if ever a woman should
    Climb to the dwelling of Peele the Goddess!
Accursed were she!

VI

One from the sunrise
Dawned on His people and slowly before him
    Vanished shadow-like
    Gods and Goddesses,
None but the terrible Peele remaining as Kapiolani
    Ascended the mountain,
Baffled her priesthood,
    Broke the Taboo,
    Dipt to the crater,
Called on the Power adored by the Christian and
    crying, "I dare her, let Peele avenge herself!"
Into the flame-billows dashed the berries, and drove
    the demon from Hawa-i-ee.

The immediate region about the crater of Kilauea, being remote from all mission stations, remained for several years under the priesthood of Pele. It was seldom visited by ruling chiefs, and the inhabitants living within the circuit of former devastations of the volcano, and in sight of the terrific action, were more deeply imbued with the heathen superstition than those whose idols had been destroyed and whose faith in them had been year after year weakened by foreign influence.

Many pages of missionary history in the Islands give stories of the life of Kapiolani, as well they should. Mr. Bingham, who knew her intimately, wrote of her historic action at the volcano: "Here was heroism of a more sublime and immortal character than that which rushes to the battle field. Here was a philosophy which might put to blush the pride of pagan Athens and Rome, whose philosophers would risk nothing in suppressing idolatry."

Kapiolani remains today one of the great heroines of Hawaiian history. Her noble deed, however, was not wholly effective, for on the lips of old Hawaiians—and on those of many white men—is whispered still the name of Pele. Despite modern Hawaii's development and sophistication, legend lingers and Pele is occasionally seen to stalk her ancient by-ways. When she does, there are those who marvel anew at Kapiolani's bravery.

THE GREAT MAHELE

Chapter X

"The hearts of kings are deep."
—HIRAM BINGHAM

THE REIGN OF KAMEHAMEHA III, following the death of Kaahumanu, began in turmoil. The King and the chiefs felt that the very keystone of the kingdom had crumbled.

Kaahumanu's later years had been considered peaceful years. Education towards civilization had been steadily moving forward. There had been little apprehension or disturbance from outside powers. But there was deeply seated trouble within the kingdom because of the unsettled question of ownership of land, and that of religious privilege. In 1827, the first Catholic missionaries arrived. They were in for a difficult time. Kaahumanu, over-zealous in her new-found faith and possibly ill-advised by the Protestant missionaries, ordered the priests to stop spreading their faith. Orders were published prohibiting the natives from attending Catholic worship. Many of the priests were forced to leave the Islands. The lay brothers who remained behind, along with their followers, suffered religious persecution for some years to come. Then, too, the chiefs were worried about the King.

From the time of the breaking of the taboo, when Kaahumanu and the Queen Mother, Keopuolani, had insisted that the young Prince, Kauikeaouli, should, with them, defy the law of the centuries and eat together, he had been under the constant restrictions of the two women. As long as Kaahumanu lived he had followed her leadership and accepted her dictates with few exceptions. In 1829, three years before the Regent's death, the young King seemed to be maturing in the proper direction. Kaahumanu and the chiefs, as well as the missionaries, were pleased when, at the dedication of the great meetinghouse in which Kalanimoku had been so greatly interested, with four thousand people in the congregation, both native and foreign, the King unexpectedly rose to his feet and addressed the assembly. Wearing his rich Windsor uniform, and with a gracious manner, the young ruler made a good impression. He spoke with clearness and decision. He said that he had built the church and now wished publicly to dedicate it to God. He said that he wished his subjects to serve God's law and learn His word. The King was but sixteen years old, and his attitude seemed to be a firm step forward and a promise for his coming reign when he should reach his majority.

Not long after the dedication of the meetinghouse, the King appeared to be taking a real interest in governmental matters. He proclaimed in his own name, and that of Kaahumanu, that the laws of the kingdom forbade murder, theft, licentiousness, sabbath breaking and gambling, and declared that these laws should be equally enforced on subjects and foreigners. The Christian marriage was established. All persons who continued to live with one partner after a certain date would be considered legally married.

In the foreign population many intelligent men, including the British consul, Mr. Charlton, were at sword's points, among other things, with the government restrictions on land-buying and transfer by foreigners. Mr. Charlton had many supporters. He claimed that all laws must first be submitted to the English King for his sanction before they could be accepted. He also asserted that he, as the English consul, had the power to remove the Regent, take the fort, and imprison the King and the members of the royal family. So the community was in a constant upheaval over conflicting measures. This all took place before Boki made his fatal expedition. In the meantime, under the influence of Boki and Liliha, of both of whom he was very fond, the King began to lose interest in the serious concerns of the government. But, after the death of Kaahumanu, he again expressed his desire to assume some responsibility and to have more to say in the council of chiefs.

During the months following Kaahumanu's death, many changes took place. There was consternation among some of the people when the announcement was made that Kinau, the King's half-sister, was to be the Regent. Although she was the daughter of Kamehameha I, she was of lower rank than the King, her mother having been of lesser rank than Keopuolani, the King's mother. It was feared that she could not fill the high office which Kaahumanu had held in the kingdom. Because of this feeling it was decided that the King and Kinau should make a joint proclamation so that the people might fully understand the situation and the matter of laws which had been declared.

The King proclaimed: "I am superior, and my mother (figuratively, meaning Kinau) subordinate. She is my chief agent. We two, who have been too young and unacquainted with the actual translation of business, now, for the first time, undertake to regulate our kingdom. Ye men of foreign lands, let not the laws by you be put under your feet. When you are in your countries, there you will observe your own laws."

Kinau, in her new role as Regent, declared: "The office which my mother (meaning Kaahumanu, even though Kaahumanu had not been her actual mother) held until her departure, is now mine. All her active duties and her authority are committed to me. The taboos of the King, and the laws of God, are with me, and also the laws of the King. My appointment as chief agent is of long standing, even from our Father (Kamehameha). This is another point I make known to you; according to the law (or violation of law) shall be the loss or dispossession of land. We are trying to make our minds mature."

Months passed. The King gradually lost interest in government affairs, leaving all decisions to Kinau and the chiefs while he spent his time spending money and enjoying himself as he never had done before. Through the influence of Liliha, he had taken into the intimacy of his court a group of young men who called themselves *"Hulumanu"* (bird feathers). These new friends surrounded the King with every possible temptation. They praised and flattered him, probably saying, "You are the King! Why not do as you please?" The Regent and the chiefs were distracted. Mr. Bingham strongly and patiently pleaded with him, but while he was polite and friendly to his old teacher, he did not change.

Looking back to the boyhood of Kamehameha III, one comes to a reasonable understanding of his reactions. He had never had any of the good times such as belonged to boys of his age. He was kept strictly under the control of Kaahumanu. All of the old-time sports of the Hawaiian people, the ancient culture of the race, had been placed under a ban by the coming of the missionaries. Kaahumanu's conversion to the Christian faith, and her great interest in education, had gone to extremes, and more and more restricted became the pattern of the young King's daily life.

Kinau, the Regent, was a woman of great ability and strong character, but she could not control the King as Kaahumanu had done. Like his father, Kamehameha, and his brother, Liholiho, he loved ships. He wanted to own a yacht and to sail whenever and wherever he pleased. The sea, and all it held, was the birthright of the Hawaiian people; it was *their* sea. When the King told Kinau that he wished to buy a yacht, she objected, and referred it to the council of chiefs. It was decided that the government could not afford to pay $12,000 for a pleasure boat when there were already pressing debts to be met. Both Liholiho and Boki with their extravagancies had so depleted the treasury that there was no money for luxuries. Kinau and the council were alarmed. The young King was following in the footsteps of his brother and of Boki. The chiefs refused to purchase the yacht. The King became angry. He had already promised to buy the boat, and he at once planned a drastic revolt against authority.

At the King's command, a crier was sent through the streets proclaiming that all laws except those relating to murder and theft were rescinded. This was not only an antagonistic attitude toward Kinau and the chiefs, but a breaking away from the widespreading control of the mission. The King and his friends, the bird feathers, were joined by Mr. Charlton and were led by him in establishing an orgy of misrule. History relates, "The royal example was followed by thousands in all parts of the kingdom. The hula and other ancient sports were revived and extensively practiced to the accompaniment of gambling, drunkenness, and other vices indulged in by both natives and foreigners in a strong reaction against the rigorous, puritanical rule which had reached its climax in 1831 and 1832."

An American trader who had lived in the Islands for many years said: "The King and his party have thrown off the ecclesiastical restraint which they have been under for so long a time. All their ancient games and customs have been revived again. We see the natives everywhere about the village playing the games of the Stone, Spears, &c., &c. Every evening large companies assemble to sing and dance all in their ancient way. Nothing bad has resulted from it yet, except a few of the lower classes of natives spending their time carousing and drinking to excess. But these and such like excesses may be expected for a time after such a 'Revolution.' They are no longer a priest-ridden people."

The revolt continued month after month for two long years. More and more foreign influence was brought to bear upon the mind of the King. The group of men following the lead of the English consul were in constant attendance at the palace and wherever the King might be. They urged him to take entire control of the government, telling him they were ready to back him up in anything he wished to do.

Kinau and the chiefs were distracted. The King had forbidden Kinau even to enter his presence. Her friends feared harm would come to her. Desperate, she finally appealed to Dr. and Mrs. Judd. She told them she could no longer bear the strain. She begged them to go with her, taking their families, to some distant country, where they could live in peace. Her friends pointed out to her that she must be strong and accept the responsibility of Regent of the nation for the sake of her people, urging her to take a firm stand for the right, assuring her that the time would come when the situation would be under control and the troubles forgotten.

The mission workers continued their teaching. While in Honolulu, especially, the meetings may not have been as well attended as formerly, there were many native Christians and new converts to the Christian faith who carried on the schools and the work of the church on all the islands. But conditions were rapidly changing and the mission program had to be adapted to the change.

It was evident that the King hoped to regain for the crown as much as possible of the power which had gradually passed into the hands of the chiefs. The King may have reasoned that his father, Kamehameha I, had controlled the chiefs, not they him. He made the laws and the people accepted them. He, Kamehameha III, would do the same.

Clouds of apprehension and uncertainty settled over the nation. No one knew what to expect. Then the King took a surprising and definite stand. He was now eighteen years old. He first met with and announced to the council of chiefs that he was taking into his possession "the lands for which his father toiled, the power of life and death, and the undivided sovereignty." He summoned a public gathering of the people. This was held in the open air. There was suppressed excitement as the people gathered, wondering what was to happen. The different groups, both native and foreign, were alert to all they could hear as they waited for the King.

It was feared by some that the King might renounce Kinau and appoint some inferior person to her high station of *kuhina-nui*. The English consul, Mr. Charlton, and his friends believed that one of their number, possibly Liliha, might be the chosen one. Many of the chiefs feared civil war. Suddenly, there was a startled movement among the people— Her Royal Highness, Kinau, made her way through the crowd and spoke to the King as he was about to begin his address. She said to him, "We cannot war with the word of God between us!" Kauikeaouli was a Kamehameha at heart. Turning to the people he first declared his sovereignty, then, lifting his hand, he solemnly confirmed Kinau as Premier of the kingdom. When he was asked why he had done so, he replied, "Very strong is the kingdom of God."

To his people, the King spoke: "These are my thoughts to all of ye chiefs, classes of subjects and foreigners, respecting this country which by the victory of Mokuohai was conquered by my father and his chiefs. It has descended to us as his and their posterity. This is more . . . All this is within it, the living and the dead, the good and the bad, the agreeable and the pleasant, all are mine. I shall rule with justice over the land, make and promulgate all laws; neither the chiefs nor the foreigners have any voice in making laws for this country. I alone am the one. These three laws which were given out formerly, remain still in force, viz., not to murder, not to steal, not to commit adultery; therefore govern yourselves accordingly."

To those who had the life of the Islands at heart, a day of hope had dawned. For a long time there had been tension and estrangement between the King and Kinau. She was older than he, and at times he was jealous of her power. But when, a few months later, Kinau gave birth to a son, the King at once adopted him as his heir, and there was great rejoicing.

When the King learned of the birth of the baby, he immediately went to congratulate Kinau. He first spoke to Kinau and then scrutinized the infant with a look of affection. When he left the room a scrap of paper was found stuck in the thatched wall which read, "This child is mine." The age-old Hawaiian custom of the adoption of royal children at birth by another high ranking family was again carried out, and Kamehameha III became the foster father of Kinau's son, who was, eventually, to become the fine ruler known in history as Kamehameha IV.

The surgeon of the U.S.S. *Peacock,* Dr. W. S. Ruchenberger, told of his acquaintance with Kamehameha III in the fall of 1835. The doctor was interested in the personality and character of the young ruler. He described him as a stoutly built young man, about five feet seven inches in height, with a broad face and mild countenance. He wrote, "He was frank and unassuming, but had a cold temperament and was not easily excited." The doctor continued, "I had the honor of an introduction to His Majesty on the night of our arrival. We found him bowling for a bottle of wine with several of his chiefs. He was dressed in white drilling pantaloons without suspenders, and a white jacket, and he wore a neatly plaited parti-colored straw hat set knowingly on one side of his head. He speaks English intelligibly but prefers his own language. After the usual salutations he seized the ball in his left hand and resumed the game with great energy. He is fond of athletic exercises; plays skillfully at billiards and bowls; rides well, hunts well, and readily joins his lowest subjects in the severest toils. Not long ago a ship was cast away at Diamond point, and the King in a Tarpaulin and sailor's shirt and trousers, assisted actively in saving the cargo. He is fond of ships and delights in navigating among the islands of his domain."

At night the billiard tables were resorted to by both natives and foreigners, and at one or the other the King was sure to be found attended by several of his chiefs. One evening when he was bowling, someone asked him to go and play pool. He led the way to the billiard room and played pool until the clock struck eleven. He threw down his cue at once, although in the middle of a game. The lights were extinguished in obedience to the curfew law which was made by himself to restrain dissipation.

The doctor wrote of meeting the King under very different circumstances. With the officers of the *Peacock* and the *Enterprise,* he was invited to meet the royal family. They were received in a coral house by a chief in a blue military frock coat. The King wore a blue coat with two gold epaulets, white pantaloons, and vest. There were present the King's sister and his two half-sisters, Kinau, the Regent, and Auhea. The ladies all wore black silk. They received the officers standing, but soon seated themselves on a sofa in front of which stood Rev. Bingham, as interpreter. The doctor wrote: "A commonplace conversation occurred, and a glass of wine was offered."

During the stay of the *Peacock* and the *Enterprise* in Hawaiian waters, there was much social entertainment, but there was also much discussion of important matters with the King and with the chiefs, especially regarding the holding and transferring of land occupied by foreigners. Kinau said that the King had never, in any instance, alienated his right in the soil, and when lots of ground were assigned to foreigners it was always understood, either on the departure of the individual from the Islands, or at his death, such ground reverted to the King, and that it must be cleared. Kinau also stated that the King would give his consent, were he asked, to the sale or transfer of houses &c., provided he should deem the person, to whom the transfer was to be made, respectable and likely to be a good citizen.

The following day Commodore Kennedy and Dr. Ruchenberger, from the *Peacock,* met the chiefs in another conference at which the King was present. The King said that if he yielded the right of free transfer, he virtually resigned his right in the soil, as well as all authority and control over it, and thus he might be deprived of all of his country.

The matter of leasing lands for the cultivation of sugar, cotton, coffee, tobacco, and silk was discussed, and the King stated he was entirely in favor of the principle, but that he wished to be expressly understood that, in recognizing the principle of lease, he did not feel bound to grant lands to all who might apply. He also said that he was unwilling to give his statement in writing, because it was a new thing and required more consideration than he had yet been able to give it. This explanation opened the trail which the Hawaiian government was to follow for years to come—the trail of land.

Changes were taking place in the King's personal life. The death of his sister, Nahienaena, dealt a stunning blow to the King. He and his sister had been closely associated in every way, and it had been hoped that some day the Princess might sit at her brother's right hand in the government.

Two months after the death of his sister the King was married to Kalama, a lesser chieftess. She is described as a "sprightly young person" who had been a favorite of the King for some time, so the marriage was promising. The wedding was held in the native church following the evening service.

The King's marriage gradually distracted him from his interest in governmental affairs, but he was interested in the building of a stone church, to which he contributed fifteen hundred dollars from his personal funds for the purchase of lumber, windows, and other needed supplies. The new church was to be called the "King's Chapel." Kamehameha III probably did not count himself a religious man, but he regularly attended divine service and always showed attention. The chiefs may have felt that the building of the church was a move in the right direction, but they were troubled and anxious over governmental concerns. As the King pursued his pleasures, more and more responsibility of running the government fell upon Kinau. The British consul in 1836 wrote that "she is entirely governed by the American Missionaries who through her govern the Islands with unlimited sway."

For years different foreign powers had been contending over the possible control of the commercial interests in the Islands, which were steadily growing in importance in the Pacific area. Foreign ships in increasing numbers were coming and going. Officers of these ships constantly advised the King and the council that the laws of the country should be changed and adapted to modern conditions, as foreigners did not understand the form of Hawaiian government.

Hawaii was no longer the Hawaii of the old days. This was pointedly emphasized by foreigners who declared that drastic changes must be made if there was to be peaceful and profitable living for everyone, both native and foreign. The debts of the nation were mounting beyond belief. The King was finally brought to realize, and to face, the situation. He summoned Dr. Judd and William Richards to talk things over with him. He told them he was anxious and coerced, and did not know which way to turn. He said that if they would stand by him he would cut his own personal expenditures, and also give of his private funds that the most pressing obligations might be met immediately. This he did. He resumed his responsibilities as head of the nation and settled down to a more normal and constructive way of life. The chiefs and the friends of the King were encouraged.

After many conferences and very careful consideration, it was decided to ask Mr. William Richards to go to Washington to present the situation of the Hawaiian government to the President of the United States, requesting him, if possible, to send them a legal adviser.

About this time a bright bit of progress evidenced itself with the opening in 1839 of a private school for young chiefs—the "Chiefs' Children's School"—under the direction of Mr. and Mrs. Amos Starr Cooke. One by one the royal children were entered in the school. The King was greatly interested in this forward step in the education of the young chiefs who would one day take the responsibility of the kingdom. A school was opened at Punahou in 1841 for the children of the missionaries under the direction of Rev. Daniel Dole. The children of foreigners who came to reside in the Islands were also admitted. The land for the building of the school at Punahou had been given to Mr. Bingham for that purpose by Boki before he left the Islands.

When Mr. Richards returned from Washington with his report, the King and the council were disappointed. They turned to Mr. Richards and asked that he, himself, accept the responsibility of adviser. To do so he was obliged to resign his connection with the mission, since the missionaries were not supposed to take any active part in the government. Mr. Richards accepted the responsibility, unwillingly, but under his guidance governmental matters moved on with more assurance.

In April, 1839, the Premier, Kinau, was stricken with paralysis and died. The nation was again in mourning. Kinau, both great and wise in her leadership, had been a stronghold in the council of the King. Like Kaahumanu, Kinau had been a mother to the nation, and the people were bereft. There was no one to take her place. The position of the *kuhina-nui* must continue, and Kekauluohi (Auhea) was appointed. She had been trained from childhood to be the repository of the history of the Hawaiian people. There was no question of genealogical interest that she could not answer. But it was Mr. Richards who carried much of the responsibility.

One of the first moves made by Richards was to organize a lecture course for the chiefs. He lectured to them every day at ten o'clock along the lines of political economy and the science of government. Dr. Kuykendall writes: "The question uppermost in the minds of the chiefs, and to which Richards had to give immediate attention, was that relating to the land and fixed property in the possession of foreigners and the privilege, claimed by the foreigners, of transferring these things from one to another."

The lecture course was a great success. The King was keenly interested. He said he wished the young chiefs to be trained in the same manner, so that when the time came for them to take their places in the council they would be prepared.

After many conferences with Richards, and within the council, the King decided there must be a decisive action in favor of the people.

Up to this time the King had owned all the land. The great chiefs were his tenants, but they could sublet their lands to retainers who would also sublet to the common people. The natives were defenseless. They were often taken advantage of by the chiefs who were landholders. Because of this, large numbers roamed from place to place with no settled homes, often attaching themselves to some landlord for the sake of food. If a man wanted a piece of land to live on, plant and culti- vate, he had to pay a heavy rent. If he planted and raised a fine crop of taro, for instance, the landlord could take it from him without com- pensation. The people often were forced to give of their time in building public roads, a *heiau* (temple), fish-pond or sea wall.

Kamehameha III was basically a kind man. He came to realize that some of the old customs were wrong, and determined to change mat- ters. In 1839 he issued a declaration which is often called "The Bill of Rights." It said that every man was given by God Liberty, the labor of his hands, and the production of his mind. The declaration announced: "Protection is hereby assured to all people, together with their lands, their building lots, and all their property, and nothing whatever shall be taken from any individual except by express provision of the law. Whatever chiefs shall perseveringly act in violation of this constitution, shall no longer remain a chief of the Sandwich Islands, and the same shall be true of all governors and land agents."

But old habits were too strongly ingrained. Abuses of power still continued. After long consideration, advice, and counsel, Kamehameha III took the most revolutionary action in Hawaiian history. He decided to divide the lands of the kingdom between himself, the chiefs, and the people. This act is known as the Great *Mahele*—land division.

The first division was between the King and the chiefs. Then the King divided his share of the land into three parts: Public Lands, Grants to Individuals, and lands to be retained by the King for his personal use and control. Following this, the chiefs' lands were also divided, part to the people, part to the state, and part being retained and known as the "Chiefs' Estates." Small pieces of land were given to those who had lived upon the land and were deserving, these to be known as *Kuleanas* (small pieces). This term is still in use today in real estate, the titles to which are often in dispute in the courts of the Islands.

A land commission was later appointed and for ten years allotted land to those who held it as tenants. This gave a feeling of security in establishing individual ownership of land. Today people speak with pride of having inherited land which was a grant from the King. The gift of the Great *Mahele* marked the century, and marked Kameha-

meha III, now settled and mature in his ways, as the first great demo-
crat and liberal in the Kamehameha dynasty.

From this time on, exciting events took place in the Sandwich Islands.
There are always men in public life who usurp or assume authority. The
English gentleman, Lord Paulet, a commander in the British navy, was
one of these. There had been some unpleasant associations connected
with several Britishers who had been unfair in their dealings with the
Hawaiian government. Out of these disturbances came the crisis of Lord
Paulet's attempt to seize the Islands in the name of the British crown.
In the meantime, Richards had gone to the United States and to England
to place before the authorities in those countries the matter of diplomatic relations between the Sandwich Islands and the foreign lands.

On the tenth of February, 1843, the British frigate, *Carysfort,* commanded by Lord Paulet, arrived in Honolulu. No salutes were given
from the ship as was the usual custom. The officials on shore realized
that something was wrong. Representatives of the King went to the
Carysfort to pay their respects, but they were not permitted to go on
board the vessel.

That night the captain of a United States ship, the *Boston,* received
a letter to the effect that the commander of the *Carysfort* was planning
an immediate attack on the Islands. At this time William Richards,
Haalilio, the Hawaiian diplomat, and Sir George Simpson, were in
England negotiating for recognition of the independence of the Islands.

In the morning the *Carysfort* was cleared for action. The English
families were taken to a brig in the outer roads. The Americans and
others, having but short notice, placed their funds and papers on board
the *Boston* and other American vessels, planning to retreat to them if
actual hostilities began. Everyone was fearful, and there was great alarm
and intense excitement in all sections of Honolulu.

Dr. Judd was the official treasurer of the government. Fearing a
seizure of the national archives, he removed the important papers from
the government house and concealed them in the royal tomb. In the
tomb at night, by the light of a lantern, using the coffin of Kaahumanu
as a writing table, the doctor kept the record for the government.

Communications were exchanged between the King, his council, and
the commander of the *Carysfort,* and resulted only in intensifying the
situation. The King was urged to cede the Islands at once to the United
States and France jointly. This he refused to do. Finally, with the advice
of the council, he decided to make a provisional surrender to England.
He saw no other way to prevent actual battle and the loss of many lives.
He trusted in the friendship of England, and he believed that, when

matters were fully explained, his kingdom would be restored to him. So, on February 25th, the King stood on the ramparts of the fort and addressed the people.

"Where are you, chiefs, people and commons from my ancestors, and the people from foreign lands! I make known to you that I am in perplexity by reason of difficulties into which I have been brought without cause; therefore have I given away the life of our land, hear ye! But my rule over you, my people, and your privileges will continue, for I have hope that the life of the land will be restored when my conduct shall be justified."

The deed of the cession was then read to the people, and Lord Paulet read his proclamation, after which the Hawaiian flag was lowered by native men. The British colors were hoisted over the fort, and the flag over the British consulate was struck.

For five long months the Sandwich Islands were under the control of Lord Paulet and his officers. But happier days were ahead. Word of the incident finally reached Rear Admiral Thomas of the British navy, who was located at the time at Valparaiso. Lord Paulet had overstepped his authority. Admiral Thomas sailed immediately for the Islands, bringing with him the assurance that the King's confidence in England had not been misplaced. Upon his arrival he declared at once that the King's sovereignty would be returned to him. He said that the Queen of England desired Kamehameha III be treated as an independent sovereign, leaving the administration of justice in his own hands.

It was a great occasion when, on the open plain not far from the town, in the park which today in Honolulu is known as Thomas Square, the restoration ceremony was held. It was one of Honolulu's perfect, sunny mornings. The marines from the Admiral's flagship, the *Dublin*, and from the *Carysfort* and the *Hazard,* were drawn up in line, with a battery of field pieces on the right. The King, escorted by his troops, and accompanied in his carriage by Admiral Thomas, arrived on the grounds. As the Royal Hawaiian Standard was hoisted, a salute of twenty-one guns was fired from the battery. The Hawaiian flag was then raised over the fort and on Punchbowl Hill. Salutes were fired from both forts and from four men-of-war which were in port. Admiral Thomas read a lengthy declaration, which announced and verified the restoration of the Island Kingdom to Kamehameha III as the sovereign of the Sandwich Islands. History was written that bright morning in the hearts of men of many nations.

At one o'clock a thanksgiving service was held in the Stone Church (Kawaiahao). The King addressed the congregation. He told the people

that, as he had hoped, the life of the land had been restored. He said
that the country from that time would be governed according to the
constitution and laws. At the close of his address, which the people had
received with great rejoicing, a holiday of ten days was announced and
the community began a happy time of celebration.

As years went by, a civilization patterned on American and European
standards was built up. The King and the people followed the leadership of white men in establishing and consolidating the government.
Many of the leading men in the time of reconstruction were from Massachusetts. The judicial procedure and many of the statute laws were taken
from that state. The words of the Massachusetts constitution, "To the
end that this may be a government of laws and not of men," was the
ideal which the men from New England sought to impress upon the
Islands. Courts were organized, and trial by jury was finally established.
Hawaii has a judicial history older than the majority of the States. The
printed decisions of the Supreme Court of Hawaii, which began in the
reign of Kamehameha III, compare well with those of any state. A new
constitution was adopted in 1852, calling for a legislature of two houses
to sit in separate chambers. The nobles were to be appointed by the
King for life and the representatives elected by the people.

The rapid development of California opened a new market for the
products of the Islands. Agriculture was pushed forward. Wheat and
sugar were successfully grown and exported to the United States. A
foundry was started in Honolulu, and plans were made to establish a
savings bank. The whaling industry brought many ships to the Islands
and a good return to the treasury.

Month by month ships from foreign countries brought supplies to
Honolulu. The people of the Islands had a choice of food such as other
countries had. Old newspapers, carefully preserved in the Territorial
Archives, tell in long columns of advertising what the citizens of Honolulu and the outside islands were supplied with: "For sale, Merrimac
prints, white flannel, checked gingham, Swiss spot muslin, fringed para-
sols, ladies embroidered handkerchiefs, bags, hats, silk cravats, and
ladies black elastic hose." The grocer advertised: "Pickles, catsup, pie-
fruit, dried apples, jams, fresh clams, English mustard, olive oil, halibut
fins, tongues and sounds, extra quality champagne, cider, butter, cheese,
currants, crackers in tins, sperm candles, lamps, sardines, corkscrews,
knives, forks and clocks."

There was a steadily increasing need for artisans of all descriptions:
"Wanted, twelve journeyman carpenters. A farmer who understands
ploughing and farming operations generally." Under the head of "Med-

ical" an advertiser stated: "The undersigned invites the attention of physicians, planters, and public generally, to our stock of American, English and French drugs, imported directly for their special use from Europe and the United States. Particular attention will be given in putting up medicine for sea use." A newspaper announced that the King had received a gift from the local jeweler of a massive gold ring, beautifully chased, and a highly creditable work of art.

During the intervening years, it is true, many of the most important offices of the government were filled by foreign men, who, however, in order to fill these offices, were obliged to become naturalized citizens of Hawaii. For a time there was considerable protest made against the employment of so many foreigners, especially by Hawaiians residing on other islands than Oahu. The King decided to make a tour of the various islands so that he might speak personally to the people regarding this. John Young, Jr., who had been a close friend and companion of the King since their boyhood, went with him.

On this trip both the King and Mr. Young explained the necessity for employing foreigners in the offices of the government. The King said he hoped the time would come when the young chiefs would have acquired a sufficient education to enable them to assist in governmental matters. On the island of Maui, the King made a special plea to the people for their trust and cooperation. He said, "I urge you to support school and cultivate the soil. We are seeking the good of the country, but the work is not done. Your hereditary chiefs have been in trouble and therefore I have chosen some to aid you. They are ministers of white skin whom you see here. This is according to the old system. They know more than we, and I have chosen them for the sake of knowledge."

There was a more settled feeling among the people following the King's addresses on other islands, and the King continued to push forward the educational program everywhere. The missionaries had laid a strong foundation in the field of education, and this Kamehameha III both acknowledged and supported. In 1848 Rev. Richard Armstrong accepted the appointment of Minister of Public Instruction, which position he held as long as he lived.

For a period of ten days in 1849 Honolulu was again occupied by a foreign power—this time, France. This act marked the culmination of the friction which existed between the government and a self-important French consul named Dillon, who had taken it upon himself to make a series of demands upon the government. These included (1) that Catholic schools be subjected to the direction of the French mission, (2) that the tariff on brandy and liquor be lowered, (3) that the law prohibiting liquor to be imported free of duty up to $200 be repealed, since most French vessels had nothing else to import but liquor, and (4) that the French language be used in all business intercourse. The demands were forwarded to the Governor by Admiral Legoarant De Tromelin, who had come to Dillon's aid aboard a French frigate. When the government rejected the ultimatum, De Tromelin landed an armed force which took possession of the fort, government buildings, and all vessels flying the Hawaiian flag. After approximately ten days of occupation and negotiation, De Tromelin finally withdrew his forces and sailed away with the understanding that the King would send an agent to France to settle the difficulties. (It should be pointed out that Dillon later received a severe reprimand for his actions from the French government, which also disavowed De Tromelin's part in the affair.)

A few days after De Tromelin's departure, Dr. Judd sailed for France, accompanied by the two young Princes: Alexander Liholiho and his elder brother, Prince Lot. Young Alexander was the heir apparent to the throne, and the trip abroad appeared to be important, not only to the mission but to the broader education of the two young men as well. They would represent Hawaii.

As the years slipped along, the matter of treaties between Hawaii and other countries became so complicated that the possibility of annexation with the United States was the question of the hour. It was an economic problem based upon the sugar and whaling industries, which were controlled largely by the Americans. These men agitated for annexation because it would provide Hawaii with a sugar market free of tariff duties and an important American supply center for whaling vessels. In 1853 a group of thirteen radical Americans had threatened "revolution and a republic" unless the King consented to annexation with the United States. The King's foreign policy, however, remained unchanged. While cultivating the most friendly relations with all nations, he recognized in none the right to interfere in the internal affairs of his kingdom, or to exercise any jurisdiction whatever within his domain. He pushed for reciprocity treaties with other countries in order to guarantee the independence of the Kingdom. There were already established consulates from other countries. A table of the King's foreign agents reads as follows:

"1845-1851

"Commissioner, London; Consul General, Chile; Consul for New Zealand; Consul General for New South Wales; Consul General, Hamburg; Consul General for China; Consul for Hong Kong; Consul for Boston; Consul General for the United States; Vice Consul for Baltimore; Consul for Bremen; Consul for Java and the East Indies."

In the latter part of the reign of Kamehameha III, the matter of annexation was again pushed forward. The King had reached the final decision that annexation with the United States might settle difficulties which were mounting beyond his control. For several months the King had not been well. His friends and the officials were alarmed. They felt he had over-taxed his strength, and were not surprised when, on the fifteenth day of December, 1854, an acute illness developed so rapidly that the King died at the age of forty-one. Dr. Kuykendall, in his great story of the long thirty-year reign of Kamehameha III, says of him: "Few kings have in their lifetime more clearly won the affection of their people, or deserved more to be held in grateful remembrance by their own and future generations."

The will of Kamehameha III proclaimed his adopted son and heir, Alexander Liholiho, to be king with the title Kamehameha IV. And to him and the people he left the heritage of a liberal constitution and the gift of the right to hold land in fee simple.

Kamehameha III is remembered by his people for his unselfish patriotism in turning his semi-feudal inheritance into a constitutional monarchy. Duplicity and intrigue were foreign to his nature; he was sure and steadfast in friendship. These are great words to say of any man, even of a king.

THE DIARY OF A PRINCE

Chapter XI

> *"I am disappointed at the Americans. They have no manners, no politeness, not even common civility to a stranger."*
>
> —ALEXANDER LIHOLIHO

THE LATE, BELOVED Kinau's sons, both of whom were eventually to become kings of the Kamehameha dynasty, sailed from Honolulu on September 11, 1849, accompanied by Dr. Judd. They were off on a grand tour of France, England, and America; they went, too, to be on hand as representatives of the royal family when Dr. Judd should attempt to draw up treaties with these countries and to settle the knotty French problem occasioned by Consul Dillon's actions.

Prince Alexander Liholiho, adopted son and heir apparent of Kamehameha III, was possessed of a good mind and the ability to express it. He was observant, courteous, and genial, and altogether an excellent ambassador-at-large for his people. His brother, Prince Lot, seems to have been at this time somewhat phlegmatic in his reactions to the outside world. Alexander, however, kept a detailed and enthusiastic journal of the trip written in clear and pleasing English.

Alexander did not enjoy the first few days of the voyage after leaving Honolulu because he suffered from seasickness. He wrote: "This is the seventh day we have been out and we all feel quite well this morning. I saw a whale ship trying to get near us so as to be able to speak us, but the Captain did not seem inclined to speak to her." The Prince reported that their time was spent mostly in reading, and that he was up late the night before with *The Last of the Mohicans*. But the two boys were also given the task of copying manuscript for Dr. Judd. Alexander was kept so busy that he neglected his journal for several days. In the evenings the boys played different games and cards, but they were not allowed to play cards on Sunday.

"San Francisco, Monday, October 8, 1849. San Francisco has very much exceeded my expectations. I found it to be a very busy place, larger than I expected to find; large buildings and the streets crowded with people from all parts of the world. The streets are not such as we see in the S.I., but houses are built on each side of the road, such as the streets we have heard of in foreign countries."

The boys accompanied the Captain to the Post Office. There they met Mr. St. John, formerly of the Islands. Alexander wrote that they lost sight of the Captain and Dr. Judd, and with St. John, he and Lot proceeded to see if they could find John Dominis "alive and kicking."

They did not like the hotel where they stopped and moved to another. Alexander noted that they had to pay $5.00 to have their trunks brought from the tender. They found the weather of San Francisco very changeable: "For the past two or three days the weather had been unusually delightful. There is, perhaps, no country in the world where the weather is so changing. Perhaps the morning will be as fine as you will find in the Islands and then, perhaps, in an hour or two, dark, heavy mist will come up and continue so for two or three hours."

The boys had their "likenesses" taken at the Daguerrean Gallery. In the evening after tea they had a game of whist. On Sunday, they attended the Presbyterian Dutch Reformed Church, and in the evening Alexander attended the Baptist church. "A good sermon. Lot was sick and could not go." The next day Dr. Judd also had his likeness taken and when he returned he gave the boys copies, along with some advice which he laid down for them to follow:

"I am sorry to find occasion to make any observations upon the course you are pursuing, and I now do chiefly with the view of putting you upon your guard and protecting you from difficulties and dangers which I foresee will follow if you pursue that course longer. I was sorry to see you both drink ale on board the *Savannah,* because it can do you no good. The use of ale will do you much harm by creating a fondness for stimulants which always grows upon a person as he grows older; and, as you very well know, ruins many persons in the Islands.

"I am sorry that you sat up so late last evening playing cards. It was Sabbath morning before you retired, and you appear to have felt the ill effects today of the late hours. My objections to cards are that they will often tempt you to neglect other and better employment and will lead you into the society of those who should better be strangers when we arrive in the United States and England. This will be the case much more often after we leave San Francisco. I expect you to listen to my advice and to improve."

Alexander discussed the treaty: "October 29, 1849. On Thursday evening last we all assembled in our room and began examining the treaty between the United States and the Hawaiian Islands, lately negotiated by the respective commissioners, who, on their way to their respective destinations, met at this place and having found their powers duly authorized them to do so, did take hold, concluded, and signed their names and affixed their seals on that day. We had been making the different copies on the preceding week, and therefore I could not have time to be regular in writing my journal."

The visits at San Diego and at Panama were interesting, but Alexander had a cold and was obliged to be attended by the ship's doctor, so the boys did little sightseeing.

The diary continues: "Irving House, New York, December 17, 1849. We have at last arrived at the great city of New York. The houses are very large and tall, and the streets wide and clean. This building opens right onto the Park as it is called. We ordered dinner in our own apartment, which was a large, finely furnished room with two beds in it, one single and the other a double one.

"We had engaged a cabman to take our baggage to the Irving House, but on our first arrival a fellow had come on board and forced tickets into our hands, and he made a great fuss about our not taking his carriage. But we soon got rid of him by jumping into the one we had engaged, and we were soon on Broadway, our wheels rattling over the paved streets, to say nothing of our alarm and consternation in the way that our driver put us through."

Alexander recorded that the Common Council called and invited them to visit the City Hall. Mr. Stewart, former missionary in the Islands, also called. The boys visited the Museum and were greatly pleased with what they saw. Alexander mentioned, "We saw some living snakes and also some wax figures of the largest couple living. The rest of the day I spent in writing home." According to the journal, the boys seem to have done little in New York, although Alexander said, "We have seen many things to please us as well as to amuse us."

They left New York and, after a two days' sailing, they reached Halifax. "The passengers were given two hours for enjoyment. We immediately sallied to hire a sleigh, having heard that there was good sleigh riding on shore. After we rode for about a mile on very poor grounds, we came upon nice riding and it being my first time in a sleigh I was a little alarmed in the way we proceeded. We have got completely out of town and were going at a terrible speed. But what was my astonishment that instead of going in a circle towards the sea, we were advancing more and more into the interior of the country, and I began to have some misgiving that our driver was treacherous. But after about an hour's ride I was put to my ease by his turning all at once and going towards the vessel in a straight line. We arrived safely on board the steamer *Canada,* just in time for the packet's leaving." Alexander took cold and was kept in bed several days.

Alexander recalled his experience in the inspection of their baggage upon reaching Liverpool: "After my shirts and other things were pulled about, and the bosoms of my shirts especially wrinkled, we were allowed to pass, and I know of no other nuisance so often met in traveling."

The sight of London was thrilling. The boys were eager to visit the Zoo, and there they saw many animals and birds entirely unknown to them. Christmas night they attended the theatre at Drury Lane. They were pleased with the pantomime, but Alexander much preferred the drama, and he wrote that he liked Drury Lane theatre better than any place he saw in London. He added, "Mr. Judd and I visited the House of Commons and Westminister Abbey. Mr. Richard's account of that most interesting place was thrown in full view by seeing it with my own eyes."

He later wrote: "Met the Greek Minister and the Chancellor and daughter (the boys had evidently attended a tea); the mother of the hostess, Mrs. Calmaster; several literary ladies and two or three reporters of different English papers. The mother of Mrs. Calmaster said that she remembered well the time Liholiho and his Queen were in England, and also the Prime Minister who was named after the English monarch at that time. This was Boki."

Alexander was sick with another severe cold and the Queen's physician, Sir James Clark, attended him for fifteen days. Admiral Thomas called, and this pleased the boys very much. Alexander wrote: "He said he would do all in his power for our cause, and that he was going to see Lord Gray that evening. Sir James intends to leave for Ireland tomorrow or next day. Day after tomorrow, the Queen holds a Privy Council, and Turkish and English ambassadors had a conference yesterday with General Lahitte, French Minister." In this way, Alexander was learning of diplomatic assemblies.

The boys were taken shopping and Alexander said, "We did not forget to visit the Daguerrean Gallery where we made some arrangements about taking a miniature, etc., to put in rings and lockets to send home."

One of the great sights was their visit to the Colosseum, which delighted both of the boys "beyond description." "About two o'clock we were conveyed to the top of the house by sliding up, or something of the sort, and in the way it was managed I could not find out. But we were supposed to be ascending in a balloon over the city of Paris. When we did get high enough it was indeed a sight. There was the whole city of Paris at our feet. Every street was visible nearly. The moon was shining and the stars twinkling; the streets were lighted and it was like being in Paris already. There was a cloud which shaded the road to Versailles, and everything seemed as natural as could be. After feasting our eyes for about an hour, we reluctantly retraced our way towards mother earth.

"About half past three a bell sounded and we were shown into a large room something like a theatre, where there was a curtain to withdraw for the scene, and seats were arranged like a theatre. There were a number of people there at the time and about thirty were awaiting the withdrawal of the curtain for the Cyclorama of the Earthquake of Lisbon. Finally the curtain was withdrawn, and we beheld the harbor of Lisbon. The view was moving, and we were supposed to be approaching the city of Lisbon, docks, houses, and men passing rapidly by. All this while the lights were put out which added to the awfulness of the scene. And everything looked so natural. There was the sun just rising above the hills, and the waters of the Tagus were brilliantly sparkling, and the whole thing was nearly perfection itself, but when the earthquake came on it was awful. There were houses thrown down and then the music stilled the grumble of the Earth. There were awful sounds and it was enough to make one faint. But then there was the hour when Lisbon was on fire, and then it was past describing. The smoke curling up in columns, and people running to and fro in the houses were discernable through the windows. But the top notch of the whole was when the ships were all swallowed up in the harbor. You could hear the roaring of the breakers, and the heaving of the sea. It was so well managed that it was perfection itself and the scene indescribable."

On leaving for Paris, Alexander wrote a note of appreciation to Sir James Clark, thanking him for his kindness in "waiting upon him."

The boys were impressed with Paris. They were delighted, when visiting the hot houses of the Champs Elyssess, to see *koa, mamani, maile, kalo, ape,* and orange and lemon trees. On their arrival in Paris they had engaged French and fencing masters and took lessons every day. Alexander wrote: "Feb. 9th, 1850. This day begins the 16th year of my life." He remained at home and at twelve the fencing master came. The French master also arrived, but did not finish his two hours of instruction.

The boys visited the Palais Royal and enjoyed the shops. They made plans to spend "$100.00 for presents, etc., to send home." They attended a carnival, and were later pleased to receive an invitation from Gen. de Lahitte to a "soireé." Alexander found his white gloves had been misplaced and had to order another pair. He reported, "At the soireé everything had the aspect of a private dinner or tea party. The General's daughter was most engaging and the conversation was of interesting topics—fashion, music, painting, dancing, etc."

A visit to the great art galleries the boys found fascinating, and they went twice to see the conjurer, Robert Houdini, and learned how several of his tricks were done. They visited the national library containing a million volumes, and they especially enjoyed the exhibition of coins; but shopping held their interest. Alexander noted, "Bought a bracelet for Victoria and a pair of studs for John Young, and a ring for the Queen." On the way to the flower market, Alexander purchased "a beautiful head dress and a couple of pins." The boys attended another soireé and there met one of the de Lahitte daughters, the Turkish Ambassador, Spanish Minister, and American and Scotch Legation. "Gen. de Lahitte apologized for not giving the attention due us."

"Did not go out this morning. I wrote to the King, Queen and John Young."

"This evening went to see a Spanish Giant in the Boulevard and paid three francs for admission. He was aged 24, measured 8 feet 3 inches and weighed 367 pounds and a half. His foot was fifteen inches long, his hand tremendous, and his little finger was more than an inch longer than my middle finger. I walked under his arm with my hat on."

Alexander attended another soireé given by the General. He met there the Greek Minister. Dr. Judd and the General discussed the matter of the Treaty and the General felt it would be settled satisfactorily.

"Attended the theatre and prepared to be received by the President of France. General Lahitte piloted us through the crowd that was pressing from all sides and we finally made our way to the President." After some presentations, the General advanced and presented Dr. Judd and Alexander and Lot. "Dr. Judd was the first taken notice of and both of them made slight bows to each other. Lot and myself then bowed which he returned with a slight bend of the vertebrae. He then advanced and said, 'This is your first visit to Paris?' to which we replied in the affirmative. He asked if we liked Paris to which we replied, 'Very much indeed.' He then said, 'I am very grateful to see you, you having come from so far a country.' He then turned towards the Doctor and said, 'I hope our little quarrel will be settled,' to which the Doctor replied, 'We put great confidence in the magnanimity and justice of France.' "

The boys sat for their portraits and attended the opera, and also a service at Notre Dame. Then they returned to England.

"London, 13th April, 1850. Fine trip and beautiful country. Traveled second class." At Plymouth they were met by Admiral Thomas and taken at once to his home. There they met Mrs. Thomas and Miss Thomas, and two young ladies who were invited to dine. Alexander wrote: "We visited the dock yards and saw several lines of battleships, also two or three frigates. Saw the sawmill, blacksmith shop, and other things all worked by steam."

"London, April 19th. Last night we went to the Lyceum theatre and were much pleased with the 'Island of Jewels' and thought the scenes were exceedingly beautiful. When we returned, we found a note on our table from Lord Palmerston asking us to come to Buckingham Palace a little before three." Lord Palmerston also explained that it was not going to be possible for them to meet the Queen, because she was soon to be confined and was not receiving, but he thought the Prince would be there to greet them. "This morning the Doctor wrote to Palmerston asking what dress we were to wear. About eleven he wrote back that a plain dress was all that was required."

Alexander continued: "After a great deal of humbug we got into the entrance to the palace. We were met at the door by Col. Seymore who accompanied us to the waiting room, a little while before Lord Palmerston arrived. I followed Lord Palmerston and the Doctor and Lot entered alternately. When we entered, the Prince was standing with Lord Palmerston on my right and Dr. Judd on my left, and then Lot. The Prince began the conversation by asking if we intended to make a long stay in Paris, to which I answered by saying that we expected to leave in about a week. Then Mr. Judd made a few remarks on business to which he replied by expressing the hope that they were not too late to mediate between us and France. His Royal Highness then asked if we had seen anything of London. To this I replied, 'Not very much.' The Doctor then said that we had been to the British Museum and had seen some idols brought from home that were not to be found in the Islands. The conversation then turned on the Islands, the Prince making inquiries of our principal exports, to which I mentioned sugar, coffee and molasses, and he then remarked that California being so near us, that we were well situated for trade between China and that place, to which I answered in the affirmative."

The next day after they had visited the Palace, they went to St. James's Theatre and sat in the Queen's box, and the following day they all went to Windsor Castle. Alexander described it: "This majestic structure, so justly termed an Emblem of the British Constitution with its strength, its grandeur and its antiquity, is built upon the summit of a hill, on the descending of which the town of Windsor stands and forms a most magnificent feature for many miles around."

The following day, the boys with Dr. Judd left for Liverpool and shortly embarked for the return voyage to Halifax.

"Washington City, May 27, 1850. Yesterday morning we arrived in this city from Philadelphia. We left Boston on Saturday afternoon about 2-½ o'clock. The week we spent in Boston was pleasant on the whole." The Mayor of the city took the young Princes to drive, and while in Boston the boys sat for their portraits. Mr. and Mrs. Bingham called and the boys met Mr. and Mrs. Hunnewell who gave a large party in their honor.

Alexander continued: "The next day our trunks arrived from New Haven" (the party having stopped there for a brief stay). "This morning we went to the House of Representatives and also to the Senate. We were introduced to Mr. Henry Clay and several other distinguished statesmen of the country. The city of Washington is a rather clean place; about 50 or 40 thousand inhabitants in it."

The boys also visited the White House and met President Taylor. "We crossed a sort of park or a lawn and soon reached the President's House which is called here, the White House. The servant who opened the door looked more like a street beggar than a porter to the President of the United States. He showed us into a neat little parlor.

"Attended the President's levee, as they call it here, although properly it was a soireé or reception. We went in our court dress. All belted and cloaked, we got into a carriage and drove to the President's."

While in Washington, the boys visited the Smithsonian Institution and "there learned its origin and history."

On the fifth of June they returned to New York City. Alexander wrote: "We arrived in the city yesterday afternoon about one o'clock from Philadelphia. We called on Captain Wilkes and his daughter. She gave us some seeds to carry home and some flowers that had been pressed. When Captain Wilkes showed us some portraits, one of them was mine and the other two were Haalilio and Father. I immediately had some daguerreotypes taken from the pictures.

"The next morning while waiting at the station for the baggage to be checked, Dr. Judd told me to get in and secure seats. While I was looking out of the window a man came to me and told me to get out of the carriage, rather unceremoniously. I immediately asked him what he meant. He continued his request. Finally he came around by the door and I went out to meet him just as he was coming in. Someone whispered a word into his ears. I came up to him and asked him his reason for telling me to get out of the carriage. He said he had his reasons. He then told me to keep my seat. I found he was the conductor and had probably taken me for somebody's servant, just because I had a darker skin than he had. Confounded fool! The first time I had ever received such treatment; not in England nor in France or anywhere else. But in this country I was treated like a dog, to go and come at an American's bidding. Here I must state that I am disappointed at the Americans. They have no manners, no politeness, not even common civility to a stranger."

It can be assumed here that the lowly conductor never knew the part he played in changing the course of Hawaiian history. The incident had a profound effect on Alexander's mind. Because of it, and similar incidents encountered in the United States, he became, subconsciously or otherwise, anti-American. In later years, after he had ascended the throne, he decisively rejected the clamor for annexation with the U. S. that had plagued Kamehameha III's last years. Alexander, as Kamehameha IV, feared racial discrimination under American rule, pointing to the Negro slave in the United States as representative of American contempt for colored races. His sentiments, instead, were always pro-British.

The days following were filled with happier experiences. The boys rode up the Hudson river to Albany. They visited Niagara Falls, and Alexander recorded some of his impressions. "The Falls was something more than I can describe. It was magnificent, it was awful, and to specialize, I was filled with wonder and with awe, and meditated on the world of Him who made the 'earth and the seas and all that in them is, and that moveth the planets in their turn, and who calls himself, 'I am that I am.' "

From Buffalo the travelers went by boat to Detroit to visit some relatives of Dr. Judd at Royal Oak, from whence they drove in a lumber wagon to the town of Troy. Alexander was greatly moved by the meeting between Dr. Judd and his mother, from whom he had been separated for over twenty-three years. At the country home of the Judds the boys had a wonderful time. They went hunting with the men and enjoyed an "Old Fashioned Picnic." Everybody filled the great lumber wagon to go to meeting. Soon the boys felt perfectly at home in the strange country, enjoying everything; but they, with the Doctor, were obliged to leave for Buffalo and Rochester, the next stop on the way home.

At Rochester, the boys secured two horses and went for a ride. Alexander wrote: "Passing by the hotel, I was riding a little behind Lot and had my pantaloons inside my boots. The lady we saw singing at the hotel came and greeted me again. 'How do you do, Sir Knight!' I carried the joke by saying, 'Well, fair one, and thanks for the kindness your ladyship has showen to a stranger.' She said nothing but took off her glove and threw it at me. I caught it and kissed it and then rode on. Looking inside there were the initials of Mrs. C. C. Wadsworth. Hang my stars and her too! Think of a married woman playing such a prank!"

Alexander's journal was a long and carefully prepared manuscript, of which extracts only have been given here. The last recording was but a brief statement: "June 29th. Attended church all day." Doubtless the time from then on was crowded with interests of the long journey back to California, but Alexander was tired of writing.

THE GENTLEMAN KING

Chapter XII

"Great and good friend."
—A. LINCOLN

As THE FIRST Hawaiian monarch to be given from birth the broadening opportunities of travel and a good education, Alexander Liholiho at the start took advantage of both to emerge as Hawaii's most brilliant King—Kamehameha IV. As a true grandson of Kamehamcha the Great, his brilliance was never gaudy; it was tempered with simplicity and the common touch, drawing him close to the hearts of his people.

On January 11, 1855, less than a month after the death of Kamehameha III, Alexander Liholiho took the oath of office, and the symbolic golden cloak of kingship was wrapped about his shoulders. He was just short of being twenty-one years of age. Aware of his inexperience to take on so great a responsibility, he had said to his privy council: "Chiefs, I have become, by the will of God, your father as I have been your child. You must help me, for I stand in need of help." To his subjects and those foreigners assembled in Kawaiahao Stone Church he delivered his inaugural address. There was a deep silence in the old church as the King began to speak. He opened his address in the ancient manner of appealing to the ancient kings of the different islands:

"Give ear, Hawaii *O Keawe!* Maui *O Kama!* Oahu *O Kuihewa!* Kauai *O Mano!* The good, the generous, the kind-hearted Kamehameha is no more. Our great chief has fallen. But, though dead, he lives in the liberal, the just, and the beneficent measures which it was always his pleasure to adopt. His monuments rise to greet us on every side. They may be seen in the church, in the school house, and in the hall of justice; in the security of our persons and property; in peace, in the law, the order and general prosperity that prevail throughout the Islands. He was a friend of the *Makaainana* (common people).

"By the death of Kamehameha III, the chain that carried us back to the ancient days of Kamehameha I has been broken. He was the last child of the great chieftain.

"Today we begin a new era. Let it be one of increased civilization, one of progress, industry, temperance, morality, and all of those virtues which mark a nation's progress. The importance of unity is that which I wish to impress upon your minds. Let us be one and we shall not fail."

At the opening of the Legislature, young Kamehameha IV again excelled in his address. He reviewed somewhat the reign of his uncle, Kamehameha III. He referred the members of the legislature to the reports of the different departments of the government, commenting and making further recommendations regarding future progress. "Weak as we are," he said, "and imperfect as our government may be, it will not be doubted, I think, that this is a country in which there is now entire security of life, liberty, person and property."

The King spoke at this time of the particular attention which should be given to the improvement of the Honolulu harbor so that all ships might be better accommodated and foreign trade with the Islands increased. He emphasized the great advantages that had come to Hawaii with the fast clipper ships which enhanced commercial interests among nations.

"Who ever heard," he said, "of winter upon our shores? When was it so cold that the laborer could not go to his field? Where among us shall we find the numberless drawbacks which in less favored countries the working classes have to contend with? They have no place in our beautiful group which rests on the swelling bosom of the Pacific like a water lily. With tranquil heaven above our heads, and the sun which keeps his jealous eye upon us every day, while his rays are so tempered that they never wither prematurely what they have warmed into life, we ought to be agriculturists at heart as well as in practice."

The King continued, saying that education in the English language should become more general. "It is my firm conviction that unless my subjects become educated in this tongue, their hope of intellectual progress and of meeting the foreigners on terms of equality is a vain one."

A severe epidemic of measles, brought to the Islands from California, had so depleted the Hawaiian population, with thousands of natives dying from the disease, that the King presented the matter to the Legislature, recommending that a hospital be at once established to care for the many dependent sick. Because of the decrease of native laborers, experiments had been made in bringing coolie labor from China. This did not prove as successful as had been anticipated, and the King, in his address to the Legislature, suggested that they try bringing another group of people from the South Seas. Polynesians, he believed, might readily adapt themselves to life in the Hawaiian Islands.

There was no point of concern connected with the welfare of the Kingdom that Kamehameha IV did not touch upon with farseeing understanding. As he closed his address, he was given the salute of twenty-one guns as a tribute from the leaders of the nation.

Honolulu was growing. It was taking on the atmosphere of the outside world. A fireproof building with a granite front was being created, the granite having been shipped to the Islands from Massachusetts. Newspapers commented upon this, saying that while a few fence posts and doorsteps had been made from granite which had come from China, never before had the beautiful New England granite been used for building in the Islands.

Business men were realizing the demand for more carefully planned business methods. The first Chamber of Commerce was organized. Every effort was made to stimulate an interest in farming. Kamehameha IV was intensely interested in the development of his kingdom along progressive lines of agriculture and good business. In a frank speech to a large assembly of citizens, he deprecated the dream of many who indulged in the expectation that a fortune could be made in a very short time. He said: "The want of perserverance is the cause of nonsuccess." "*Oiaio no*" ("true, true") broke from many parts of the house. Prizes were offered by the two agricultural societies for special development in raising crops. Rice seed had been brought from South Carolina, and the experiment of raising rice was so successful that large shipments were exported.

Travel between the different islands had always been difficult and unsatisfactory. Because of this, as life in the Islands became more and more a matter of interchange between the merchants in the island group, it was decided to have a steamship built for inter-island shipping and travel. A vessel, the *Kilauea* was built in New London, Connecticut, and its arrival was a great and celebrated event. Business was marching forward in the Sandwich Islands.

Newspapers printed extracts of foreign news from all over the world. Kamehameha IV was keenly interested in what was going on in different countries. He constantly encouraged a larger development of world interests through the press. People, generally, were at this time eagerly watching for news from the great war in Crimea. Mails were slow in coming. The newspaper announced, "No mail yet!" But while waiting for the mail, the citizens went cheerily along about their business and their pleasures.

The King's interests at this time centered on the matter of treaties with foreign countries, especially those concerning the United States. He hoped that it would be possible for the Islands to export sugar, coffee and other products to America free of duty. A treaty to this end was submitted, but it failed to be ratified because of a bloc put forth by several southern sugar states. This was the America that had once ordered Alexander Liholiho from his seat in a public carriage because he was dark-skinned.

The newspaper of the day recorded, "Grand vocal and instrumental Concert." This notice was a reflection from the bright and gay social life of the city of Honolulu. It was becoming fashionable to have one's picture taken. The "Daguerrean Gallery" offered special rates to ladies. To have these little pictures suitably encased in gilt bordered frames, or placed in gold lockets to be worn about the neck suspended from a gold chain, was the last word in artistic circles. Every ship coming to the Islands brought different varieties of food for the markets. "Fifty dozen Baltimore Fresh Cove, now landing from the barke *Frances Palmer,*" announced the delicacy of fresh oysters. The little city of Honolulu fared well in those days.

During the reigns of Kamehameha III and Kamehameha IV the whaling industry was the outstanding commercial interest in the Islands, and Hawaii became the transhipping center for the oil and whalebone. It is said that at times the ships were moored so closely together in Honolulu harbor that a person could walk from one end of the harbor to the other on the decks of the vessels without going ashore. There were, of course, thousands of sailors in port. Business was prosperous and interesting. The sailors were free with their money, and the ships were supplied with such Island-raised products as firewood, Irish potatoes, bananas, molasses, sugar, coffee, hogs, turkeys, goats, coconuts, pineapples, melons, breadfruit, cabbages, taro, oranges and leather. The ships required many other products—such as copper, ropes, tar and rosin —which had to be imported from foreign countries. Kamehameha IV understood the value of business, but he also was interested in people. It was his interest which developed the plan to build a sailor's home, which for many years was called the "Seamen's Institute." The cornerstone was laid on Restoration day. An editorial in the morning paper told about it:

"We saw it from our window. It is not often that the makings of news come so near to our newspaper office. It was quite pretty looking down on the well-dressed crowd of people in carriages, on horseback, and on foot. We could see everything without stretching our necks and seeing nothing. The trustees and officers having escorted His Majesty to the corner where the stone was to be laid, the ceremonies were commenced with prayer.

"The president then announced the contents of the box to be buried under the stone. They were the Bible in Hawaiian, handsomely bound; Jarves' *History of the Islands,* copies of Dauguerreotype of Kamehameha I, II and III, and two portaits of Kamehameha IV; various copies of the 'Polynesian' and 'The Friend,' 'New Era,' and 'Elele'; the *Hawaiian Phrase Book;* 'School Report'; various publications relating to the home, and several coins of the reign of Kamehameha III, stamped with the bust and bearing his superscription. The corner stone laid, the King addressed the multitude. After stating things concerning the kingdom, he said: 'The hardships with which the sailor contends, and the danger which he braves, bring us assured security. Had he not steered his ships into our waters, Honolulu might simply have retained its position as a fishing village, or become by this time a deserted beach.' "

Kamehameha IV greatly opposed the annexation of his kingdom by the United States, and feared the growth of American financial interests in the kingdom. He was English in his thought and feeling. This was not strange, because England had been the friend of the Island Empire since the time of Kamehameha I. Although very young, Kamehameha IV, when in England, had been impressed with both English institutions and government. The form and ceremonies of the English church and court interested him. It was to these things that he turned when the time came for him to accept the kingship of the Islands. The King was European in temperament and his court took on the aristocratic grandeur and grace of the Court of St. James. He was a gentleman, but he was also a canny politician. Determined to remove the factions which strove for annexation with the United States, he gently but firmly began to remove from their positions of influence in governmental matters first the missionary group and gradually, but finally, all Americans. At the end of his reign, there was not a single American in the King's cabinet.

Two years after his inauguration, the King married Emma Rooke, a granddaughter of John Young. Through her mother's line, Emma was a descendant of the ancient Polynesian kings. When she was a small child she had been adopted by Dr. C. B. Rooke, an English physician. For years, the doctor had been a resident of the Islands and had been closely associated with governmental matters, and so, with the King. Emma had been a student along with the two Princes, Alexander and Lot, at the Young Chiefs' School. Later, she had an English governess in the home of Dr. Rooke. When she was still older, it was decided that she should go to England. While there, she was received at court and, eventually, became a great favorite of Queen Victoria. Returning home, she was well prepared to take her place as the wife of the King.

The wedding of the young couple was held at Kawaiahao, the old Stone Church. The Rev. Richard Armstrong performed the ceremony, using the ritual of the English church. Among the writings of Sanford B. Dole is found a description of the wedding. At that time Mr. Dole was a boy of twelve and a happy guest at the party. He wrote that the King was tall, well proportioned, and possessed of elegant manners. He noted that Emma's veil was of Honiton lace and was a gift from Queen Victoria. There were three bridesmaids: Victoria Paki, Liliuokalani and Mary Pitman. Mr. Dole, describing the scene, said: "There were many gorgeous *kahilis* made from the feathers of tropical birds, some red, some white. Some of the *kahilis* were so tall that they had to be lowered to enter the archway to the entrance. I do not know of any regalia in the traditions of the courts of civilized or mediaeval times of equal magnificence."

The bridal party walked slowly down the broad aisle of the old church. The *kahili* bearers led the way. Everything in order, the ceremony took place, the guests eagerly watching every move and listening to every word of the sacred marriage service. There occurred, however, a somewhat startling incident. The King had forgotten to bring the wedding ring. Perhaps the guests were not aware that Chief Justice Allen had quickly and quietly slipped his own gold ring to the King as the ceremony proceeded. The wedding party walked to the palace from the church. The walks were covered with fresh greens, and soldiers in uniform bordered the way while the guns from Punchbowl Hill gave the salute of honor. After the wedding, the Chinese merchants of Honolulu tendered the royal couple a reception and a gala ball.

As time passed, the King and Queen gave their close attention to educational matters and their personal support to every movement which promised good for the Islands. They were delighted when Punahou School was given a charter as Oahu College. This was a step ahead. But with all of the changing conditions for the better, nothing so moved the people as the birth of Albert Edward Kauikeaouli Leiopapa A Kamehameha, the Prince of Hawaii. At last the nobles were able to feel that the Kamehameha dynasty was firmly established. The baby was at once officially declared heir to the throne of the Kingdom.

From time to time there had been expressed by those who were connected with the Episcopal Church the wish to have the services of that denomination established in Hawaii. The King and Queen hoped that an English bishop might be sent to organize the Church of England in Hawaii. Their personal desire was that the bishop might supervise the education of the royal Prince. England responded to the call and a bishop and two clergymen were sent to the Islands.

In 1859 the King and Queen determined that a hospital should be built as soon as possible. Honolulu had no greater need. The "Polynesian" published this comment: "His Majesty, notebook in hand, is seen in the most frequented parts of the town, soliciting subscriptions to the hospital for his poor subjects." Members of the Legislature were disturbed as reports of the King's doings reached them. The daily papers announced that the King and Queen were going from door to door begging money for the hospital. The legislative members conferred one with another. It was an appalling situation. "His Majesty is pressing the matter of the hospital at tea parties, telling our wives that the Hawaiian race will die out if an institution isn't established." The monarchs likewise canvassed funds during the whaling seasons when captains were ashore and generally in a cheery mood after the long Arctic cruise.

The Legislature met and were amazed to learn that the King had collected the fine sum of $13,000, and they voted him the necessary balance to build the hospital. In response to this gift, the King addressed the Legislature: "I confess that the act of your two houses which I regard with the most complacency is that in which you commit the public Treasury to the aid of hospitals. I wish to take this public occasion to express the almost unspeakable satisfaction with which I have found my efforts successful beyond my hopes. It is to the subscribers, as a body, that I should bear witness to the readiness, not less than the liberality, with which they have met my advances. When you return to your several places, let the fact be made known that in Honolulu the sick man has a friend in everybody. Nor do I believe that He who made us all, and to whose keeping I commend in now dismissing you, has seen with indifference how the claims of common humanity have drawn together in the subscription list names representative of almost every race of men under the sun."

The laying of the cornerstone to the new hospital was a great event. The entire community, and friends from other islands and from far countries, joined in the celebration. For many years Kamehameha IV had been closely associated with the Masonic Lodge. He was elected the Master of the *Lodge le Progres de Oceanie* for three separate terms. He was honored by the Supreme Council of France with the thirtieth degree for his Masonic activities. It was suitable that the King with his brother Masons should have laid the cornerstone of the hospital. The King gave it the name of "Queen's Hospital" in honor of Queen Emma. The building was completed and dedicated, and the ladies of Honolulu hemmed the sheets as their daughters made the pillow cases.

The following letter, written by Kamehameha IV to his friend, Judge Robertson, who was absent on the coast, tells of the laying of the cornerstone of the hospital:

"Palace
"July 12th, 1860

"My dear Judge Robertson

"I received your letter from Victoria, V. I. with much pleasure, and I will willingly grant the extension of your leave of absence to such time as will be sufficient to the full recovery of your health. If the climate of Vancouver Island does not agree with you, why not come down to San Francisco and spend a month or two there?

"We are moving along slowly in the Legislature, Kamakau and Ukeke are great stumbling blocks.

"Lot has been down with congestion of the brain, and for a time was in a very critical state, but he has turned the point as it were, and is improving. His recovery, though, will be very slow, as his head had received such a severe shock. It was at first thought that it was brought on by imprudent self treatment, of what he thought was a cold in the head &c, but his physicians are now of the opinion that it is, and was from the beginning, congestion of the brain. He was always troubled with affections in the head while a boy, and his great size at the present time would accelerate any little cause that might present itself. As I said before, he is recovering slowly, his mind being very weak, as well as his body, and I should not be surprised to find that the doctors ordered him to Vancouver or California.

"We had an interesting ceremony yesterday in laying the corner stone of Queen's Hospital. You will, I dare say, receive full particulars of the ceremony from your other correspondents from the Islands.

"If it is thought impracticable to import Salmon, Trout, or Deer from Vancouver, to the Islands, will you oblige me by ascertaining whether the different kinds of game birds such as the grouse, pheasant, quail, etc., could not be introduced here with success.

"Hoping your health will speedily recover,

"Yours truly,

"The King."

During the ten days following September 11, 1859, a rumor, passed by word of mouth in hushed whispers, said that Kamehameha IV was considering abdication. In all that time, only one newspaper made reference to the affair, and that in an oblique manner. The truth of the matter was that the King, in a blind rage, had shot a man in cold blood.

Despite his brilliant mind, Alexander Liholiho, as he matured, became possessed of a violent uncontrollable temper; and always his reaction was just as violent, hurtling him into the depths of abject despair and remorse. The incident in question occurred at Lahaina on the island of Maui, where the King and his party were vacationing. Mr. H. A. Neilson—"a gentleman of independent fortune, well-educated, refined"—was the King's private secretary and constant companion. At Lahaina, someone in the King's retinue made subtle insinuations of Neilson's having "betrayed the King's domestic rights." In a hasty moment—and there were rumors that the King had been drinking heavily—Kamehameha IV seized a loaded pistol, rushed into the house occupied by Neilson, whom he found lying on an extension chair, and fired point blank at his breast. The bullet entered one of his lungs, but he did not die immediately. The King soon learned that his mistrust of Neilson was unfounded. The remorse and despair set in, and thereafter he did everything within his power for the wounded man. Neilson remained an invalid for many months. Each time word was received in Honolulu that Neilson's condition had taken a turn for the worse, Kamehameha IV sailed for Lahaina to be at his side. In March, 1860, the King brought Neilson to Honolulu, assigned him to his personal seaside cottage, and lavished on him every care and gift that a king's remorseful ken could summon. On February 12, 1862, Neilson died.

On only one other occasion was the King's personal sorrow greater than that he had suffered over the Neilson affair. It occurred in 1862, and this time it carried him to the brink of suicide. The four-year-old Prince of Hawaii was the light of his eye and, to the Hawaiian people, the beloved link who would carry on and perpetuate the Kamehameha dynasty. A short time after Neilson's death, the child was taken with brain fever, sickened, and died.

The death of the Prince of Hawaii left Kamehameha IV a stunned and broken-hearted man. His health failed rapidly. Before he became too ill to take an active part in governmental matters, he kept in close personal touch with all details concerning his own government and those of foreign powers. His voluminous correspondence over the world yielded one letter, at least, showing that his efforts were not in vain.

"To His Majesty, Kamehameha IV

"Great and Good Friend:

"I have made a choice of Mr. James McBride, one of our distinguished citizens, to reside near the government of the Kingdom of Hawaii, in quality of Minister Resident of the Republic of the United States of America.

"He is well informed of the relative interests of the two countries, and of our desire to cultivate and strengthen the friendship and good correspondence between us, and from a knowledge of his fidelity and good conduct, I have entire confidence that he will render himself acceptable to your Majesty, by his constant endeavor to preserve and advance the interest and happiness of the two countries. I therefore request your Majesty to receive him favorably and give full credence to whatever he shall pay to you on the part of the United States, and most of all when he shall assure you of their friendship and wishes for the prosperity of your kingdom.

"And I pray God to have your Majesty always in His safe and holy keeping.

> "Written at the City of Washington,
> "the sixteenth day of March, in the
> "year of our Lord, one thousand,
> "eight-hundred and sixty-three.
> > "Your Good Friend,
> > "Abraham Lincoln.

"By the President—
    "William H. Seward
    "Secretary of State."

There were many important developments in the Islands during the brief reign of Kamehameha IV, in all of which he took a leading part. The deepening of the Honolulu harbor, the building of the prison replacing the old fort which had served as a jail for the community, and the erection of a new customs house. The waterworks were greatly enlarged. A system of pipes was laid at a cost of $45,000. Pipes were also installed for gas, but were given up for want of patronage. The English language was taught in all government schools. The old American mission was placed on a self-supporting basis. No more missionaries were sent to the Islands from the United States, but native churches with native pastors continued to carry on the missionary work on all of the islands. The Episcopal Church was fully established.

Following the death of the Prince of Hawaii, the King retired very largely from public life. His health did not permit him to attend large functions of the government. During his retirement he devoted his time and thought to translating the English Book of Common Prayer and the Litany into the Hawaiian language. Then, on November 30, 1863, he died at the age of twenty-nine.

THE LAST KING KAMEHAMEHA

Chapter XIII

> *"I will never sign the death warrant of my people."*
> —LOT KAMEHAMEHA

PRINCE LOT HAD COME to the throne. He had not been a popular prince, for his disposition was reserved and unresponsive. But he was the next in line of the great house of Kamehamehas because, after the death of the Prince of Hawaii, he had been named heir-apparent by his younger brother, Alexander Liholiho. This fact alone gave him the allegiance of the nation. Although as well educated and as well-traveled as his brother, Lot lacked the sparkle of greatness and the human touch that had marked Kamehameha IV. Lot's mind ran in channels of practicality, whereas Alexander's had run in those of brilliance. The fifth King Kamehameha was never to be the close friend and idol of his people that the fourth had been.

There was intense interest on the part of the ministers of the kingdom, and considerable apprehension, as to what course the new King might take. It was well known that he was not in sympathy with the current administration, and that, like his brother, he was bitterly opposed to annexation with the United States.

As Prince, Lot had filled the office of Minister of the Interior during the reign of Kamehameha IV. In that position he had shown both ability and political acumen. He was recognized as a man of force, and, like Kamehameha the Great, he hoped to protect the Islands from foreign influence.

Kamehameha V believed that the constitution which Kamehameha III had adopted was not a good one for the Hawaiian government. He said the Hawaiian people were not far enough advanced in civilization either to appreciate or to profit by such measures; that they did not know what to do with such liberty as was given to them. He said the majority of the people were like children and must be protected. He believed strongly in royalty and that a king must remain the father of his people. This attitude was not necessarily selfish, inflated, or personally despotic. Even while his brother and, particularly, the young Prince of Hawaii lived—at which time his own chances of becoming king were very remote—he had fought at each session of the Legislature for a revision of the constitution which would strengthen the power of the throne. He was a Hawaiian, and the strengthening of the power of the throne meant a lessening of the power of foreign influence. This was his course. All of this and much more was known to the officials of the government, but when the new King refused to take the oath to support the Constitution they were not only surprised but alarmed.

The King did not call the Legislature together as was the usual procedure, but issued instead a proclamation asking for the election of delegates to a convention to consider some changes in the Constitution. The King himself, with Mr. Wyllie, a Britisher and a prominent member of his cabinet, made a tour of all the islands that they might explain to the people the King's plans regarding the Constitution.

The convention met in July, 1864. There were present sixteen nobles and twenty-seven elected delegates. The session was a stormy one. Most of the delegates were opposed to the King's plans. After a week of lengthy discussions, the King lost his patience and dismissed the convention, saying that he would set aside the old constitution and write a new one. This he did.

At the first meeting of the Legislature following the convention, the King gave his reasons for taking such a drastic step, and expressed his ideas regarding the future responsibility of the government. "In calling a national convention I was influenced by the firm conviction of its being necessary that the system under which a people lives should be strictly adapted to its genius and traditions. The right to the throne of this country, originally acquired by conquest and by birth, belongs hereditarily to the family of Kamehameha I. The Constitution of 1852, by its ninety-fourth article, left the heir to the throne free to take an oath to support the constitution or to refuse to do so." The King then explained that Kamehameha III would never have signed that constitution unless he had believed that it might be changed to suit the needs of the people and that the King would hold the controlling power in all matters of the Kingdom.

Returning to his discussion of the convention, the King further explained that he had called the convention so that the representatives would have opportunity to discuss the proposed changes in the government, but that the convention had shown antagonistic elements which prevented the very ideas of improvement which he, the King, hoped for. And so, he had dismissed it. The King then spoke specifically of different important matters—of education, of foreign policies, of the control of the growing menace of leprosy, and of the care of the health of the people generally.

An important measure in the King's new Constitution was that concerning the privilege of voting on governmental matters. Only those would be allowed to vote who owned a certain amount of property, and who, if born since 1840, were able to read and write. Another striking innovation was the discarding of the old and important office of *kuhina-nui,* thus preventing for a number of years to come the participation of high-born Hawaiian women in governmental affairs.

Many problems confronted the new government. More and more of the natives were dying from diseases which had been brought to the Islands from foreign countries. Between the years of 1853 and 1866 the Hawaiian population dropped from seventy thousand to fifty-seven thousand. The whaling industry, which had been the great commercial asset of the Islands, declined because of the use of kerosene oil in the place of whale oil all over the world and because of the passing from style of the hoop skirt, for which quantities of whalebone had been used. But to offset these discouragements, the demand for Hawaiian sugar was steadily increasing. The Civil War in the United States had cut off from the North its supply of sugar, previously obtained from the South. Plantations were started in the Islands, and these called for more laborers. This situation led to the organization of Hawaii's first Bureau of Immigration.

The methods of Kamehameha V in dealing with the government were original and striking. For instance, several months before the Legislature was to meet, the King would hold a cabinet meeting nearly every day. He said, "I want my cabinet to know before the Legislature meets what I will support and what I will not support. And I wish the cabinet to show me beforehand the reasons why the government should bring forward certain measures, then there will be no surprise to my cabinet during the session of the Legislature from not knowing what my views are."

The royal household was conducted in the same careful manner. The King was very particular about details, and he was especially careful regarding money matters. He kept an account of all purchases made by himself or others of his establishment, entering every item in a memorandum book. After breakfast he would call his people together and, looking over his book, he would pass the money out to those who had made purchases for him, saying, "You promised that such and such an article would be paid for today; now go and pay for it." Business men said that they could always be sure of their money when the King had ordered the purchases.

Unlike the chiefs and kings of olden times, who gave little or no consideration when dealing with their serfs or dependents, Kamehameha V was both just and generous when dealing with his people. The story is told of a visit he made to the island of Hawaii. During his travels, he lodged in the small house of a native man rather than in the home of a chief. When leaving, he gave the owner of the house a present of twenty dollars in gold. The man was amazed. He said, "What is this for?" The King replied, "I have turned you out of your house for two days, and I wish to make you a little present for your kindness to me." The man refused the money, saying, "You are my king and everything belongs to you. I do not wish anything." The King answered, "I am not the king to get everything I can out of the people. I receive my salary so as to pay for what I need. I am not giving this to you as pay, but as a small present." He then walked away, leaving the money on the mat.

Kamehameha V was a bachelor, and through the years he became more set in his ways and ideas. One of the first things to feel his censure was the hula. He may have encouraged the hula in his younger days, but, for several years before he came to the throne, he found the natives on his lands on Oahu traveling thirty miles a day to see hula dancers, and, when at home, sitting around their houses in the daytime neglecting to plant and cultivate food for their families. He was indignant and forbade any more dances on his land, and turned away the dancers. At the next session of the Legislature he used all his influence having a law passed prohibiting the Hawaiian hula unless a license was first obtained, and forbidding any license to be granted outside of Honolulu. It was the usual thing to have hula dances around the palace at the time of the death of a member of the royal family; however, when the father of Kamehameha V died no hulas were performed, but instead the native choirs were allowed to sing.

In his youth Kamehameha V had acquired a predilection for drink, but when he came to the throne, and as long as he lived, he promoted the cause of temperance in the kingdom. If his servants broke the laws, or were arrested for drunkenness, he either paid their fines or left them in jail as he thought best. In 1865 a bill was brought before the Legislature to repeal the law which called it a penal offense to sell or give intoxicating liquor to natives. Alcohol had been one of the White Man's contributions to the Islands, along with firearms and disease. The Hawaiian population seemed to wilt to an alarming degree as a result of all three commodities, and drastic actions had had to be taken in years previous to Lot's reign. Kamehameha surprised the supporters of the bill by saying, "I will never sign the death warrant of my people." The measure was defeated in the second reading.

To Kamehameha V there was no thing of greater importance in the Kingdom than the continued effort to establish the educational program which had been so carefully planned. He envisioned the day when Hawaiians would be able to fill all offices in their own government. But he was always practical. He said over and over again that the children and young people should be taught to work with their hands as well as with their heads; that if the children were not taught to work while in school they would not work when they left school. The King said, further, that if young men did not work with their hands they would think they must be lawyers, or something of the kind, and perhaps get their living by rascality if money did not come fast enough to suit them.

The year 1865 brought several important matters to a head. Through the Bureau of Immigration, established early that year, a representative was sent to China, India, and the Malay Archipelago to procure laborers for the Islands. In July, 1865, five hundred Chinese laborers arrived in Hawaii. The representative was to learn, if possible, something further regarding the treatment of leprosy. Leprosy first made its appearance in the Islands in 1853. By 1864 the disease had spread to an alarming extent. It was decided that something more definite must be done about it at once. Accordingly, a bill was passed to isolate the lepers, providing a separate establishment for them and their care. The first hospital for the treatment of leprosy was opened at Kalihi. About this time, a permanent location was selected at the present site of the leper settlement on the north side of the island of Molokai. This is a peninsula comprising some five thousand acres, surrounded on three sides by the ocean, and shut in on the south side by a steep precipice rising to a height ranging between two thousand and three thousand feet. In 1866 one hundred forty lepers embarked for Molokai.

The same year, the King's sister, the Princess Victoria, heir-apparent to the throne, died at the age of twenty-seven. A newspaper of 1866 gives the following notice:

"Assembly: Minister Hutchinson presents a letter from His Majesty— 'To the Nobles and Representatives of my people, it has pleased God to again afflict myself, my family and the nation by recalling to Himself my beloved sister, Her Royal Highness, Princess Victoria Kamamalu Kaahumanu, who died at her residence this morning at 10 A.M. While bowing submissively to the will of the Almighty, your love and sympathy for myself and my father, your venerable president, of which we feel assured in this hour of bereavement, will be our chiefest earthly consolation.'

"Signed, Kamehameha (R) Iolani Palace.
"May 29, 1866."

The death of the father of Kamehameha IV and Kamehameha V, the Hon. Kekuanaoa, soon followed, and the King again addressed the

Assembly of nobles and friends. He spoke of the loss to himself and to the kingdom, adding: "The best wish that I can have for you is that I may ever preserve the remembrance of his precepts and follow his example of pure patriotism."

It was an old custom, after the death of a monarch or someone in authority, for the native people to stop all work and spend the days in idleness. This custom Kamehameha V determined to change. Following the death of Kekuanaoa, he called his father's retainers together and said to them: "You have mourned with me for my father and now it is time for you to go to work, and if you need money to buy clothes I will advance it on account, and I will pay you so many dollars for your work."

The men did not like this. They replied, "Your father fed us all the time and did not make us work, and you should do the same." Kamehameha answered firmly: "I am not the king to teach the nation to be idle, but it is my place to teach the people to work and support their families. I do not want anybody to work for nothing. Those who want to work for me will be paid for it, and those who do not want to work must go elsewhere to live, as after a certain time no food will be given out to those who are able to work and will not work. You have shown great respect for my father and now you cannot do him or the nation any good by sitting in idleness and saying, 'We do this in *aloha* for your father,' " The King put the men to work reclaiming marshes at Waikiki, planting and fishing.

It was about this time that, through the continued interest of the King and his officials, the first Board of Education was founded, and, following the work of Mr. Richards, the office of Inspector of Schools was created. A reformatory school was opened, and a special school for Hawaiian girls was started, filling a need in the Hawaiian community.

The Treaty of Reciprocity, so long pending between the United States and Hawaii, was still in question in Washington. This was a constant worry to the King and his cabinet. There was encouragement, however, in the rapid development of ocean travel between Hawaii and America, and from Australia to the Islands. Kamehameha was emphatic regarding the need of the greatest possible promotion of interchange of commerce between Hawaii and other countries. He told the Assembly that he wished to commend to their fostering care the matter of steam communication between the islands of the Hawaiian group, believing that liberality in this respect was the wisest economy.

While serious and concentrated thought and attention were given to these government and national concerns, Honolulu and the Islands did not want for excitement. The people never knew when to expect an eruption from old Mauna Loa, and an eruption of great magnitude took place in March, 1868. In March, preceding the actual eruption, there were earthquake shocks; in April, a terrific earthquake shook down every stone wall and nearly every house in Kau. All Hawaii was affected. Historians give the following story:

"In eastern Kau the earthquake, which is known as a 'mud flow,' an enormous mass of marshy clay, detached itself from the bluff at the head of the valley, and in a few minutes a stream about half a mile wide and thirty feet deep in the middle, swept down for a distance of three miles. It moved so swiftly that it buried thirty people, and more than five hundred horses and cattle."

Immediately following the earthquake, a tremendous tidal wave, said to be forty or fifty feet high, rolled in upon the coast of Kau, sweeping away villages and killing more than eighty people in a few moments. At the same time, the crater Kilauea emptied its lava through the underground. The floor of the crater fell in, forming a pit three thousand feet long and five hundred feet deep. The following month, Mauna Loa again erupted on the southwest slope of the mountain, spreading over the Kahuku country from five thousand six hundred feet above the sea. Great masses of lava, forming fountains several hundred feet high, flowed ten miles to the sea, destroying thousands of acres of good land, numerous homes, and many people. The government at once sent help to the island of Hawaii. The King, personally, accompanied the *Kilauea,* which was loaded with supplies for the stricken area. Large sums of money were contributed by private citizens, and a second ship was soon on its way to relieve the suffering of the people.

The years were bringing many improvements in Honolulu. The government building, which had been greatly needed, was finally completed at a cost of $130,000. Everybody was elated when the new Post Office was opened on Bethel Street. In the early days, when mail, which seldom reached the Islands, did arrive, it was dumped on the floor and people were at liberty to look it over for possible personal letters. It was around this time, too, that the first lighthouse flashed its welcome to the ships at sea. Kamehameha V had been concerned about the lighthouse; he said there was no more important thing on the government's agenda than its building. When the first Royal Hawaiian Hotel was completed—at Richards Street and the byway now known after it, as Hotel Street—Honolulu at last became a city where visitors could be properly accommodated and entertained.

Notwithstanding his royal responsibilities, Kamehameha V did not ignore the social side of life. A newspaper reported: "The ball given at the court house by His Majesty's staff was a most brilliant affair. It is not disparaging other elegant entertainments given in Honolulu in years past to say that, with the exception of the ball given by His Majesty in honor of the Duke of Edinburgh, this was the most brilliant entertainment we have seen in Honolulu. The decorations were splendid; beautiful fancy colored lanterns were placed along the walks, and special lights were used at various points. Eight hundred guests were invited. . . . Her Majesty, Queen Emma, honored the Occasion. The Queen arrived shortly after His Majesty. There was a formal reception followed by a great ball, which opened with a quadrille in which sixty couples took part. Dancing continued until very late. At five o'clock in the morning the guns from the *Mohican* gave the signal to close the party." No one seemed to enjoy the festivities more than did the King, whose health had been drunk by many friends during the supper hour.

Lot Kamehameha was known as the Bachelor King of Hawaiian history. The status, apparently, was not of his own choosing. It is said that, in his youth, he was in love with, and expected to marry, Bernice Pauahi, herself a descendant of Kamehameha the Great. In her childhood, according to the ancient Hawaiian custom, Bernice had been "adopted out" to Kinau, the *kuhina-nui*. This made her Lot's foster-sister. She was the wealthiest and most eligible maiden in the Kingdom. But against her parents' wishes (and they refused to attend the ceremony), she married Charles R. Bishop, a young adventurer from Glenn's Falls, N. Y., who had become a naturalized citizen of Hawaii in 1849 to accept the position of Collector General of Customs for the port of Honolulu. It was a happy marriage. Through the years she and Lot remained close friends. Since Kamehameha V was not a voluble man, history can offer only conjecture regarding his inner emotions. The only clue to those emotions is the fact that, on his deathbed, he named Bernice Pauahi Bishop his heir-apparent, which honor the lady gently declined.

In an old book of travel, *Seventy Thousand Miles with Shakespeare,* Daniel Bandman, the English actor who visited the Islands in the late seventies, told of being entertained by Kamehameha V at the plantation of his friend, Mr. Cummins, at Waimanalo. Mr. Bandman described the dangerous ride over the Pali trail, when each moment seemed an eternity and every inch of the way a jeopardy to life and limb. The party of gentlemen and ladies rode horseback. When they reached the plantation, they were royally received. Musicians had gone before them and greeted them in the Hawaiian fashion. At three o'clock the King arrived. Kamehameha V was a large, heavy person, and he often found it difficult to get around. He purchased a small steamboat in which he often visited the plantation at Waimanalo. He also had a bit of railroad laid for his special use, traveling with ease from the boat to the plantation. Mr. Bandman wrote that the King wore a navy blue suit and a crimson sash. "He looked like a true knight of medieval times and welcomed the friends by saying, 'This is Liberty Hall here.' "

During the dinner hula dancers entertained the guests. It can be assumed that the dancers had been duly licensed by the King. Mr. Bandman was requested to give a recitation; he, in turn, asked what the King would like to hear. The King replied: "Something earnest; it will do my people good."

Among the treasures in the deep vaults of the Territorial Archives in Honolulu is a small collection of letters written personally by Kamehameha V. Their pages are crisp and yellowed by the passing of the years. They are beautifully penned in a fine, delicate script, and bordered in black because of the official sorrows which had come to him. But the letters are cheerful, giving interesting details of his everyday life.

The first letter is written to the King's intimate friend, John Dominis:

"13th May, 1867

"My dear Dominis: The soldiers who want some clothes given them, tell me that they received some clothes before they went up with me to Hawaii last September, but no woolen blankets.

"They want blankets and some other things; supposing you come down here. You will be able to settle the matter then in a more satisfactory manner.

"Yours &c.
"Kamehameha."

A second letter to Mr. Dominis was written from the island of Hawaii, where the King was spending his vacation. It describes how he has settled down to country life in "perjamoners" and "colored shirts." The King wrote: "We are somewhat crowded but will try to manage to live. I am going to build a little grass house about as large as your little house at Waikiki, in order to have you and Cummins when you come up. The grass here is glorious, everything green, and the cattle close to our houses are very fat and with that peculiar bright color of their skin."

The King evidently enjoyed country life.

Two personal letters written by Kamehameha V to Governor Nahaolelu of Maui throw an interesting and important light upon the King's mind and time.

"Iolani Palace
"Feb. 20, 1869.

"The Hon. P. Nahaolelu,
    "Greetings to You.

"Your note was received. If you are thinking of a new horse from California for your carriage, then I will send for it. But you must give me the money.

"I have postponed our trip to Molokai until next month, because there is so much to do here. I have heard that some Haoles here in Honolulu wish to build a sugar mill at Hilo, if some land owners will make an agreement to let them plant seven hundred and fifty acres of sugar cane. I thought of talking to ask what they thought about building a sugar mill at Lahaina (on Maui), and to have some of the people there to plant the number of acres mentioned above with sugar cane. This may be exactly what you want, but I will ask first and when I know I will let you know about it.

"Here is the *Kamaile* sailing to Lahaina with a new captain. If it is possible and proper, I wish to help the captain of the *Kamaile* by hiring men temporarily to help put the freight on board, while the ship is at Lahaina. Show him some strong men who are able to do that work, because they may be strange to Lahaina.

With love,
Aliiolani."

Another letter, written several years earlier, is also addressed to Governor Nahaolelu. It speaks of various matters of local interest: of the planting of trees on the government lands on Maui, and of the King's desire to have *olona* and *awa* planted on special fields or lands which were of the crown heritage along the Koolau range. The letter tells of the damage done to property at Lahaina by an unusual flood, and the illness and recovery of the Princess Victoria Kamamalu. In it, too, the King reports of the important historical occurrence when the remains of Olohana (John Young) were exhumed, and of the reburial at the Royal Mausoleum. He wrote: "The remains of Olohana and others have been exhumed and taken up sometime during the past few days. Fanny (John Young's daughter) was one who were there to witness the exhumation as directed by the Minister of the Interior. The remains of Olohana and others were encased in new caskets."

It was Bernice Pauahi Bishop who had provided the funds for the building of the Royal Mausoleum in Nuuanu Valley. It was her wish that the early chiefs and kings of the Kamehameha line—the remains of whom the whereabouts were known—be assembled in one plot of ground. The bones of Kamehameha the Great, of course, could not be laid together with those of his confreres and royal descendants. But on a certain night, by torchlight, an eerie procession wound its way up Nuuanu Valley. Crowds, awed and silent, lined the streets as the remains of their ancient *alii* proceeded to their final resting place. The remains of lesser nobles, such as John Young, followed within a short time to take their places as guardians of the royal tomb.

Agriculture had taken on a new trend through the later reign of Kamehameha V. With additional laborers from other countries, the sugar industry was steadily increasing. From records one learns that, in 1872, eleven thousand tons of sugar were produced. This increase in production was very encouraging. However, the hoped-for Reciprocity Treaty with the United States did not materialize, and its failure caused constant anxiety to the King and his cabinet.

Meanwhile, Honolulu was growing cosmopolitan. For many years it had been a port of call for ships from many countries. Someone wrote an account of a trip which he made to Hilo in the whaling ship *Roscoe,* Captain Macomber in command. The traveler noticed that there were several men of different nationalities in the crew. He asked about it. The Captain said he would make a check-up, which he did. In the crew of the *Roscoe* were men from the following countries: Russia, Finland, Holland, Germany, Scotland, France, Ireland, Portugal, the United States, New Zealand, Strong Island, Ascension and the Sandwich Islands. One man, who had recently died, belonged to Hope Island. Captain Macomber said he had never had a more efficient crew. And so, the Kingdom of Hawaii and the city of Honolulu were known to many parts of the world, at least through the eyes of world mariners.

Kamehameha V was not a High Churchman, but he had the greatest reverence for sacred things and for the religious life of his people and country. He was not a member of the great Masonic fraternity as his brother had been, but he frequently attended the more social meetings of the Masonic lodge. His name appeared on the register, showing, perhaps, his underlying interest and kindly feeling.

The following note, which the King received from missionary friends, pleased him very much:

"To His Majesty, Kamehameha V.

"Sire: The undersigned have the honor to present to your Majesty the accompanying volume of the Holy Bible, from the American Bible Society. This is the new edition of the entire sacred scriptures in the Hawaiian language, with marginal references. It is printed in several forms and will be sold at cost to the people. This, however, does not include the cost of over $10,000 for the electrotype plates, which are a donation to the nation.

"Believing that your Majesty will take a deep interest in this new effort for Christianizing your people,

We remain

Your Majesty's O'bt Servants
S. C. Damon
L. H. Gulick"

The gift was accepted by the King with the following response:
"Gentlemen:

I receive with pleasure and gratitude the volume of the Holy Bible you present to me on behalf of the American Bible Society. Their efforts for the Christianization of my people are well known and fully appreciated by me, and for the new proof of their interest in my people and kingdom, I pray you to tender them my sincere thanks. I remain, gentlemen,

Gratefully yours,
Kamehameha."

It was an evening in mid-December, 1872. The King, evidently, was sitting alone at the palace, the last of his family. It may be he was writing a letter to some friend, or only passing a lonely hour putting his thoughts into written words as he penned the lines: "The Anglican Church bell is ringing, calling its members to church at twelve o'clock to begin its service to commence on Christmas itself. The Roman Catholic church is illuminated. It will hold divine service on the commencement of Christmas. The public will, undoubtedly, crowd these places of worship."

Notwithstanding factual disturbances, the daily life of the people of the Islands went along rather smoothly. While Kamehameha V was not very popular, personally, outside of intimate friends, his people appreciated his allegiance to them and gave their loyal support in return. In celebration of the King's birthday, a national holiday had been declared for December 11th. Flags floated from the public buildings and from the masts of the ships anchored in the harbor. The people from the country crowded into the town, and the townspeople were decorating business houses and private homes in honor of the day. Everyone was wearing *leis* of flowers and festooning even the horses with garlands of sweet *maile* from the forests.

But while all of this preparation was taking place, the officials of the government and the friends of the King were gathered in his chamber, for the court physician had announced that the King had suddenly been taken alarmingly sick. The King had been told that he should arrange his important matters at once, and he was urged to announce the successor to the throne. For some time he refused to do this, but finally he turned to Bernice Pauahi Bishop, who was sitting by his side, and said, "I wish you to take my place, to be my successor."

Mrs. Bishop replied, "No, no, not me. Do not think of me. I do not need it."

The King then said, "What makes this room so dark?" He asked who all the people were who were standing in his room. Some of them were sent away. The King again spoke to Mrs. Bishop, "I do not wish you to think that I do this from motives of friendship, but I think it is best for my people and for the nation."

Mrs. Bishop replied, "Oh, no, do not think of me. There are others. . . . There is Queen Emma; she has been a queen and is therefore fitted for the position."

The King answered, "She was queen by courtesy, having been the wife of a king."

This closed the conversation.

It had been generally known that the King had not been in good health for some time, but when the newspaper announced that he was feeling well and in excellent spirits, the people entered into the celebration of his birthday with merry hearts. The cannon on the slopes of Punchbowl were loaded, ready to give the royal salute at noon. The people were astounded when, at ten o'clock they heard the mournful minute guns announcing the death of the King. An old record of that hour says, "National festivities, scattered over many a league, were checked and hushed with the ominous warning. . . ." And the King had not officially named a successor to the throne.

Every evening for several days, as the King lay in state at the Palace, crowds of people poured through the gates bringing their offerings of tribute while the Royal Troops stood guard.

Kamehameha V, throughout his life, has been in his heart loyal to the old regime. This the people understood and appreciated. "The old time custom of wailing for the dead stirred the night air to plaintiveness and sorrow. The *hula* drums kept up their solemn beating, and the Hawaiian musicians sang their sacred chants to the accompaniment of the gourd and bamboo timebeaters. Great *kahilis* waved over the head of the dead king, and the beautiful throne room became a place of mournful awe." Hour after hour, marching feet passed the couch of the sleeping monarch, marking the close of the reign of Prince Lot— Kamehameha V. A deep and strange loneliness settled at the heart of the nation. The King was no more. The last Kamehameha was dead.

A MAN OF THE PEOPLE

Chapter XIV

"I like the man."
—MARK TWAIN

THE THRONE WAS WAITING. The black *kahilis* were still waving at the palace, and the mourning and the wailing continued night and day, for the funeral of Kamehameha V, delayed by a severe and unusual lightning and thunder storm, had not yet been held. It was an unprecedented situation. Since the beginning of the Kamehameha dynasty, a direct descendant of Kamehameha I had succeeded to the throne. But Kamehameha V had neither left an heir nor officially declared a successor. According to the constitution of the country, the duty of selecting and appointing some high chief as the ruler of the Kingdom belonged to the Legislature.

Prince William Lunalilo was the son of the noble chieftess, Kekauluohi, who had been Premier of the Kingdom under Kamehameha III, following Kinau. Lunalilo held the highest rank of any chief in the Islands; although he was not a direct descendant of Kamehameha I, he had, through his mother, inherited Kamehameha blood. Because of his high rank, the throne was offered to him by those so authorized under the Constitution, but he refused to accept it, saying that he felt the people should be allowed to choose their king. This was a departure from custom and an amazing attitude, even to the foreign members of the legislature. However, Lunalilo won their cooperation and prepared his program.

Six days after the death of Kamehameha V, Lunalilo sent broadcast over the Islands a printed manifesto declaring his right to the throne, but giving the people the opportunity to express their choice as to whom among the high priests they would prefer as king. A date was set for the people to meet at the polling places on the different islands and cast their votes. In the meantime, the Legislature had called an Extraordinary Session for the eighth of January, 1873, when the matter of the succession would be permanently settled.

Feeling ran high as everyone discussed the situation. The names of the different high chiefs were on everybody's tongue—Prince Lunalilo, Dowager Queen Emma, Bernice Pauahi Bishop and David Kalakaua. All, by rank, were eligible for election.

Prince Lunalilo, personally, was popular with all classes of people. His simple sincerity and friendliness had won him many friends. The declaration in his manifesto that, if elected to the throne, he would restore the constitution of Kamehameha III, "of happy memory," making only such changes as would adapt it to present laws and thus giving to the people the rights and privileges which had been theirs in the past, was received with enthusiasm. The majority of the Hawaiians were loyal to him, and called him "The People's Prince."

Mrs. Bishop was a Kamehameha, and Queen Emma also had Kamehameha blood. Both were greatly beloved, and, as women of highest rank, fine intelligence, and wide interests, they stood well in line for support, but neither pushed her claims to the throne. Colonel David Kalakaua was a high chief, but not of the Kamehameha line. He was descended from a long line of Polynesian chiefs of the Island of Hawaii. He had been born in Honolulu, had held different governmental positions (his title having come from his commission in the Hawaiian army) and was considered by many to be an able administrator. He, too, was popular in the community.

Colonel Kalakaua and his party secretly prepared a paper attempting to show that Lunalilo was not a true Kamehameha. This document was headed "This is the Truth" and was signed "By the Skillful Genealogists." Historians agree that they cannot rely on the genealogical records of the Hawaiians, but, whatever the truth may have been, this paper aroused widespread opposition to Colonel Kalakaua and rebounded to the favor of Lunalilo. Many people considered it an attack on the Prince, and many who before this had not taken sides one way or another came over to his camp. Every steamer and sailing vessel brought people from the outside islands to Honolulu, all interested in the coming election. Mass meetings were called in Kaumakapili Church. This church was used for large assemblies and had, it is said, acquired the character of Faneuil Hall in Revolutionary days. When the church bell, which hung in a low, wooden belfry by the churchyard gate, was rung, the people dropped whatever they were doing and hurried to the church to see what was happening. Politics ran at a high pitch in Honolulu.

The first meeting preceding the election, which was called for the purpose of offering resolutions of sympathy to the surviving sister of the late King, ended in a public expression of allegiance to Lunalilo, which came about in the following way:

From the platform was told the story of his baptism. When the Rev. Mr. Bingham, who was about to perform the ceremony, asked, "What shall we call the child?" Kanaina, the father, replied, "William

Charles Kanaina." "No," objected the baby's mother, Kekauluohi, "he is the highest chief in all the Islands; therefore, his name shall be Lunalilo, 'out of sight, above.' " Hearing the story, the people stood waving their hats and handkerchiefs, shouting their acclaim for Lunalilo.

Kalakaua, learning what had taken place at the church and thinking to influence the older Hawaiians in his favor, at once sent out an appeal to the people. This document was posted everywhere, written in the oldtime phraseology:

"O my people! My countrymen of old! Arise! This is the voice! Ho! all ye tribes! Ho! my own ancient people! The people who took hold and built up the Kingdom of Kamehameha.

Arise! This is the voice!

Let me direct you, my people! Do nothing contrary to the law or against the peace of the Kingdom. Do not go and vote.

Do not be led by foreigners; they had no part in our hardships in gaining the country. Do not be led by their false teachings."

Then followed a long, detailed attack upon Lunalilo and his adherents, ending with the exhortation:

"Arise, O People!

To the front!

Drink the water of bitterness.

Signed, David Kalakaua."

Press reports of the day tell that Kalakaua's elaborate message accomplished nothing and was received with derision. Lunalilo's party continued their advertising. Posters appeared everywhere, printed in English and Hawaiian, urging everyone to cast his vote for the king. No property ownership was necessary; only citizenship.

The election was set for New Year's Day. For the first time in their lives many people were to cast a vote, and never before had anyone voted for a king. The houshold troops went quietly in a body to the polls and deposited their ballots. Following them came a large company of Mormons from the other side of Oahu. They had made the long trip to Honolulu, most of them walking all the way. Great numbers of people from outside districts crowded into the city, all eager to vote. Three thousand votes were cast in nine hours—two thousand seven hundred by Hawaiians and the remainder by naturalized citizens. The excitement was almost beyond bounds. Crowds remained at the polls hoping that the final count would assure the election of the Prince.

Lunalilo, fearing a demonstration, sent word to the polling places that, if the people would be quiet until after the election was officially

declared, they could call upon him at the Palace. This message was received with great rejoicing, and the crowd dispersed, shouting and
singing. That Lunalilo had not taken the throne when the opportunity
was open to him had completely won the hearts of the people.

A week later, Colonel Kalakaua, depending largely upon the vote of
the Legislature, which he regarded as his stronghold, was entertaining
at breakfast the most influential members of the community. The Prince
was grave and anxious. The final decision was yet to be made. The
Legislature was to sit at noon. As the time drew near, crowds of people
moved towards the court house and surrounded the building. Many
were armed with stones and cudgels and some with revolvers. The
situation was alarming.

The assembly convened at twelve o'clock, and, after some prelimi-
naries, proceeded with the election. Lunalilo left the hall and waited in
another room for the returns. Kalakaua had written to each member of
the Legislature asking for his vote. And so these opponents, who had
been friends from boyhood, awaited the turn of the tide.

The counting of the votes began. It was a tense and thrilling hour.
A writer who was present wrote of the anxiety of the people: "The
crowd outside as well as audience in the assembly were as silent as the
grave, and almost breathless from excitement. The first ballot was told
off. 'Lunalilo for King!' The next was the same, and the next. As each
one was reported, the result was signaled by those who thronged the
open windows to the people below. So the telling went on in the hushed
stillness of the great assembly until as the number of votes reached a
bare majority and thus far all for Lunalilo, a cheer came up from the
grounds and, gathering strength, burst in a deafening roar which rose
and fell like the crisis of a storm; the outskirts of the crowd took up the
refrain, and the streets leading into the square sent out their answering
shouts. Never before had the capital been the scene of equal enthusiasm."

Lunalilo soon made his appearance on the balcony of the courthouse.
The crowd gave him an ovation. They had made him their king! He
spoke in both English and Hawaiian, then, refusing to ride in the carriage which was waiting for him, he joined the crowd and set out on
foot for Iolani Palace.

Journalists of the time further relate that there was no military
cortége; no drums and bugles announced his triumphal march. "Bare-
headed and reverently he walked, with the Chancellor of the Kingdom
at his side. The great crowd surged around him in a solid mass as he
went, and the imposing procession moved through the streets, citizens
all, vanguard and rearguard, heralded only by the hearty hurrahs of the

populace." Other writers, describing the great day, say that, when evening came, the town was illuminated and a huge torchlight procession wound its dazzling way through the streets for hours.

The events of these few days are vividly brought to mind in the diary of a young girl of the period. In the delicate tracery of the handwriting of the times she recorded her personal experience of those stirring events. She wrote:

"Tuesday, January 7th
1873

"Went down this morning to see the funeral of Kamehameha V, but on account of the rain it was postponed till Saturday.

Wednesday, 8th

"Prince William C. Lunalilo was elected the King today by the Legislative Assembly. Every vote was for him. Governor Dominis declined to vote as David was his brother-in-law.

"Spent the evening at the hotel and saw the torchlight procession and the illumination in the honor of the King.

January, 9th

"Went to Kawaiahao to see Prince William take the oath of office. There were over 3000 people in the church and many more outside. He walked to and from the church, saying that he had no carriage of his own and he was not going to borrow one. He appeared very finely dressed in black."

January, 10th

"The national hymn sung yesterday was composed by Lunalilo.

Ten years ago it took the prize among fifteen or twenty others. It is a translation of 'God Save the King.' "

A more formal account of the coronation is given in different newspapers of the time:

"Yesterday at 12 o'clock, His Majesty, King Lunalilo, took the oath of office. He was simply but elegantly dressed and wore no decorations save a broad scarlet ribbon and silver star of Royalty. He was met at the entrance to Kawaiahao Church by Chief Justice Allen, and members of the cabinet of the late King.

"The scene was most impressive. An immense crowd filled the church and grounds. In the church the pulpit had been removed and in its place a wide platform had been erected. Before it was placed a table upon which was laid the Holy Bible. A throne chair stood at one side covered with a royal mantle of golden feathers. In the rear of the platform and at either end the Royal Standards of Hawaii Supporters, wearing feather capes and bearing the royal *kahilis,* guarded the royal chair.

"The seats nearest the platform were occupied by members of the Legislature, former representatives, officers of the *Benesia,* Queen Emma, the Hon. Mrs. Bishop, and the Hon. Mrs. Dominis. Also present were members of the old *Alii* families.

"Precisely at noon, His Majesty, escorted by members of the staff of the late King, entered the church. The immense audience rose and greeted him with enthusiastic cheers. During the prayer, offered by the Rev. Mr. Parker, His Majesty remained standing.

"The certificate of election was read in English and in Hawaiian. The King again rose from his seat and the oath of office was administered by the Chief Justice. At once the King stepped forward and addressed the members of the legislature as follows:

—THE KING'S ADDRESS—

" 'This is the first time in the history of this kingdom that the Legislative Assembly has been convened for the purpose of electing a sovereign, and I tender you my thanks for the cordial unanimity and good will which has characterized your proceedings.

" 'But before adverting to any considerations of duty or responsibility, it is becoming as well as in accordance with the promptings of our hearts to express our sorrow at the sudden death of the illustrious Chief, whose successor I am, and whose funeral rites are so soon to be celebrated.

" 'The late King had decided traits of character. He was enterprising and labored to develop the resources of this country and extended his protecting hand to the Hawaiian people!'

"The King continued his comments upon the development of the country under Kamehameha V, and then added:

" 'Governments may be said to enter upon a new era at the accession to the throne of every sovereign. The commencement of my reign is auspicious. Our relations with foreign governments are of the most friendly character, and I am satisfied will continue so if we faithfully discharge our duty in conforming to the principles of justice and comity recognized among nations. May the blessings of our Heavenly Father, without which there can be no permanent success, attend our efforts to promote the best interests of our government and people.' "

After his long address to the Legislature, the King spoke to the people expressing his thanks for their loyalty and kindness to him, closing with the words: "I need not assure you that my heart is filled with gratitude." Hawaiian voices filled the great church with song as the choir led the people in the beautiful anthem, "God Save the King." As they sang, King Lunalilo quietly left the church.

All this time the mourning of many of the native people had continued at the palace, where Kamehameha V was lying in state. Mark Twain, who was in Honolulu at that time, wrote the following sympathetic description: "It is two o'clock in the morning and I have just been up towards the palace to hear some of the singing of the numerous well-born watchers (of both sexes) who are standing guard in the chamber of death. The voices were pure and rich and blended together without harshness or discord. The music was exceedingly plaintive and beautiful."

The great storm was over and the funeral of Kamehameha V was finally held, with King Lunalilo acting as chief mourner. It was a strange situation, or so it seems in these more modern times. "When the funeral services were ended, the last prayer said, the volley fired, the black *kahilis* placed standing before the mausoleum doors, then the prevailing joy and gladness broke forth as Lunalilo rode back to his palace with the jubilant acclaim of a spontaneous ovation of his subjects."

Prince William, as Lunalilo was called by his intimate friends, had not been popular with Kamehameha V. Although his very high rank automatically gave him a seat in the House of Nobles, he had been shown no honor by the late King. The young Prince was a songster, and Kamehameha V did not sing. Genial, generous, and friendly, "Prince Bill" was beloved by the people. Stories are told of his lavish entertainments and extravagant manner of living, both of which so troubled the King and his cabinet that, at one time, he was declared a spendthrift and was allowed only a small portion of his rightful income. His house was shabbily furnished, and he had little money to spend. However, this did not lessen his friendliness and good humor, and his hospitality continued to be generous and warm-hearted no matter how limited it might be.

Lunalilo was born a prince, the highest in the land. His mother died when he was only eight years old. He was brought up at court, petted and spoiled, receiving little or no discipline. He was finally placed in the School for Young Chiefs, where, along with Alexander, Lot and other royal youngsters, he received his education. He was a good student, and, as he grew older, his scholarly mind won him many laurels. He loved poetry and wrote creditable verses, expressing his love of the beauty of the Islands. He was especially fond of Shakespeare, and his mind was stored with quotations from English classics and from the Scriptures.

An editor in Honolulu, who knew Prince Lunalilo well, once wrote: 'I was present at an old-fashioned one ring circus which had come down for a season from San Francisco, while the fleet wintered in Honolulu. Prior to the opening act, Lunalilo, who occupied a ringside seat, was in characteristic mood, laughing and talking rather loudly. A circus attendant in passing, not knowing who he was, peremptorily told him to stop his noise and keep still. Instantly the attention of the audience was fixed on Lunalilo who arose slowly to his full height, threw his head back slightly, fixed his penetrating gaze on the attendant, extended his right arm, and, with his index finger slightly sawing the air in a menacing, chiding manner, and in an oratorical voice began speaking in the present idiomatic English somewhat in this fashion, without quoting literally:

" 'Sir! Thou fillest my soul with weariness. 'Tis ever common that men are merriest when they are away from home. Perhaps you are too far from home to be merry.

" 'I would rather have a fool to make me merry than experience to make me sad.

" 'Let my liver rather heat with wine than my heart cool with mortifying groans.'

"By this time the attendant was in a daze, not knowing what he had worked up, and slunk away while the audience rocked with laughter. With a benignant smile and wave of the hand to the people, Lunalilo resumed his seat as the band began to play and the procession entered the sawdust ring."

Mr. Bandman, the English actor who became a close friend of Prince Lunalilo, wrote that, with Dr. and Mrs. McGrew and friends, he drove to Waikiki to call upon the Prince. As they neared his home they saw him high up in a coconut tree, dressed only in his very brief *malo*. Knowing that it would be embarrassing to the ladies, who were strangers in Honolulu, if he so received them, they did not stop, but drove on, planning to call upon their return. Lunalilo had seen them and, divining their purpose, he scurried down the tree, and, when later the visitors arrived, he was ready to welcome them in conventional dress. They were ushered into his parlor, where they found upon the table copies of the New York *Herald*, the London *Times*, and the latest fashionable society papers of both England and America.

Mark Twain, in his notes which were written the same night that he listened to the singing of the watchers at the palace, said of Lunalilo: "Prince William is a man of fine, large build, is thirty-one years of age, is affable, gentlemanly, open, frank, manly; is as independent as a lord and has the spirit and will of the old Conqueror himself. He is intelligent, shrewd, sensible; is a man of first-rate abilities in fact. I like the man. I like his bold independence and his friendship for and appreciation of American residents." It was so that many men spoke of Lunalilo.

The Kamehamehas had received certain recognition from different European countries, but Lunalilo was not well known abroad. He had traveled no further than California, but he had always had an intelligent interest in matters concerning government. Although he was a Kamehameha by inheritance, his reign was to be an independent one.

When Lunalilo was a young man he attended, with Kalakaua, a great celebration in honor of the restoration of the Hawaiian flag. Kalakaua was the speaker of the day, but Lunalilo acted as toastmaster at the great banquet. A newspaper reported: "We have space for but one speech, the one delivered in English by Prince William Lunalilo." This was a lengthy address covering the experience of the loss of the Island Kingdom and its restoration by Admiral Thomas. The Prince spoke of the short but impressive address which had been given by Kamehameha III at that time, and then continued:

"Well do I remember the scene when, standing within the walls of the fort with His present Majesty (Kamehameha III) and his two late brothers, we witnessed the lowering of our flag. On that day the Islands were ceded to Great Britain and on that day the meteor flag of Albion waved triumphant over the group. England boasts of her mighty navy, of her colonial possessions all over the world. It is truly said that the sun never sets on her domain. France has boasted of her Bonaparte and of how all Europe trembled once when that hero of a hundred battles sat on the French throne. The Roman Empire once boasted of her strength and wealth. The United States of America has boasted that during her struggle for independence she has gained her freedom and, during the few years past, rebellion has been crushed and slavery no more exists.

"Have we anything to boast of? I must surely say we have; for in the few years since the light of the gospel has reached our shores, the tree of knowledge and of wisdom has been planted; it has taken root, its branches have spread, and we are now sending seed to be planted among the yet heathen nations of the vast Pacific Ocean. Our light has been increasing in brightness day by day, and I am proud to say that we now rank among the civilized and enlightened nations of the globe.

"In conclusion I would say, let us give thanks unto Him, the Ruler of all things, for His unbounded mercy to us during our hours of affliction and of prosperity and happiness. May God in His infinite mercy save the King."

Years passed and, in 1873, the hour came to Lunalilo when he, as King, for the first time addressed the Legislative Assembly. His speech is recorded in the *Roster of the Legislature of Hawaii, 1841-1918*.

"Nobles and Representatives, you were called to meet in an extraordinary session.

"Your promptness and decision in accomplishing the business to which your attention had been directed have made you a model Legislature. I am confident that in the future your example will be cited as worthy of praise and imitation.

"I congratulate the nation on your unanimity in recommending certain amendments to the Constitution. Ample time will now be given to the people to consider the propriety of their final adoption so that the next Legislative Assembly will be prepared to act upon them with a decision and intelligence worthy of your own. The public mind has been for some time agitated on the subject of amendments to the Constitution, and I trust that the course now taken will lead to a satisfactory result.

"I desire that the Constitution shall secure to my subjects all the rights which shall best promote their improvements and happiness.

"Nobles and Representatives, by your choice, which is in accordance with popular suffrage, I have been made King, and my efforts will be unceasing to prove myself worthy of that high trust.

"In parting with you I renew the expression of my thanks for the cordial good will and support you have rendered me.

"May the blessing of our Heavenly Father be continued to our Kingdom.

"I now declare this Legislative Assembly prorogued."

In his papers, "Thirty Days of Hawaiian History," Sanford Dole reviewed the political situation in the years preceding and following the reign of Lunalilo. He said in his opening address: "History derives less interest from the magnitude of its events than from the principles involved therein; less from the number of its hosts than the causes and character of their movements. The uprising of a small people may be as inspiring as the uprising of a great nation. To the lovers of liberal institutions the accession of King Lunalilo to the Hawaiian throne was full of propitious omens. A step towards popular government, even in a comparatively insignificant state, belongs to the world and is part of universal progress. To Hawaiians it will ever be an era of great political moment. It was a serious crisis in affairs and fortunately terminated favorably for Hawaiian citizenship."

In such a review Mr. Dole presented the situation at the time of the election of Prince Lunalilo. Unfortunately, the reign of the young ruler, so full of promise, lasted but a short time. Attacked by pulmonary tuberculosis, King Lunalilo's decline was rapid, and death soon ended the life and career of the spirited young monarch. Officials had urged him, as they had Kamehameha V, to declare a successor to the throne, but, steadfast to his principles and his democratic feeling regarding government, he refused, insisting that the people should be allowed to choose their ruler.

It was in his own home, a short distance from the Palace, that, surrounded by his friends and members of his cabinet, Lunalilo's benevolent career came to a close. The press reported that news of the King's death flashed over the town, and by ten o'clock that evening hundreds of people had gathered in the grounds of the beloved King's home.

The following letter was written by Mr. Curtis Lyons to his father at Waimea soon after the death of the King:

"Feb. 14, 1874

"In the evening we had company and at nine o'clock we heard the bugle call at the barracks for the artillery men. I immediately said, 'The King is dead!' and in a moment or two we heard that it was so. Everything was quiet; not a wail nor a loud spoken word. In the dim moonlight forms of people glided quietly into the lane toward the back gates of the palace. Julie and I walked down there and back; people were gathering at the gates and messengers were flitting to and fro; no noise whatever. We returned and retired for the night."

Recorded, too, are other events of the fateful evening: "At one o'clock, as was the Hawaiian custom, the body of the King was moved to the palace to be laid in state. The crowd of spectators opened to the right and to the left, when the solemn procession of the government officials and the staff of the late King, with the shrouded bier in their midst, moved slowly along. The moon shone with unclouded brightness and the deep silence was broken only by the sound of the marching steps of the procession. It was a scene for the painter or the poet."

At midnight when the King's body was to be placed in the casket and the attendants started to remove the beautiful yellow feather mantle upon which the King was lying, his father stopped them, saying that he wished the cloak to be wrapped about his son: "He is the last of our family and it belongs to him." (This was not the Kamehameha State cape, however, but one of Lunalilo's own.) As the King's body was carried across the room to the casket, it is said that the great gathering of native people, silent until then, broke into a most terrible wail.

At eight o'clock the next morning the minute guns were fired from Punchbowl and from the ships in port. Flags on all government buildings and on all ships in port were placed at half mast. In front of the palace the Honolulu Rifles were drawn up as a guard of honor. Within the palace the Cabinet Ministers, the Judges of the Supreme Court, and the Members of the Privy Council, all in attendance as his devoted followers, one by one passed through the room to look for the last time on the face of their chosen King. Only the sounds of repressed grief broke the stillness.

A beautiful tomb of classic lines, erected in memory of Lunalilo, stands in the grounds of the Old Stone Church—Kawaiahao. It was built by his father during the year following the young King's death and according to his request. The story is told that, when the remains of past kings and chiefs had to be transferred to the Royal Mausoleum in Nuuanu Valley, those of Lunalilo's mother, herself a high chieftess, had been overlooked, either by thoughtlessness or uncertainty as to the exact location of her grave. Nevertheless, Lunalilo had been offended by this slight by the Kamehamehas to his mother and preferred for his own last resting place a spot near her, rather than one among the royal dead in Nuuanu Valley.

Few governmental changes were made during the brief reign of Lunalilo, but those which were made were of great importance. Much progress was made in the care of the leprous people, which had been of vital concern to Lunalilo. Further steps were taken by the government for possible reciprocity treaty with the United States, and it was at this time that the Hawaiian government first proposed to offer to the United States the exclusive use of Pearl River on Oahu as a coaling and repair station for their ships of war.

Lunalilo specified in his will that the greater portion of his large estate was to be used for the building and maintenance of a Home for Aged and Poor Hawaiians. This Home is the pride of the Hawaiian people today, "a tribute to the generosity and loving kindness of the understanding heart of Lunalilo"—Prince and King.

THE MERRY MONARCH

Chapter XV

> *"My great object is to strengthen the foundation of My power as guardian of the people."*
>
> —KALAKAUA

As THE "Merry Monarch" is Kalakaua, the last King of the Sandwich Islands, most frequently remembered. No ruler of any country enjoyed himself more than he did. Notwithstanding his supposed responsibilities and the grave political and governmental situation, David, King Kalakaua, made his life a matter of continuous entertainment. He not only enjoyed himself, but he wished everyone about him to do the same. With a charming manner, which was distinctly royal, and with his warm and genial personality, he set the pace for his reign, which he believed would be long, happy and successful. Thereby hang many tales, both historical and legendary, which make up the story of King Kalakaua.

Yet, with all his merriment and frivolity, his reign from beginning to end was marked with intrigue and hatred. Loved by his intimate friends, hated by his foes, defeated overwhelmingly by Lunalilo one year and elected to the throne the next—this was Kalakaua.

Since no declaration of an heir to the throne had been made when King Lunalilo died, the Legislature was again, for the second time, obliged to elect a ruler for the kingdom. Upon the death of Lunalilo, Kalakaua lost no time in advertising his claims to the throne; he even placed placards at the entrance to the Old Stone Church, asking the people to vote for him.

In the meantime, Queen Emma had been strongly advised to assert her own claims to the throne and thus oppose the election of Kalakaua. This brought about a distinct political and governmental situation. It was believed that the election of Queen Emma, who was definitely British in her feeling and allegiance, would result in making British interests paramount in the Islands, and this, it was felt, would greatly damage the commercial life of the country. Many men from America and elsewhere, believing in the progress of commercial interchange between America and the Orient by way of Honolulu, had placed their financial and personal interest in the development of the Islands and had become citizens of the Hawaiian kingdom in order that they might better serve the country and, perhaps more so, provide for their own future.

Considering all this, the Assembly had been called. The leaders of the government decided to push the claims of Prince Kalakaua. He was a high chief and had many friends among the foreign population. It was expected that he would attract a large foreign vote. The campaign opened. Many mass meetings were held and the contest became tense and bitter. The adherents of Queen Emma brought from the outside islands many simple native people, and several hundred of these men, with many others, surrounded the courthouse where the Legislature was meeting and where the election would be decided. When the votes were counted it was found that Kalakaua had won the election by thirty-nine votes, only six votes having been cast for Queen Emma.

Mr. Lorrin A. Thurston, in his book of Memories, gives a vivid description of what happened that day. He tells that suddenly a man rushed from the building and through the crowd shouting at the top of his voice, "Kalakaua is King! Kalakaua is King!"

"The people in the yard received this news with an angry shout, which speedily became a roar of angry execration, as though a stick had been twisted in a giant beehive. Immediately a committee of three members of the Legislature appointed to announce the election of Kalakaua came down the stairs and to a carriage which had been drawn up for their use. They wore long-tailed coats and plug hats. Irresolutely the crowd watched the committeemen start to enter the carriage. With a snarl they fell upon the vehicle and the span of horses. Almost before one could think, the hats of the committeemen were knocked off, their coats were torn from their backs, the carriage was wrecked, and the harness was detached from the carriage; after a bang upon their quarters the horses tore up the street. Thereupon the crowd, roaring, rushed upon the double doors at the foot of the inner stairs.

"In a doorway, facing the mob, stood Sanford B. Dole and C. C. Harris, each with a hand upon the shoulder of the other, warning the crowd back. There they stood, two men only; by sheer moral courage they held the rioters off for twenty minutes or so. But other rioters got out a whaling spade, climbed the outside stairs and dug a hole through the panel of the locked doors at the top. Thus they gained access to the legislative hall. That place was gutted. Some members of the legislature were mobbed because they had voted for Kalakaua and pandemonium ensued. A rain of books, chairs, tables and other furniture poured from the doors and windows of the court house, upstairs and downstairs. Some members of the legislature crawled from the windows and hung on the outside of the building by their hands. The mob stamped on their fingers so that they fell into the street below. Some were seriously injured and one died."

Officials of the government finally appealed to the representatives of the United States and Great Britain for assistance. The response was immediate. One hundred and fifty marines from the warships in the harbor were landed. They marched along Queen Street and up Fort Street to the courthouse. The mob retreated and the marines took charge. They remained on shore several days guarding the government buildings and the palace grounds, until it was assured there would be no more trouble.

In reviewing the strange happening in the usually quiet and orderly community, the newspaper commenting on the occurrence expressed strongly their regret and mortification that such a thing could have taken place. Mr. W. R. Castle, in his *Sketch of Constitutional History of Hawaii,* in referring to the riot following the election of King Kalakaua, says, "This riot was caused by adherents of Queen Emma, and the participants were almost without exception native Hawaiians who objected to Kalakaua as representative of the foreigners, and desired Queen Emma as more particularly representative of the native people." Mr. Castle also observed that Queen Emma had been very unwisely advised in her attempt to gain the throne.

On the night of the election, Queen Emma was at the Priory with the Sisters. Directly following the election, the official notice was carried to Kalakaua who had waited at his residence for the returns. It was a great moment when, the dream of his life fulfilled, Kalakaua could say, "I am the King."

Kalakaua was born November 16, 1836, at the foot of Punchbowl Hill, where the minute guns had sounded through the years. He was descended from ancient high chiefs of the island of Hawaii. Through his father's line, as through his mother's, there were chiefs who had been distinguished counselors of Kamehameha I. In 1863 Kalakaua married Princess Kapiolani, the granddaughter of Kaumualii, the last king of the island of Kauai. She was named for the same Kapiolani who had defied the goddess Pele long years before.

The inauguration of King Kalakaua was held on the 13th of February, 1874, at Kinau Hale—the House of Kinau—near the palace. Kalakaua had expected the inauguration, as was the custom, to be held in the Old Stone Church, Kawaiahao. He had planned an elaborate installation ceremony, and was greatly disappointed when advised by the councilors that, because of the recent disturbance, it would be best to have a simple ceremony performed as quietly and quickly as possible. The cabinet ministers of the late King, the foreign diplomatic and councilor representatives of the kingdom, the native and foreign citizens to the number of two or three hundred, and the officers from the ships of war in port were present to witness the inauguration. A few minutes before twelve o'clock the King appeared on the veranda. He addressed the audience:

"Nobles and Representatives: You have been called to assemble at this time with the representatives of foreign governments to witness My assuming the sacred trust of the Constitution. I am sorry that on account of the present disturbance I cannot, as I had designed, give My people a new Constitution as a blessing to them, and to establish the independence of our Kingdom, the Throne of Hawaii *nei*. But this is a time of commotion, and My great object is to strengthen the foundation of My power as guardian of the people. I am conscious that it is a high responsibility and one that demands great caution in the possessor, but at this time, as the disturbance is over, and as I see the consequences of the riot upon the representatives in My presence, I ask that you will aid me in My trust."

His Honor, Judge Hartwell, Vice Chancellor of the Kingdom, then administered the following oath, His Majesty repeating it sentence by sentence after Judge Hartwell, and both resting their hands on the Holy Bible held by H. R. H. Leleiohoku:

"I, Kalakaua, solemnly swear, in the presence of Almighty God, to maintain the Constitution of the Kingdom whole and inviolate and to govern in conformity therewith."

The Rev. H. H. Parker offered a fervent prayer appropriate to the occasion. The audience gave three cheers, which were repeated by the crowd outside, while the guns on Punchbowl fired the first royal salute to King Kalakaua and his Royal Standard, which was responded to by H. B. M.'s Ship *Tenedos* and the U. S. ship *Tuscarora* in the harbor.

One of the first acts of Kalakaua was to appoint a successor to the throne and to provide for a continuous succession through his own family, displacing the Kamehameha line, which was practically extinct. Kalakaua appointed his younger brother, Prince Leleiohoku, as heir apparent. This met with the approval of the people generally, the Prince being a popular member of the Royal family.

At the beginning of his reign Kalakaua realized that he must regain his friendship and prestige with the Hawaiian people, many of whom felt that he was too closely associated with foreigners. He soon decided to make a tour of the Islands to meet as many of the people as possible. He went first to Kauai. A representative of the press accompanied the King's party and later reported the details of the fine reception given to Kalakaua on Kauai:

"Bay of Hanalei: His Majesty landed at one o'clock under a royal salute of twenty-one guns from the shore—not precisely guns but big *ohia* logs, which the loyal people of Hanalei had placed in line on the bluff overlooking the landing place, bored and charged with powder. As soon as the boat, bearing the Royal Standard, left the steamer, the improvised cannon were fired by a long fuse or powder train, each going off with great regularity, bursting and splitting the logs into firewood with a report that doubtless seemed grand to the populace of Hanalei who were out *en masse* to see the King.

"A large red and white banner waved from a tall flagstaff over the battery on which was the motto, '*Hookahi puuwai*' (one heart). Everybody from the two plantations in the valley made a holiday. Noticing, on one of the tall peaks that overlook the valley, a white speck on the deep green of verdure, we learned that it was one of the many telegraph flags by means of which our arrival had been signaled from point to point over the island. The moment the King stepped ashore the entire assembled population broke into repeated cheers as the band played the national anthem."

The King's visit to the different islands gave the people renewed confidence. They accepted Kalakaua. He was to them the great chief. He had said he would build up the Kingdom, and in him they put their trust.

The matter of the constitution was an everpresent problem. Each king wanted a new constitution. In his paper, which he read before the Historical Society, Mr. Castle further commented: "There is no question that when Kalakaua took the throne the respect felt by all people for the authority of the constitution had been very much shaken. By various means, not always of the most creditable character, he sought to establish himself firmly as a friend of the people." He could not give a new constitution, but by increasing friendliness must win the loyalty of the nation.

Upon his return from the tour of the Islands, Kalakaua faced the necessity of keeping his promise to push the matter of the Reciprocity Treaty with the United States. After much discussion it was decided to send two representatives to Washington to further negotiations. An invitation had been extended to the King to visit Washington as the guest of the nation, and the steamer *Benicia* had been placed at his service. He left for Washington on Nov. 17, 1874, stopping at San Francisco on his way to the capital.

On the sixteenth of November, which was his birthday, Kalakaua sent out a proclamation calling upon the people to attend a religious service in the different churches to pray for his safe return from Washington. His Majesty first attended the St. Andrew's Temporary Cathedral and received the Holy Communion at the hands of the Lord Bishop, in company with Her Majesty, Kapiolani, and Dowager Queen Emma, all kneeling together at the same altar; according to a press report, this was "a happy assurance of the peace of Hawaii."

On leaving the Islands the King was accompanied by the American Minister and important members of his own staff. This was not Kalakaua's first visit abroad. In company with Prince Lot and Prince Lunalilo, when they were all young men, he had visited San Francisco. But this trip to Washington was his first adventure in traveling as a monarch. He looked forward to this experience with great anticipation.

The San Francisco *Chronicle* of Nov. 29, 1874, gives an account of the reception to the Royal guests:

"The city was aglow with excitement yesterday. It isn't every day that a king comes to San Francisco, and she evidently made up her mind to celebrate the occasion.

"By ten o'clock a perfect swarm crowded the thoroughfares. By half past ten the wharfs in the vicinity of the landing were alive with the throng. Ships lying at their berths were overrun. Boys clambered to the rigging and clustered like flies on the spars and masts. A dense crowd surged at the gates of Broadway wharf when it was announced that His Majesty and suite would make that landing.

"The King was attired in a suit of black broadcloth of the latest fashion. He wore no jewelry but three massive gold rings. On the lapel of his coat was pinned a small strip of parti-colored ribbon including the Royal Order with which he had been vested."

In San Francisco the King and his party were received by the officials of the city, as he had been by the military forts when entering the harbor. The King was entertained at the California Club, where he surprised the members by a brilliant play at billiards.

The trip of the royal party across the country was made in a luxurious palace car, the same car that was built for President Grant. The train was a special, provided by the government of the United States, and made no stops en route except at Omaha.

Kalakaua was the first Hawaiian monarch to cross the United States, and his reception was flattering. It was said that all political parties, and all classes of men, vied with each other in paying the King suitable honor. In one report of Kalakaua's stay in Washington it was stated, "A becoming kingly dignity without pride, pretense, or ostentation, gained him universal admiration."

The King was received in State by President Grant. Those were the days which delighted the heart of Kalakaua. He had come to Washington on a great mission. He expected to speak before the House of Representatives and the Senate regarding the hoped-for Reciprocity Treaty between the United States and his kingdom. However, because of a severe cold he was unable to speak; he was present at both houses, nevertheless, his address being read for him. In the address the King said:

"Today our country needs the aid of a treaty of Commercial Reciprocity with America in order to insure our material prosperity, and I believe if such a treaty can be secured the beneficial effects will soon be apparent to all classes, and our nation under its reviving influence will live again."

Kalakaua made a great impression in Washington both diplomatically and socially. On Christmas Day he attended St. Thomas's Episcopal Church, and at five o'clock gave a reception in his private parlor at the hotel to many old acquaintances whom he had known in the Islands.

Negotiations were immediately reopened for a treaty of commercial reciprocity with the United States. This was ratified in June, 1875, by King Kalakaua, and, in spite of great opposition in both America and the Islands, the laws necessary to carry it through were enacted in September, 1876. With an extension of the treaty in 1887, Pearl Harbor Lagoon became the property of the United States.

With the Reciprocity Treaty, a new world was opened to the people of the Islands, bringing untold prosperity and a change for the better to both countries. It is said that this treaty was the great event of Kalakaua's reign, and perhaps the most important event in Hawaiian history since 1843, when France and England united in a joint declaration recognizing the independence of the Kingdom of Hawaii. The fact that Kalakaua's ratification of the treaty made possible its passing has been to his credit at those times when his critics have attacked him.

The King and his officials returned from Washington well satisfied with what had been accomplished, and for a few months matters seemed to move along more smoothly. Then, the following April, the King's brother, Prince Leleiohoku, the heir apparent, suddenly died. His sister, Liliuokalani, was proclaimed heir to the throne. She was in entire sympathy with the plans and ideals of Kalakaua, and as heir apparent she held an important position and great influence with the Hawaiian people.

As time passed Kalakaua became more and more dissatisfied and was in constant disagreement with his ministers. In his inner soul was engrained a deep sense of racial prejudice—that self-same blot which has always caused parts of the outside world to look askance at U. S. culture and its avowed democratic spirit. It may well be said that this feeling of prejudice—so alien to the native Hawaiian, whose innate feeling is one of tolerance and *aloha* for all men—was one of the last evils, after guns, disease, alcoholism, and a certain naive greed, to be inflicted upon the Hawaiian by the White Man. Kalakaua, flattered by the white man and seeking the white man's political support in his own not-too-stable kingdom, fell prey to the white man's vices. The result was somewhat ironical. From his inheritance through the high chiefs of the Polynesian world, Kalakaua believed in the ruling power of great chiefs. He was determined to break the control of the white man wherever possible. He did not believe in constitutional government, although he was supposed to be a student of international law. It was learned that influences were in operation to control the votes in the Legislature. It became evident that this opposition came in an underhanded way from the King himself. In 1876, the year the treaty had been adopted, Kalakaua suddenly dismissed his cabinet and appointed men who would do as he wished. Historians record: "This making and unmaking of cabinets soon became the rule." There was a great upheaval throughout the government. The King ran rampant in his attempt to raise more and more funds, accepting bribes, setting up a lottery, pushing the opium trade, and giving away crown lands. The men who were carrying the real responsibility of the government finally revolted. A strong committee waited upon the King demanding the dismissal of his cabinet and a radical change in his own attitude and behavior. The men who had been his close associates deserted him. He was suddenly left to his own devices and knew not quite which way to turn. Deeply in debt, he finally decided to accept the demands of the men in power, knowing he was helpless to do otherwise, and to allow a new cabinet to be formed.

The Reciprocity Treaty brought many important changes in the Islands. Uppermost was the demand for laborers on the sugar plantations, which were rapidly increasing in number. In this connection, Kalakaua developed a bright idea. He decided to make a tour around the world, supposedly to study the matter of immigration. This would give the opportunity to meet the rulers of other countries and, perhaps, secure more laborers for Hawaii. Anyway, he would have a fine trip and a good time. He said to Mr. Armstrong, his Attorney General, "Now that my troubles are over, I mean to take a trip around the world and I want you to go with me." The governmental officials agreed to this plan with the understanding that the King would meet the expenses.

His sister Lydia Liliuokalani, was appointed Regent. The night before sailing, Kalakaua gave a banquet to one hundred of his white subjects, feeling that it would be a diplomatic move. The King also invited Col. C. H. Judd, his Chamberlain, to accompany him. Col. Judd and William Armstrong had been boys together with Kalakaua. The three men were lifelong friends and evidently Kalakaua wished their company in this great adventure. The King's suite, therefore, consisted of Col. Judd, as the King's Chamberlain, and William Armstrong, as Minister of State and Royal Commissioner of Immigration, with the King's valet, Robert, to care for many details.

Mr. Armstrong, in his story, *Round the World with a King,* explains that Robert, the valet, was a man of fine presence who had met with reverses. He was a German and claimed the title of Baron, which was later verified in Europe. He had arrived in Honolulu from a sailing vessel upon which he had been the cook. Eventually he landed in the kitchen of the palace as Kalakaua's chef. He was an educated man and a remarkable linguist. Kalakaua decided to take him on the tour, since he might prove useful as an interpreter. His great failing was the bottle, but he promised faithfully to keep sober.

Before leaving, the King announced that he would give a farewell address in the Old Stone Church. On this occasion, he impressed upon the audience of native people that his one great hope was to bring back many things of benefit to the Islands, especially laborers for the sugar plantations. He was going, he said, only in the interest of his country. The native people wept and were proud. He was their King, and he was going to travel around the world on a mission of duty such as no other monarch had ever done.

The King had decided to travel incognito, using the title of Prince. It would then not be necessary to take with him a large and costly retinue. He would be free, also, to enjoy himself with less responsibility. Mr. Armstrong, though, noticed that Robert was carrying a long canvas bag, and he surmised that it held the Royal Standard. The King would be ready if, later, he desired to step back to his kingly setting.

When the ship entered San Francisco Bay the Captain urged Kalakaua to hoist the Royal Standard, and, as he had already begun to feel restricted by the role of Prince, he consented, and the royal ensign was soon flapping in the breeze. Recalling the fine reception which had been given him in San Francisco six years previously, he was quite alert to whatever honor might be his during his stay in California. The Royal colors were almost immediately recognized by the Federal officials, and there quickly followed a salute of twenty-one guns. The greeting from the city of San Francisco was both cordial and elaborate.

The Legislative Assembly was in session in Sacramento, and the King and his suite were invited to visit the gathering. That evening a dinner was given in his honor at which some fine, complimentary speeches were made by American men of prominence. One member greatly impressed the King with his eloquent address, and gave him something to remember and to think about. He discussed the Hawaiian kingdom and its great importance in the rising commercial interests of the Pacific Ocean, and predicted the final union of all Oceania and Polynesia under one rule, and declared that rule would be under King Kalakaua, the "Colossus of the Pacific." That title, "Colossus of the Pacific," was stamped upon the mind of Kalakaua. It had a pleasing sound.

When the King and his party returned to San Francisco, they were honored with an entirely unexpected banquet. This was held in Chinatown and given by the Consul General of His Majesty, the Emperor of China. Twenty tables were laid, covered with heavily embroidered crimson satin with fringe of gold bullion and silver stars. From the ceiling hung scrolls of silk. These were inscribed with the wise saying of Confucius. American, Hawaiian and Chinese flags were entwined around the large pillars of the room.

The King was seated at the right of the Consul, who, when he gave the toast to Kalakaua, said he was speaking for all Chinese. He thanked the King for the just treatment which the Chinese had received in his kingdom. He said that there was but one place in Christendom, beyond the precincts of the British Empire, in which Chinese immigrants could live without fear of unjust assault, and that was in King Kalakaua's dominions. Kalakaua acknowledged the compliments with dignity and appreciation.

The King presented an impressive appearance in his military dress, wearing orders which had been presented to him by European rulers when treaties had been exchanged. He wished there might have been some suggestion of the Islands in the dress of the members of his suite. In the old days, high chiefs wore the magnificent feather mantles, but those cloaks could not suitably be worn over the modern diplomatic uniform. He had, however, brought with him a handsome feather cloak worn only by the Hawaiian kings, thinking it might be of interest to the members of the foreign courts. This cloak he had put in the care of Robert, with the understanding that it was never to be worn unless so ordered, and that he was to give the greatest care to the valuable garment at all times.

The King recalled that he had also brought with him some very handsome material which had been made in England for a former ruler of the Islands, but which had never been used. The design was of the beautiful *koa* leaf and that of the *taro* plant, both representative of Hawaii. So, while in San Francisco, he had a tailor make a very fine uniform for his Minister of State, Mr. Armstrong, who tells us that the uniform was greatly admired in every European court, much to the satisfaction of Kalakaua.

During the stopover in San Francisco, Robert was entertained very often at the bar of the hotel, and he was seen walking down the corridor wearing the King's silk hat askew on his head, bowing and tipping the hat to everyone he passed. It was discussed by the members of the suite whether he had not better be dismissed at one, but the King said he needed his services and so Robert was allowed to proceed with the party to Japan on the *Oceanic*.

On the fourth of March, the party reached Japan, entering the Bay of Yedo. The King hesitated about displaying the Royal Standard. He was advised not to do so, since no word had been sent to Japan of his coming, and he might be humiliated if no notice was given of his entrance. A fellow passenger had been requested to secure accommodations for the King and his suite at some hotel in Yokohama, but no official notice had been planned. However, Captain Metcalf (the chances are very remote that he was in any way related to that Captain Metcalf who, in 1790, had transported John Young to the shores of Hawaii) was very anxious to announce that he was carrying a distinguished guest and the King seemed pleased to agree with him. Robert was ordered to take the Royal Standard from the canvas bag. It was soon fluttering in the breeze. Mr. Armstrong tells the story of their entrance to the harbor of the great Japanese port, Yokohama:

"While we leaned over the rail looking at the Bluffs of the foreign settlement of Yokohama, we saw a number of warships in the harbor; seven Russian, two British, one French, and three Japanese. It was an imposing sight of sea fighters stretching for a mile before the city. They rode at their anchors in silence and without a sign of life. As our steamer crossed the bows of the first ironclad, a Russian, there was a sudden discharge of saluting guns from her batteries. At the same moment the Hawaiian flag was broken out on the mainmast. Swarms of sailors sprang aloft and manned the yards; that is, stood in line along them each man extending his arm to the shoulder of the next one. As if by magic the ship was dressed from stem to stern with the flags of all nations. The report of the first gun was followed slowly by a royal salute of twenty-one guns, and our Royal Standard dipped in response. Within a minute we passed the bows of the next warship. From her mainmast also the Hawaiian flag was unfurled; her crew also manned the yards and the ship was dressed with flags as had been the Russian, and her slow discharge of saluting guns swelled the volume of noise. The Royal Standard on the *Oceanic* was again dipped in response, and as we crossed the bows of all the warships, in succession, the same ceremony was repeated, the crews mounting and manning the yards, cheering as we passed; the roar of the hundred and seventy-three guns, the smoke rising in dense clouds and rolling away towards the bay; the innumerable flags with which the warships were dressed, appearing and disappearing in the smoke, made an extraordinary brilliant scene and a startling one because so unexpected. The King stood impassive, lifting his hat as we passed each vessel, while our Royal Standard dipped in response."

Mr. Armstrong relates that, very soon after reaching port, an Admiral and two Imperial Commissioners, with other officers, arrived bringing an invitation from His Imperial Majesty for the King and his suite to be his guests as long as they were in the Empire. The King received the delegation with gracious dignity and said that he would be pleased to accept the Emperor's invitation for both himself and his friends.

Crowds of people swarmed on the docks of Yokohama, and, to the utter amazement of the King and his party, there suddenly burst forth the strains of "Hawaii Pono'i," a compliment from the Emperor's military band. A young music teacher from the Islands, it was later learned, had the music of the national anthem which she lent for the occasion. This was a great day. A monarch from another country had come to visit the Empire, and the government and the people turned out *en masse* to greet King Kalakaua from the Sandwich Islands.

Mr. Armstrong continues: "The government of Japan was well aware of the importance of the Hawaiian Islands, situated at the crossroads of the Pacific Ocean, while its treaty with the little kingdom gave the latter the arbitrary and 'extra territorial' power which the European nations held in the treaty with Japan. Besides, her trading ships and navy found the port of Honolulu most convenient."

The King and his friends were given a residence—a palace reserved for the Emperor's special guests—overlooking the city of Yokohama. The Emperor had appointed his Chamberlain, Mr. Nagasaki, to attend the King during his stay in the Empire. Mr. Nagasaki, a graduate of Ann Arbor University, Michigan, being familiar with American language and customs, was an interesting and helpful companion.

In response to the question as to how it came about that the King of Hawaii should be given such an unexpected reception, Mr. Nagasaki explained that the Imperial Consul General in San Francisco had telegraphed that King Kalakaua was to visit Japan. This placed the Japanese government under an obligation to receive the Hawaiian King as it would the ruler of any country under treaty and friendly relations with Japan.

With all the honors given to the royal party, Robert was not overlooked. His office of "Standard Bearer" and "Keeper of the Royal Feather Cloak," titles which he, himself, assumed, greatly impressed the servants and the lesser officials, and, instead of being placed in quarters, he was assigned, much to his joyful appreciation, a richly furnished room with servants to wait upon him.

The following day, Mr. Nagasaki accompanied the King and his suite when they called upon the Emperor in Tokyo. They were first received by an Imperial Prince, who had also been appointed to attend the King while he was a guest of the nation. They found His Majesty standing alone in a reception room of the palace waiting to greet them. The King's suite, with the Prince and the officials of the Imperial household, remained a little removed as the Emperor and the King shook hands in American fashion.

The Emperor then led the way to the Room of Audience, asking King Kalakaua to walk by his side. This was an unheard of proceeding, since no one was ever allowed to walk with him, not even the Empress. This was the Emperor's first experience in meeting a monarch from another country, and he set aside custom in order to be especially gracious to King Kalakaua. The officials following, the whole party proceeded to the Room of Audience, where the King presented the guests to the Empress, who remained seated but acknowledged the presentation with a bow.

The Empress was magnificently dressed in Japanese costume. The guests were told, however, that she wished her ladies to follow American styles, she, herself, doing so on all informal occasions. The King was interested to find that a very charming girl, wearing a Parisian dress and a Gainsborough hat, acted as interpreter for the interview. The daughter of a Japanese diplomatic official, she had been educated in England. Turning to the King she said in perfect English and with a quaint manner: "Her Imperial Majesty wishes to welcome you to this court; she hopes you had a pleasant voyage." The King replied that the voyage was long but pleasant. In response to the further hope of the Empress that he would enjoy his stay in Japan, he gave a gracious reply. He had enjoyed the visit to the Palace very much and expressed his warm appreciation.

When the Emperor was told that the King and his friends were to remain but two or three days in Japan, he persuaded them to make their stay longer since he desired to hold a banquet in their honor. The days following were filled with entertainment. If Kalakaua had started out with visions of enjoyment, Tokyo was doing her best to make his dream a reality. Banquet after banquet, and one entertainment of music, dancing, sports, and the theatre followed another.

The splendor and magnificence of Japan was almost beyond belief. To the King it appeared a country of beauty and joyous living. He loved it all. A touch of home, however, delighted Kalakaua when he received an invitation from the Japanese Christian people in Yokohama to visit their church and to receive from them a copy of the New Testament in the Japanese language. Learning that the Emperor had no objection to the plan, the King, accompanied by his Chamberlain and Minister, went privately to Yokohama. There, in the Protestant church, built partially through Hawaiian Christian aid, he received the gift, and from the pulpit spoke of the fine work done in his Kingdom by Christian missionaries.

During the stay in Japan, several official conferences were held to discuss the matter of immigration and the possibility of sending laborers from Japan to Hawaii to work on the sugar plantations. Kalakaua felt that his plan had worked well.

Mr. Armstrong speaks of one surprising incident, which he says was the only time the King did not consult with the members of his staff when an important matter was to be considered. One morning the King slipped away, having asked for a private interview with the Emperor. The Emperor's Chamberlain later hinted to Col. Judd the import of this interview. Kalakaua had suggested to the Emperor a matrimonial alliance between Japan and the Hawaiian Kingdom through the marriage of one of the Imperial Princes of Japan with his own niece, Princess Kaiulani. The Emperor had said that such a thing would be a startling disregard of tradition and would need very careful consideration. (It was not until the King reached home that his friends knew the real story of the interview, when a document, brought by the Emperor's Chamberlain in person to Hawaii, stated that such an alliance would be impossible. It was believed that Kalakaua was fearful lest his kingdom be absorbed by the United States and had hoped that by such an alliance this might be prevented.)

The last days in Japan were filled with glorious entertainment. The climax was a grand banquet given by the Emperor, at which Kalakaua had the privilege of meeting the important men and ladies of the Empire. When all the guests were seated, the Emperor rose and, from a lacquer box held by his Minister, took the Star and Broad Scarlet Cordon of the Order of the Rising Sun. With his own hands he affixed these to the King's uniform. Col. Judd and Mr. Armstrong, Chamberlain and Minister of King Kalakaua's court, were also decorated. In response, Kalakaua nominally invested the Emperor with the Grand Cross of the Order of Kamehameha, and conferred upon the Ministers of the Emperor's court decorations of a lesser degree. They were all to be made in Paris and forwarded to Japan. It was a splendid party and Kalakaua was radiantly happy. This was the life!

When the time finally came for the King and his party to leave, Princes of the Imperial house met the King's company in Yokohama, and the people of the city gave the visitors the same fine ovation on their departure as that given on their arrival. They were showered with rich and beautiful gifts from Tokyo, a tribute from the Emperor and his people. Kalakaua expressed a most grateful *aloha,* and as the ships left the shore he looked long at the hills of Yokohama with misty eyes. The grand tour was just beginning.

Mr. Armstrong begins his story of the travels of King Kalakaua and his friends by explaining that they were received as guests, or in formal state ceremonies, by the Emperor of Japan; General Li Hung Chang of China; the governor of Hong Kong, in the name of the British Queen; the King of Siam; the British Governors and Commissioners of Singapore, Penang, the Malacca Straits, and of Burma; the Vice-Regal Court of India; the Viceroy of Egypt; the King of Italy; the Holy Father in Rome; the British Queen; the King of Belgium; the court of Emperor William of Germany; the officials of the Austrian Empire; the officials of the French Republic; the officials of the Spanish Court, whose Regent was absent; the King of Portugal; and, finally, the President of the United States.

As the weeks passed, Kalakaua became weary of royal attention and honor. He was homesick for the Islands. But when he reached Siam his spirits revived. There he found coconut palms with their feathery tops gently blowing in the breeze. He drank coconut milk until he was satisfied. Lying on the *lanai* to rest one late afternoon, he suddenly began singing an old Hawaiian *mele,* sacred to his people. His rich vibrant voice stirred the hearts of those who listened. The natives heard the singing and gathered nearby to enjoy the music, delighted that the visiting King was so pleased that he could sing.

The King of Siam was charmed with Kalakaua. They became friends at once, finding they had much in common. The King asked Kalakaua many questions, for instance: "What is the religion of the Sandwich Islands people?" Kalakaua replied that his government encouraged all religions, and that his people were not restricted in their form of worship. The King said that was very good. Throughout the long conversations of the two monarchs, they learned that they were indeed brothers.

When the King was told that the Hawaiians had Malay blood in their veins, he replied, "The Siamese are also partly Malay. We are related!"

Bracelets of sweet jasmine were wound around the arms of the guests, and bouquets of other fragrant flowers were placed in their hands. All of this verified to Kalakaua his relation to the Siamese King. He was especially pleased when the elephants were brought to the palace and he was invited to take a ride on the sacred elephant used only by the King. Then, too, six lovely young girls from the harem of one of the royal princes who owned the theatre (to which only members of the court were admitted) came to dance and sing for Kalakaua and his friends. The visitors were suddenly amazed to hear the English words of an old hymn:

> "Keep your lamps all trimmed and burning,
> For the midnight bride is coming."

The dancers may not have understood the meaning of the words they sang, but the lilt of the old song accompanying the dance they thoroughly enjoyed. It was later explained that one of their music teachers had lived in India, and it was she who taught the girls the missionary hymn.

His Highness Sri Abu Bakar, the Maharajah of Jahore, a kingdom under the British protectorate, invited Kalakaua and his party to visit him. They were taken fourteen miles in the Maharajah's steam yacht to Jahore. Their reception was most flattering and gorgeous and elaborate in every detail. Mr. Armstrong tells that the elaborateness of the reception so impressed Kalakaua that he wished to create an effect on his own account. So, after speaking to Robert very emphatically about the sin of intemperance, he ordered him to carry the beautiful feather cloak on his arm with dignity and sobriety. When the King and his friends stepped from the yacht, Robert appeared in evening dress, white gloves, white helmet, and the gorgeous cloak over his shoulders. It was at once assumed by the Maharajah's officers that the valet was a person of superior importance, and they placed him in the royal procession. Kalakaua told him to go to the rear, but still thinking he must be of great importance the officers made up a special procession with which he marched to the grand reception room. The Maharajah caught sight of the cloak and asked to have it brought to him. He asked who was permitted to wear it in Hawaii. Kalakaua explained that only the great chiefs of the kingdom were permitted to wear the cloak. He was then asked the rank of the white man who was wearing it. The King evaded this question by saying simply that sometimes a servant was ordered to carry the cloak for his chief. The episode over, it was the last time that Kalakaua attempted to show the cloak in public.

Kalakaua and his party finally reached England. The Prince of Wales immediately called upon him, and there followed many calls from members of the British court. Receptions were given to Kalakaua and his suite by notable men and ladies of the Empire. When Kalakaua was a young prince he had received and entertained the Duke of Edinburgh and Lord Charles Beresford when they visited Hawaii. Returning this compliment, Lord Charles, with the Prince of Wales, arranged the royal welcome in appreciation. The Prince also gave a ball at Marlborough House in honor of Kalakaua, at which Kalakaua danced the opening quadrille with the Princess. The Prince of Wales was careful to respect the precedence of Kalakaua as a King, even over the heir apparent, the Crown Prince of Germany, who with the Princess were guests at the ball. Later, there was considerable adverse comment made regarding the event throughout Germany.

On the day of Kalakaua's arrival in England, Queen Victoria had sent an invitation to the King and his suite to attend a review at Windsor Park, at which they met many of England's highest ranking members of the court. The following day the King and his suite were received by the Queen, who expressed her special pleasure at meeting Kalakaua, the King of the Sandwich Islands, and assuring him of his welcome to London.

The highlight to Kalakaua of his visit to England was attending the Royal Italian Opera to hear Madame Patti sing. His friends said that Kalakaua paid no attention to the many glasses which were turned on the royal box, but seemed to be oblivious to everything but the voice of the great artist. At the close of the evening he said that he would like to present his compliments to Madame Patti and personally to express his appreciation. This word was sent to her and she asked that King Kalakaua and his friends be brought to her dressing room.

The King presented flowers to Madame Patti, which she accepted with as seeming pleasure as she did his admiration of her voice. Mr. Armstrong, in writing of that evening, says, "It was for Kalakaua a supreme moment." For years following, the King referred to that evening with deepest feeling, for he was a musician at heart.

The King was very anxious to reach Italy. He hoped to have the privilege of meeting the Pope of the great Church of Rome. This, to Kalakaua, seemed more important than to have met the ruler of any country. The visit to the Vatican proved to be more easily arranged than he had anticipated. The King and the members of his party were awed as they were led to the room of audience. Only a soft light came through the beautiful stained glass windows. The Cardinals entered silently. A door opened and His Holiness, Leo XIII, moved slowly across the room while all bowed in reverence. A chair was placed for the King. Around the Holy Father the Cardinals were grouped, and the King's suite stood near the King. The Pope carried the conversation. He asked several questions about the Islands. He said, "Do my people in your country behave well?" Kalakaua replied that they were good subjects. "If they do not behave," said the Pope, "I must look after them." Then he asked, "Why do you have white men in your government?" The King turned to Mr. Armstrong to make the explanation. Mr. Armstrong said, "The Kings of Hawaii chose educated white men to assist them as they were better able to deal with foreigners who held most of the wealth of the country." The Cardinal then asked if there were any Catholics in the Hawaiian government. Mr. Armstrong also replied to this question. He explained that the American Protestants came to Hawaii before the Catholics settled there, and they had kept control of public affairs, but that no efficient Catholic was excluded from high office by reason of his faith.

The interview closed. As the visitors were leaving, the Pope said to King Kalakaua, "Your country is far away. I shall pray for your safe return."

More days of travel and entertainment followed the visit to Rome, and the time arrived when Kalakaua and his friends were to sail for America on their return to the Islands. When they were leaving England, the King was asked if he had not been greatly thrilled in visiting so many countries. He replied that it had been interesting and important, but that he longed for the beauty and the quiet of his own kingdom. He said, "We are glad to be going home."

New York, Washington, Philadelphia, Chicago, San Francisco, and across the blue Pacific to Honolulu. Kalakaua's return was as picturesque as his departure had been. The band played, the guns were fired in salute, and the people literally covered the King with sweet *maile* and fragrant flowers. Again the native people wept for joy. The Great Chief was home. Kalakaua was radiantly happy. It was a good homecoming.

The world tour had had a very special influence upon the mind of Kalakaua. The pomp and ceremony of foreign courts had interested him tremendously. He determined to strengthen and enlarge his own position as King. He would have a real coronation and wear a crown as other monarchs were doing. Accordingly, before he left England, he had ordered two golden crowns set with precious jewels, one for himself and one for Queen Kapiolani. They would take their rightful place, properly crowned, before their people. As he neared the Islands, Kalakaua planned the great ceremony that would take place immediately upon his return.

The idea of another coronation ceremony for the King was not well received by the ministers of the government. Several members of the cabinet finally resigned, among them William Armstrong. The Legislature, however, was composed largely of Hawaiians who supported the King in his plans. Accordingly, invitations were sent to all the countries which the King had visited in his travels.

A fine new palace had been in process of building for several years and was completed the year Kalakaua returned from abroad, the cornerstone laid by his Masonic brethren, he having had solid silver tools made with which to lay the stone. The completion of the palace was one of the accomplishments of Kalakaua's reign.

Before the great day arrived a pavilion had been erected in front of the palace steps where the coronation ceremony was to take place. There was a large attendance at the coronation. Several representatives from foreign countries were prominent guests. England, France and the United States sent ships of war to honor the event. Dignitaries of court and state were present, but Queen Emma and Mrs. Bishop, the High Chieftesses, did not attend. Many important citizens likewise declined the invitation.

The coronation ceremonies were long and elaborate. When the time came for the actual crowning of the King and Queen, Kalakaua lifted from the satin cushion, presented before him, his own golden crown, the diamonds, the rubies, the emeralds, and the opals glistening in the sunlight as he placed the crown upon his head, crowning himself as the King of Hawaii *Nei*. Then, turning to Queen Kapiolani, he placed upon her head the smaller crown, which she acknowledged with a gracious bow. Doubtless Kalakaua felt more important than at any previous time in his life, but to the thinking men of affairs the coronation was a mockery which proved to be the beginning of the end of monarchial government in the Hawaiian Islands.

Iolani Palace gave to King Kalakaua and to the community of Honolulu the background and setting for the splendid and elaborate social life which Kalakaua cultivated and enjoyed. The palace was, and still is, a beautiful building, largely French in design, with the interior finished in rare Hawaiian woods. Kalakaua's personal apartments were very elegantly decorated to suit his taste. The rooms were hung with pale blue silk, and the furniture was ebony and gold. The small brass knocker especially pleased the King. It was finely carved, the design showing a pair of cupids carrying between them a garland of flowers, beneath which was a medalion bearing the King's insignia, K.K., one letter partially overlapping the other. It was, perhaps, symbolic, as were the pale blue hangings, of the King's idealism and love of beauty.

Kalakaua's first banquet at Iolani Palace was given in honor of his Masonic friends, the invitations to which were printed on silk. The King had a long career in Masonry. Masonic records tell that story, which warrants inclusion here because it sheds an interesting light on his character and diligence. Kalakaua was initiated into the oldest Masonic organization west of the Missouri River, the first degree of Masonry being conferred upon him by Kamehameha IV early in 1859. He was raised to the third degree later that year by John O. Dominis, consort of Princess Liliuokalani. Wearing the purple of the order, he became Master of the Lodge Le Progress de l'Oceanie in 1875. Joining the York Rite of Masonry in 1874, he became Eminent Commander of the Knights Templar in 1877. Scottish Rite of Freemasonry was instituted in Hawaii during 1873, and, in 1874, Kalakaua became a charter member and was the first Wise Master of Rose Croix. Coronated a Thirty-third Degree Mason in 1878, he was elected as Grand Cross of Honor on December 13, 1880.

Iolani Palace was the center of the gay social life of Kalakaua's court. There were brilliant balls in the throne room, with its beautiful rose colored satin brocade hangings and magnificent crystal chandeliers. The court of Hawaii had always had the dignity of the Court of St. James. This Kalakaua carried out to the letter, continuing the formal etiquette through the years. The court of the Hawaiian Kingdom was well known all over the world, and many important and noted guests were there received and entertained. King Kalakaua was lavish in his hospitality and, personally, was always genial and friendly.

His grand tour and his association with the crowned heads of the world had provided Kalakaua with yet another idea—dream of empire. In 1883 he sent two commissioners to the Gilbert Islands and the New Hebrides in the hope of consolidating them under a Hawaiian protectorate. In 1886 he sent a commission to Samoa to promulgate an alliance between those Islands and Hawaii. The King purchased a small steamer and had it converted into a warship. This vessel represented the Hawaiian Navy and served to insure his interests in a Polynesian Empire.

King Kalakaua was a yachtsman and a gambler. It was he who first instituted modern yachting in the Islands. His boathouse "down on the waterfront" was a popular entertainment place. To be invited for an evening at the boathouse of the King was a compliment greatly to be appreciated by the local sportsmen. The evening parties were largely given to playing poker, which Kalakaua enjoyed. Many tales are told of his losses and of his good sportsmanship on all occasions. One sea captain tells in his correspondence of a poker game he attended at the boathouse which continued for forty-eight hours. He said: "It was a unique game; the players were a king, lawyer, a butcher, and a naval officer." From a naval officer's diary comes another story of a late party at the boathouse, with four hula dancers to entertain the guests. The officer wrote: "Left about two and went to a friend's house where we kept it up all night. The King sent some champagne and ice cream and came over himself with a party of gentlemen. Guests were served champagne, hot punch, and dancing continued until daylight. We then bade the girls an affectionate farewell and rode to the wharf in the King's carriage." About Kalakaua has often been told the following tale: cornered in a certain poker game with four aces, he produced four kings and, proclaiming himself as the fifth, raised a question which has never yet been settled in gambling circles.

Affairs in the Kingdom, however, were not always so pleasant. There developed a slow but serious breakdown of relations between the officials of the government and the King, who continued to refuse all cooperation with his old friends, carrying things with a high hand to suit himself and the unreliable men in whom he had placed his confidence. He had become increasingly resentful of the growing wealth and power of the White Men in the Kingdom. He had alienated his former advisers and filled his cabinet with men, some of them foreigners, who praised and flattered him while securing from him large sums of money and valuable crown lands in return. Political matters were in confusion. The government debt had risen to fantastic figures. There was the great scandal of the notorious opium trade and the attempt to establish the Louisiana Lottery in the Islands, both of which the King approved and sanctioned, hoping through them to obtain the funds which he so greatly needed, since it has been estimated that Kalakaua's indebtedness at one time amounted to a quarter of a million dollars.

All this resulted in rebellion—the Revolution of 1887. Day by day matters grew so tense and alarming that a secret league was formed by his subjects, a large number of them foreigners, who determined that measures should be taken to demand of the King a change in his attitude and in governmental procedure. This movement resulted in the reformation of all governmental matters. A new constitution, virtually stripping him of the personal authority he sought and enjoyed, was written and presented to the King for his signature and oath. A revision of that of 1864, this constitution sought to abolish, once and for all, Kalakaua's increasingly dictatorial powers and to make the cabinet responsible only to the legislature. In place of the King's appointing members of the upper house, the constitution stipulated that they were to be elected for terms of six years by electors possessing minimum property qualifications. After a stormy session in the Blue Room of the Palace, where hour after hour the King stood his ground in refusing to accept the new regime, it is recorded that suddenly his attitude changed and, with a pleasant smile and gracious manner, he reached for the pen and attached his name to the document, "whereby he was reduced from the status of an autocrat to that of a constitutional sovereign." The document has come down in history under the appropriate and prophetic appellation of "The Bayonet Constitution."

Peace was eventually restored. Kalakaua was still the King, but his wings of fancy had been clipped. There was a great celebration on his fiftieth birthday, and the friendliness of the people gave Kalakaua the courage to face the future. Outwardly, he became again the affable, charming and entertaining friend of his subjects, and the gracious host of all Hawaii. Although he made several attempts to regain his former status of absolute ruler, his ministers were able to hold the reigns of control in the government. Meantime, his dream of empire had vanished. Nothing ever came of his plan to establish a protectorate over the Gilberts and New Hebrides. Immediately following the "Bayonet Constitution," the Samoan embassy was recalled, and the solitary warship of the Hawaiian Navy was put out of commission.

As time went on, a staid but assured future seemed to be in store for him and Kalakaua was resigned merely to grasp at whatever fun it might offer. But one cannot help suspecting that, in his secret soul, the King was a lonely, embittered man, trapped between his love of power and his own ill-aimed political acumen.

Mention has been made of the ill-feeling that existed between Kalakaua and Dowager Queen Emma during and following the election that made him king. The ex-Queen's bitterness was so great that she had refused to attend Kalakaua's coronation. An interesting sidelight on the formal ending of their feud is provided by Isobel Field, stepdaughter of Robert Louis Stevenson, in her charming autobiography, *This Life I've Loved* (Longmans, Green & Co.). She says:

"We were invited to a reception and dance on the U.S.S. *Adams*. . . . The deck of the *Adams*, like all the old-fashioned ships, was wide and clear of obstacles, for the cannons had been turned neatly aside and covered with canvas, leaving a fine floor for dancing as there were no brass things sticking up to trip over. The portholes, draped with bunting, were large enough for two to sit in very cozily. On that day the quarterdeck, with its gay awnings and brass rails, was like a stage set for a scene; under a canopy of American and Hawaiian flags, was a large chair draped in bunting—a throne prepared for King Kalakaua.

"We walked about the deck, meeting many friends, and then we heard excited whispers, 'Queen Emma is here, and Kalakaua is coming! How will they meet?' Looking up at the quarterdeck we saw a black robed figure in a group of officers that stood about the throne prepared for her rival.

"Guests came pouring over the side, and then, exactly on time, for the King was always punctual, the ship shook with the boom of cannon that announced his arrival. Twenty-four guns, when you are on the ship that is firing them, make a tremendous din. As His Majesty stepped on the deck, the ship's band burst into 'Hawaii Pono'i.' Kalakaua and his handsome equerries, Captain Haley, the Hawaiian Major and several others, all in flattering uniforms, made a fine-looking group. We, the assembled guests, opened a line to the companionway, the men bending from the waist, the women sinking in deep curtsys as the King walked slowly along, bowing graciously to right and left, his companion gazing straight ahead haughtily ignoring our presence.

"Breathlessly the crowd below watched His Majesty mount the companionway; when he reached the quarterdeck he was greeted by the Captain who motioned toward the throne where Queen Emma stood. Kalakaua stepped forward, a gallant figure in white and gold, bowed low to the lady in black, and offered her his hand, which she took and was about to kiss. With a quick dextrous movement he gave her a little whirl and a push that seated her on the throne. Queen Emma's surprised face was almost comic when the King bowed again before her. Then she smiled sweetly; he leaned over and they talked together with such evident friendliness that we all felt like applauding. After that the two were friends and I often saw Queen Emma at the King's formal parties."

Throughout Kalakaua's whole life he had been a student; from the time he had been a scholar in the missionary school he had loved books. An old resident states that he had never seen the King without a book in his hand. He carried one wherever he went. It may have been Kalakaua's interest in books which won him the friendship of Robert Louis Stevenson. During Stevenson's residence in Honolulu, he knew Kalakaua well and they became close friends. Before Mr. Stevenson left the Islands he presented the King with a beautiful and rare pearl, and with it was the following poem:

"TO KALAKAUA
(With the gift of a pearl)

The Silver Ship, my King—that was her name
In the bright islands whence your fathers came—
The Silver Ship, at rest from winds and tides,
Below your palace in your harbour rides,
And the seafarers, sitting safe on shore,
Like eager merchants count their treasurers o'er.
One gift they find, one strange and lovely thing,
Now doubly precious since it pleased a king.

The right, my liege, is ancient as the lyre
For bards to give to kings, what kings admire,
'Tis mine to offer for Apollo's sake;
And since the gift is fitting, yours to take,
To golden hands the golden pearl I bring,
The Ocean jewel to the island king.

Honolulu, Feb. 3, 1889."

Kalakaua was himself a poet and a musician. The national anthem, "Hawaii Pono'i," was his composition, but he asked the band master, Mr. Berger, to set the words to music, which the latter did by adapting them to a German air which had been and still is the music of "Hawaii Pono'i." This song, beloved by the people of the Islands, is played by the Royal Hawaiian Band on the arrival and departure of ships and at the close of all important gatherings, along with the "Star Spangled Banner."

In 1888, Kalakaua published his interesting *Legends and Myths of Hawaii.* This is a compilation of legendary lore which the King himself collected throughout many years. He frequently called the older Hawaiians to the palace to tell him the tales of the past. He became greatly interested in collecting the traditions of his people, his plan being to preserve them for posterity.

Then, two years after the Revolution of 1887, which had divested Kalakaua of most of his powers, occurred a counter-revolution, fomented by a group of Hawaiians led by Robert W. Wilcox. The insurgents occupied the grounds of the palace and government buildings. They invited Kalakaua to come up from his boathouse and proclaim a new constitution. This, oddly to say, the King declined to do. He had, perhaps, a premonition that his dreams of glory were doomed. He was right. Wilcox and his 150-odd men were surrounded by volunteer troops and citizens—predominantly Americans—who opened fire upon the insurgents, killing seven of them and wounding many more. The abortive Insurrection of 1889 did not give the Hawaiians, as they wished, a king untrammeled by foreign interests; instead, it served only to heighten the race hatred that had, in recent years, deepened its roots in Hawaii. At this point, David, King Kalakaua, must have tasted of his own bitter waters.

As the years slipped along, Kalakaua's health began to fail. His physicians and friends were alarmed, and it was decided that he should go at once to the mainland for further medical advice and care. He sailed on the *Charleston* as the guest of Rear Admiral Brown, and when he reached San Francisco old friends gave him a warm welcome. He had not been forgotten. His Masonic brethren gave him their highest honors, and the city of San Francisco did everything possible for his pleasure and comfort. The best physicians attended him, but his health continued to fail and he died quietly in his apartment at the Palace Hotel on January 20, 1891.

In Honolulu the people were preparing for the King's return. The Palace and the city were gay with decorations of welcome for Kalakaua, since no word had been received of the seriousness of his illness. The day came when the *Charleston* was sighted, her flags at half mast. The word spread like a pall over the city and the Islands—Kalakaua was dead.

All manner of legends survive the fabulous Kalakaua. He remains, still, a controversial figure. One might say that he was, if not Hawaii's greatest king, at least her most ebullient and colorful king. On only one point does everyone agree: Kalakaua was rightfully named the "Merry Monarch."

BORN TO RULE

Chapter XVI

> *"She has suffered defeat and humiliation. We should now consider her former exalted position, and accord her some special regard and kindness."*
>
> —THE FRIEND

THE THRONE was vacant and Liliuokalani stood waiting. As heir apparent she would be installed, as she had long hoped to be, Queen of the Hawaiian Islands. She was 52 at the time.

The ceremony was held in the Blue Room of the Palace on January 29, 1891, with Liliuokalani signing the same constitution which her brother had signed—the Bayonet Constitution of 1887—and taking this oath:

> "I solemnly swear, in the presence of Almighty God,
> to maintain the constitution of the Kingdom whole
> and inviolate, and to govern in conformity therewith.
> So help me, God."

With this, she embarked on one of the shortest reigns, and certainly the most tumultuous, in Hawaiian history. With all of her brother's driving ambition, she possessed, additionally, a tenacity and strength of character lacking in Kalakaua. She and Kalakaua were much alike in temperament and understood each other perfectly, but hers was the stronger will. Her indiscriminate desire to make her kingdom one of "Hawaii for the Hawaiians," coupled with her unshakeable determination to diminish the power of the foreigner within her own domain and to re-establish the throne as an absolute monarchy, proved within a short time to precipitate the Queen's downfall. But first, let us look into the caverns of Liliuokalani's character and background.

Liliuokalani was born on September 2, 1838, at the family home near the foot of Punchbowl Hill, in what was then the village of Honolulu. She was the great-granddaughter of the old warrior chief Keawe-a-Heulu. Keawe-a-Heulu was an own cousin of Keoua, the father of Kamehameha I. It is said by some historians that it was Keawe-a-Heulu who advised Kamehameha in his plans for the Kamehameha dynasty. In any event, he was one of his councilors and an important chief. While this did not give Liliuokalani the Kamehameha inheritance, it did give to her and to her brother the background of Kamehameha influence.

The men of the family were powerful and high chiefs on the island of Hawaii before Kamehameha's conquest of the island of Oahu. Following his last and victorious battle, Kamehameha brought to Honolulu several of his most responsible chiefs to assist him in the work of reconstruction. Among them was the high chief Aikanaka, the grandfather of Liliuokalani. For many years he had charge of the guns of the fort on Punchbowl, and so it was that he settled his family at the foot of the old mountain.

Liliuokalani, in her book, *Hawaii's Story by Hawaii's Queen,* told of her own father, Chief Kapaakea: "As was the custom of Hawaiian chiefs, my father was surrounded by hundreds of his own people who looked to him, and never in vain, for sustenance. He lived in a large grass house surrounded by smaller ones which were the homes of those most closely connected with his service." Liliuokalani's mother was the high chieftess Keohokaloloe, one of the fifteen councilors of Kamehameha III. But Liliuokalani was not reared by her parents. In this connection she wrote as follows: "Immediately after my birth I was wrapped in softest tapa cloth and taken to the house of another chief by whom I was adopted. Konia, my foster mother, was a granddaughter of Kamehameha I, and was married to Paki, also a high chief; their only daughter, Bernice Pauahi, afterwards Mrs. Charles R. Bishop, was, therefore, my foster sister."

Liliuokalani's own father had had a large family; there were ten children, and most of them had been adopted by friends. She wrote: "Although I knew these were my own brothers and sisters, yet we met through my younger days as though we had not known our common heritage. This was, and indeed is, in accordance with Hawaiian customs. It is not easy to explain its origin to those alien to our national life, but it seems perfectly natural to us. As intelligible a reason as can be given is that this alliance by adoption cemented the ties of friendship between chiefs. It spread to the common people and it has doubtless fostered a community of interest and harmony."

As did all the royal children in missionary days, Liliuokalani attended the mission school conducted by Mr. and Mrs. Cooke, and so received her education along with her brother and the Princes Alexander, Lot and Lunalilo. She was entered in the school at the age of three, crying bitterly about the fact as she was turned over to the Cooke's care. Liliuokalani proved to be a good student and was especially interested in music. She told that she learned to read music very readily and that she and a young boy, Willie Andrews, who also attended the school, often led the singing and, since they could read music and sing by note, the other children learned the songs from them. Her only complaint concerning her life at the school she recorded many years later, saying that she never got enough to eat, and that she and other royal children were forced, surreptitiously, to beg extra rations from the cook or else to find berries or succulent roots from the surrounding grounds.

Liliuokalani also recorded the good times which followed school days; of the fine parties at the home of Paki, where Bernice and Liliuokalani, princesses of the realm, were the young hostesses. Their home was the social center of Honolulu, and Prince Lot, Prince Alexander, and Prince Lunalilo were frequent guests. Queen Emma was younger, but it was she who married Prince Alexander, Kamehameha IV. Prince Lot, before he became king, had wished to marry Bernice, but Mr. Charles R. Bishop appeared and it was he who had won her hand.

In 1862, Liliuokalani had married John Dominis. They were engaged for two years. They set their wedding date, but had to postpone it for two weeks because the court of Kamehameha IV and Queen Emma was in mourning for the young Prince of Hawaii. When they were children, John attended a private school just over a high stone fence from the Royal School. "The boys used to climb on the fence of their side to look at the royal children, and among these curious urchins was John C. Dominis. His father was a sea captain who had originally come to Honolulu on Cape Horn voyages and had been interested in trade both in California and in China. The ancestors of Captain Dominis were from Italy, but Mrs. Dominis was an American, born in Boston, and a descendant of one of the early English settlers."

Washington Place, which today is the official residence of Hawaii's Governor, was built by Captain Dominis to be his family home. He and his wife, who did not approve of the marriage between her son and Liliuokalani, had lived at Kapalama. The Captain did not live to enjoy Washington Place, for he was lost at sea on the way to China. John Dominis and Liliuokalani therefore took up abode in the new house. John Dominis became an important and trusted official in the Kingdom. He was Governor of Oahu and also the island of Maui. Under appointment of Kamehameha V, and later, during the reign of Lunalilo, he served as Commissioner of the Administration of Crown Lands. He held the title of General in the military world and was, in many ways, both efficient and popular. Liliuokalani, as his wife, was a popular young matron, one of the social arbiters of the Honolulu of her day. And she was ambitious.

In 1877, young Prince Leleiohoku, the heir to the throne, suddenly died, and Liliuokalani was named heir apparent. This changed the direction of her course of life. It was decided that she must immediately make a tour of the Kingdom so that the people might know her, since she might one day be Queen. Of this trip Liliuokalani wrote: "In some nations the leaders, the chief rulers, have gone forth through the districts conquered by the sword and compelled the people to show their subjection. Our progress from beginning to end was a triumphal march. They welcomed me as Hawaiians always have their ruling chief."

During the following year Liliuokalani spent a month in California—her first visit to the United States. She enjoyed the trip, but her responsibilities were increasing and she was soon to give most of her time and thought to governmental matters. Her brother, the King, was leaving for his trip around the world, and during his absence she was to take his place as Regent. He explained to her that he had held a meeting with the cabinet council at which it was proposed that there should be a council of regency of which she would be the head, but that the action of the council should be required for the full excercise of authority. Liliuokalani's concept of royalty, nurtured since her birth but given new stimulus by the fact that she was now heir apparent, guided her reaction to the proposal. Of this interview with Kalakaua she wrote: "As the King had sent for me with the express purpose of asking my opinion, I gave it in terms too plain to admit of the least misunderstanding between us. I told him that I did not admit either the necessity or the wisdom of any such organization as that of a council of regency; that to my view, if entrusted with the government in his absence, I ought to be the sole regent. I then proceeded to explain my reasons for this opinion saying that if there was a council of regency there would be no need for a regent. In case such a body were to be commissioned to govern the nation, who, then, would be the chief executive? In fact, why was any such individual required at all? To these considerations the King gave careful attention and appeared to see that my views of the situation were well founded upon reason and justice. The result of this informal conference was that, before his departure, I was appointed sole regent."

Kalakaua sailed on his world tour, and Liliuokalani held the high position of Queen Regent. Governmental matters continued to move smoothly along. Nothing extraordinary took place in which the Regent had to act authoritatively except in one instance, which greatly troubled her. The court had decreed the execution of a criminal and the time came when the sentence must be carried out. Liliuokalani, as Regent, was asked to sign the death warrant. She refused until, finally, she was informed that it must be done. She was Queen Regent, but she was also a woman, and that particular duty appalled her.

It was at this time that Liliuokalani, in a carefree moment away from the affairs of state, achieved an immortal fame that would have lasted through the years throughout the world had she never become Queen at all: she wrote a song. Liliuokalani was the most gifted of a family of musicians. David Kalakaua had written the verse of the Islands' national anthem, "Hawaii Pono'i," which Henry Berger had set to music, but Liliuokalani had had a formal musical education which enabled her to write both the verses and the music of the hundreds of songs she composed.

It was in the summer of 1878 that Liliuokalani was visiting friends on Windward Oahu at the foot of the Waimanalo Pali. As the party mounted their horses to return to Honolulu, she noted with amusement that an officer in her retinue remained by the gate, lingering in a parting kiss, loath to leave his sweetheart. As the party rode up the pali road, Liliuokalani began to hum snatches of a song forming itself in her mind. When they paused at the top of the pali, she repeated her song by request. By the time they reached Honolulu, the whole party was humming and singing her new song, "Aloha Oe."

Shortly after Kalakaua's return home, it was decided that Queen Kapiolani should go to England to attend the Golden Jubilee celebrating the fifty years of Queen Victoria's reign. Liliuokalani, at this time, was greatly depressed over the death of her sister, Likelike, the wife of Hon. A. S. Cleghorn. Kalakaua arranged for her to accompany Queen Kapiolani. Since John Dominis was to be a member of the party, Liliuokalani was glad for the opportunity.

After a week's rest in San Francisco, where the royal party received many attentions, they found the trip across the United States to Boston, New York, and Washington delightful in every detail. In Boston, Liliuokalani wrote of having the chance to meet the relatives of her husband. She was charmed with the Parker House, and there received her guests. In Washington, Queen Kapiolani and her attending friends made a formal call at the White House, where they were greeted by President and Mrs. Cleveland, who on the following evening entertained the Queen and her party at dinner. Of a visit to Mount Vernon Liliuokalani wrote: "Although it is but a humble resting place for one so honored in the remembrance of mankind, yet, the sight of the sarcophagus of the General and his wife as they lay side by side, the fresh warm sunlight streaming through the iron bars which formed the gateway to the tomb, made a great impression on me; and although the Queen's party were silent and exchanged no comments it seemed to me that we were one in veneration of the sacred spot and of the first President of this country."

The royal party left New York aboard the *City of Rome,* bound for England. On reaching Liverpool, they were delighted to be greeted by familiar faces. Among these friends were Hon. Theophilus H. Davies, the British Vice Consul to Hawaii; Mr. R. G. Armstrong, the Hawaiian Consul at London; Rt. Rev. Bishop Staley, formerly American Bishop of Honolulu; and Mr. Janion, of Janion, Green & Co., long in mercantile relations with the Hawaiian Islands. When the party landed from the steamer they were greeted by one hundred soldiers of Her Majesty, Queen Victoria, detailed to honor the Queen from Hawaii. As the carriage passed the long line of soldiers, arms were presented and a salute was given while the band played "God Save the Queen." After the official welcome by the Lord Mayor at the entrance to the city, Col. Iaukea and Col. Boyd were given a separate carriage, while Queen Kapiolani, Liliuokalani and General Dominis rode in the coach with the Lord Mayor.

Queen Victoria received the Hawaiian royal party in a friendly and pleasant manner, assuring them they were welcome in England. The London air was filled with excitement. Everyone was talking of, and looking forward to, the great celebration. The city was filled with people, including visitors from all over the world. Westminster Abbey was crowded on the great anniversary, and the throngs filling the streets were almost beyond credence. The Archbishop of Canterbury opened the service with prayer as the people from many lands knelt in reverent worship. Liliuokalani wrote: "The inspiring anthems, as they were so grandly and harmoniously rendered by the great choir, lifted all hearts to the Ruler of the Universe, and the solemn tones of the great organ hushed every thought inconsistent with the devout worship of the occasion."

Liliuokalani fully appreciated the privilege of attending the grand Jubilee celebration, every detail of which was stamped firmly upon her mind. Of her final interview with Queen Victoria, she wrote: "We bade adieu to our royal hostess, wishing for her with all our hearts many, many more years of prosperity as a sovereign, and contentment and peace as the woman whose name is respected and loved wherever the sun shines throughout the wide, wide world."

The festivities were over and the visitors from Hawaii were anticipating a brief European tour before returning home, when word was received of serious trouble in the Islands. Queen Kapiolani and Liliuokalani, with their party, resolved to return immediately to Honolulu. Upon reaching Hawaii they learned that King Kalakaua had accepted and signed, though under protest, the "Bayonet Constitution of 1887"— a constitution which deprived the throne of most of its power. Liliuokalani, as heir apparent, was both amazed and angry that her brother had signed such a document, saying that if she had still been acting as Queen Regent it would never have happened. When she fully realized the concessions which had been made to the men whom she considered aliens, her anger knew no bounds and she was determined to wrest back from them the privileges which they had secured through this new constitution.

The next four years were years of discord and turmoil. From the date of Kalakaua's agreement, and his promises to abide by the constitution, there was a constant struggle between the King on one side and the Legislature on the other, with the King endeavoring by every possible means to evade or to ignore his promises, hoping to regain his former powers.

Liliuokalani could not accept this loss of the personal power of the King. She began secretly to gather about her men who, with their own political irons in the fire, would follow her. Among these was young Robert Wilcox, who occupies a prominent place in this period of Hawaiian history. Some years previously, Kalakaua had sent Robert Wilcox and Robert Boyd, two part-Hawaiian young men whom he considered promising, to Italy for military training. Kalakaua hoped, eventually, to build up a strong military power in the Kingdom. As time went by, the King's finances became so involved that he ordered the two men to return; they did so, accompanying Liliuokalani when she returned from England. Liliuokalani decided that Wilcox should assist her in her plans. Secret meetings were held at her residence in Palama, a suburb of Honolulu, she evidently making no objections to whatever was developing under Wilcox's leadership. It has been said that Wilcox finally asked her whether, if Kalakaua were put off the throne, she would be willing to take his place as the ruler. This was evidently not a new idea to Liliuokalani. While she gave a somewhat evasive answer, there seems to have been little doubt that she would approve, for she had continually and openly criticized her brother for what he had done, accusing him of cowardice in having signed the new constitution. But the revolutionary attempt by Wilcox was defeated by voluntary military forces of the government. It was not the Wilcox machine, nor Liliuokalani's opposition, which removed the King—it was death.

From the start Liliuokalani insisted upon appointing her own ministry, and after much discussion the Supreme Court ruled that the terms of the Kalakaua cabinet had expired with his death. Again, like Kalakaua, she surrounded herself with men who, to gain their own ends, would do her bidding. The ministry was continually changed; one cabinet after another was formed, the Queen dismissing as many as possible of those who refused to comply with her wishes. During these months the Queen was at work on a new constitution. She was determined to write, present, and enforce a new constitution under which only Hawaiian subjects would be allowed to vote, the guaranties of the independence of the Supreme Court would be removed, and the property of all aliens would be subject to confiscation by the government. The latter clause would have wreaked havoc among American financial interests in the Islands. In the meantime, John Dominis had died, and, with his death, Liliuokalani had lost a level-headed adviser in the cause of her own surety.

The Legislature of 1892 was purposely continued by the Queen for eight months. Because the members were worn out from long service and some were obliged to return to their homes and business affairs, the Queen succeeded, as she had planned, in passing the bill to license the opium traffic and to establish a lottery in the Kingdom, thus replenishing the treasury.

The Legislature was scheduled to adjourn on January 14, 1893. Of this day Sanford B. Dole noted in his memoirs: "At noon the Legislature was prorogued with the usual ceremony. The royal salute from the Punchbowl battery sounded as the Queen left the palace for the legislative hall, attended by her ministers, the court chamberlain, court ladies, and the *kahili* bearers. She was elaborately dressed, and wearing on her head a coronet of diamonds. The royal feather cloak covering her chair made a regal throne. With great dignity she read the address of prorogation. It was an impressive function. There was, however, only a slim attendance of the legislators. As the ceremony ended, the Queen's chamberlain announced to the local officials and foreign representatives included that a meeting would be held in the palace that afternoon to which they were all invited."

The Queen had planned to proclaim a new constitution, but the plan was thwarted by the refusal of her ministers to support her. A large group of Hawaiians had arrived at the meeting, carrying a copy of the constitution which the Queen had prepared and had ordered to be brought to her as a petition from the Hawaiian people. When her ministers refused to sign the document, the session became exceedingly stormy. The Hawaiian delegation was dismissed, the Queen telling them in an impassioned address that she would, in a few days, declare the new constitution.

Hours passed while the Queen and the cabinet were closeted in the Blue Room, she insisting that the members of the Cabinet sign her constitution. Meantime, conferences of some leading men of the community (mostly civic-minded Americans) were called to consider what might be done to prevent the Queen from carrying out her plans. Public records of the day said that it was decided to form a "Committee of Safety," a group of men authorized to take whatever measures they might consider necessary to protect the "public interest," or, as was more specifically the case, American financial interests in the Islands. To this end a mass meeting was called. The Queen, determined and angry, also called a meeting in the public square to present her side of the matter.

A glance at the economic set-up of the Islands at this crucial point in their history does much to clarify the political turmoil that was to follow. The moneyed foreigners (with the exception of Theo. H. Davies, an Englishman who held large financial interests in Hawaii's growing sugar industry, but who placed personal integrity above personal gain and sided with the Monarchy) were not so much concerned with local politics as they were with far-reaching finance. The McKinley tariff of 1890 had abrogated the Hawaiian advantage over other foreign sugars in the American market. It spelled the eventual bankruptcy of the Hawaiian economy as seen from the viewpoint of American financial interests in the Islands. The only method by which these interests could circumvent the tariff barrier was annexation. Accusations against the Queen were made by them to a gullible American press, which picked up and reported the Hawaiian situation not so much as an economic or political problem as it was the persecution of stalwart Americans by a wicked Polynesian Queen.

Meanwhile, meetings continued to be held. An Annexation Club was formed and, because of the great unrest and alarm in the American community, the Committee of Safety asked Mr. John L. Stevens, the United States Minister (and former newspaper partner of James G. Blain, President Harrison's first Secretary of State) to land a force from the U.S.S. *Boston,* then in the harbor, in order to prevent possible violence by the Queen's party. A detail of sailors and marines came ashore that afternoon, and a guard was placed at the United States Legation. Conferences were held by the Committee and plans were laid to use force if necessary to combat the plan of the Queen and her adherents. Records show that the members of the Committee of Safety were unanimously in favor of setting aside the monarchy and establishing a republican form of government, with the view of eventual annexation by the United States. Sanford B. Dole was urged to take the lead in the plans to suppress the monarchy and organize a new government. It was in this way that the Provisional Government was established on January 17, 1893, Mr. Dole consenting to take the chairmanship in the hope that annexation would be accomplished.

The Provisional Government setup consisted of an Executive Council of four members with Sanford B. Dole acting as president and foreign minister to take the place of the Queen and her Cabinet, and an Advisory Council of fourteen members. In view of the landing of American troops from the *Boston* at the request of American Minister Stevens, Liliuokalani surrendered under protest and immediately appealed to the United States government for the restoration of her power. Meantime, the American flag had been run up on all government buildings. The Provisional Government meant to operate as such only until a treaty of annexation with the United States could be effected. With this in mind, a commission left for Washington on January 19 and, with the Secretary of State, drew up and signed the treaty in mid-February. It was sent to the United States Senate, but not acted upon before the end of the session. Harrison was defeated and Cleveland, several days after his inauguration, withdrew the treaty from the Senate and sent Col. James H. Blount to Hawaii to investigate all facets of the Queen's downfall.

There seems little doubt that Blount, if not exactly pro-Liliuokalani, was at least anti-Provisional Government. His first act was to replace the American flag with the Hawaiian on government buildings. The Provisional Government accused Blount of playing politics, since they had expected to achieve annexation under defeated ex-President Harrison, and, since he had been a Confederate colonel, of being unfair to Hawaii, which had supported the North during the Civil War. Nevertheless, Blount's report to the Secretary of State, sent on July 17, clearly placed the blame for the revolution on the Americans. He stated that the "Committee of Safety" had been meeting for two years planning ways and means of bringing about annexation and that the Committee had been actively supported by American Minister Stevens and by American troops landed from the *Boston* at the time of the revolution. In *Anatomy of Paradise* (Wm. Sloane Assoc.), J. C. Furnas captured something of the feeling prevalent among the Americans in Hawaii at that time when he wrote: "In Honolulu, when Blount sailed back to the mainland, the Royal Hawaiian Band played him, Georgian and former Confederate, off with *Marching Through Georgia.* The Provisional Government insisted it was just a natural mistake on the part of dear old Henri Berger, German-reared bandmaster."

In the course of events in Washington, an order was given for the recall of Minister Stevens and the appointment of Mr. Albert S. Willis in his place. Mr. Willis arrived in Honolulu with orders from the President to negotiate with the Queen regarding the whole situation. One distinct condition was exacted by President Cleveland, which was that, if it were decided that restoration might yet be made, the Queen should grant full amnesty to all persons who had taken part in the revolution. This provision Mr. Willis carefully explained to Liliuokalani. According to the Provisional Government's version, the Queen "promptly and stubbornly refused to grant amnesty," and, furthermore, "her savage demand was that those chiefly instrumental in the organization of the Provisional Government should be beheaded." In her autobiography, Liliuokalani later recalled this meeting with Mr. Willis as follows: "I told him that, as to granting amnesty, it was beyond my powers as a constitutional sovereign. That it was a matter for the privy council and for the cabinet. That our laws read that those who are guilty of treason should suffer the penalty of death. He then wished to know if I would carry out that law. I said that I would be more inclined personally to punish them by banishment, and confiscation of their property to the government."

The vast bulk of existing historical records covering these tumultuous days is highly colored pro and con. Adherents of the Provisional Government presented Liliuokalani to the American press as a fierce and blood-thirsty tyrant. Liliuokalani in her autobiography, tried valiantly to justify what had been, in reality, her strong-willed and somewhat vindictive course of action. The truth, probably, lay between two extremes.

Mr. Willis, meanwhile, had exacted the desired promise of amnesty for the revolutionists from Liliuokalani and demanded her restoration. He backed his demands with American warships in the harbor, prepared for action on the Queen's behalf. The Provisional Government knew the warships would never fire on those of American descent, and they knew they were still in power. They flatly refused to turn over the government to Liliuokalani. Mr. Willis could do no more.

As the months passed, Liliuokalani had accepted her situation with resignation. She lived, under surveillance, at Washington Place. She was seemingly happy in her old home with old friends about her, whatever may have been her profound disappointment. And as hope dwindled for early annexation to the United States, the Provisional Government called a constitutional convention in 1894 to draft a constitution for the Republic of Hawaii. The constitution, patterned after that of the United States, was completed, and on July 5, the Republic was proclaimed with Mr. Dole as its first president. The Queen's forces, all this time, were moving about stealthily and cautiously. Late that year, a cargo of arms and ammunition from San Francisco was secretly landed east of Diamond Head. And, on the evening of January 6, 1895, it happened.

A group of insurgents, led by Samuel Nolwein and Hawaii's most inveterate revolutionist, Robert Wilcox, planned to strike at midnight to overthrow the Republic and restore the monarchy. Bad luck overtook them. By accident the plot was discovered that evening, by which the government forces were able to get the upper hand of the situation. Several men from each side were killed, but the revolution was successfully aborted and its leaders captured by the government. Liliuokalani was found to be involved, and, on January 16, she was arrested on charges of treason against the Republic and held prisoner in the palace for about nine months. At this time she renounced all claims to the throne, asking clemency for those who had taken part in the insurrection. Liliuokalani was granted a conditional pardon on September 7, 1895, and by the following New Year's Day, all of the remaining prisoners had been freed.

As the old century was drawing to a close, Liliuokalani made a trip to Washington. The purpose of her trip was to press claims for a pension from the United States government on account of the loss of her crown lands in Hawaii, the income from which would have netted her, ordinarily, between $50,000 and $100,000 a year. Senator Clark of Wyoming was her ardent champion, claiming that she had been dethroned with the aid of the armed forces of the United States. The Senate rejected his proposal that she be paid an outright sum of $250,000 for resigning her claim to her former lands.

Liliuokalani returned to Hawaii on June 4, 1900. *The Friend* reported sympathetically that the ex-Queen was inflicted with an incurable cancer of the neck and predicted her early demise. It editorialized: "We are in favor of a kind contribution being made by the Legislature to the ex-Queen's comfort, in the form of a liberal pension or perhaps of a specific grant. We are among those who in 1893 deeply resented her course of action. But she has suffered defeat and humiliation. We should now consider her former exalted position, and accord her some especial regard and kindness."

The Friend had erred in two ways: in reporting an illness from which Liliuokalani did not suffer, and in assuming that she would soon die. They reckoned without her ancient tenacity and strength of will. She lived on for seventeen more years, but her spirit had been shaken. She was interested in world affairs and spent much time in reading. She continued her musical studies and writing. She gave careful consideration to matters of education, especially for young Hawaiian girls and for orphans. Thinking, perhaps, of the Queen's Hospital and the Lunalilo Home for the aged, the Queen provided under the terms of her will the Liliuokalani Trust Fund for the care of orphan children, which is still carried on today.

Miss Mary Krout, who came to Honolulu in the interest of the Chicago newspapers which she served, wrote of her interview with Liliuokalani, first noting her impressions of Washington Place: the beauty of everything surrounding the home of the ex-Queen, the tall *kahilis* at the entrance, and the great number of tuberoses, their fragrance filling the air. She was finally ushered into the presence of Liliuokalani, who was waiting for her, having made a special appointment to receive her at eleven o'clock in the morning. "She was seated on a sofa but rose when I entered the apartment, and extended her hand, greeting me with the utmost informality. She requested me to be seated, and, as the conversation progressed, I had an opportunity to study her face. It was strong and resolute. Her hair was streaked with gray and she had the large, dark eyes of her race. She spoke remarkably pure and graceful English. Her manner was dignified and she had the ease and authoritative air of one accustomed to rule. The Queen was wearing a black and gray serge dress and wore no decorations or jewelry of any kind."

In conversation Miss Krout spoke of the beauty of the country, the charm of the climate of the Islands, and the cordial hospitality of the people. Liliuokalani replied, "Yes, we love our beautiful country and we love to hear it praised." They talked of education, Miss Krout saying that she had visited the Royal School and that people in the United States were surprised at the excellence of the Hawaiian schools. The Queen replied, "It is very gratifying to me when foreigners are able to see our schools for themselves. The Hawaiians are a well educated people; there are few, if any, who cannot read and write." It had been a pleasant interview, touching many points of interest. As Miss Krout was leaving, a group of Hawaiian women who had been waiting passed into the house with their fragrant *leis,* a daily offering to the Queen.

As years passed, Liliuokalani grew more kindly in feeling. Mr. Lorrin Thurston, who took an important part in establishing the Provisional Government, and whom Liliuokalani considered one of her chief opponents, tells in his *Memories of the Hawaiian Revolution* of attending a formal reception at the residence of Prince Kuhio in Waikiki in honor of a delegation of commissioners from Washington. Mr. Thurston had neither met nor spoken with Liliuokalani since her dethronement. At the reception he found the former Queen seated at the head of the receiving line. She held out her hand to him saying, "I am very glad to see you here, Mr. Thurston," showing that the bitter waters of her life had receded somewhat.

Only once after her dethronement did Liliuokalani enter the old Palace, and that was on Balboa Day, September 19, 1915. It was she who introduced the annual celebration. "She received from the hands of the delegates from all Pacific lands the flags of their countries, to be presented in turn by her to the Pan Pacific Union. With her own hands, she had sewn together the silken flag of Hawaii. This gave Liliuokalani great satisfaction, as did the *aloha* of the large audience and the appreciation they expressed."

Life closed for Liliuokalani, eighth and last monarch of the Hawaiian Islands, at her old home, Washington Place, on November 11, 1917. Thousands of people, many of them native Hawaiians, who loved the Queen, together with officials of the government, strangers from foreign lands, and sailors from ships in the harbor, silently watched the great funeral procession as it slowly made its way from Kawaiahao Church, where as a private citizen Liliuokalani had lain in state, to the Royal Mausoleum in Nuuanu Valley. With honor and affection Liliuokalani was left to rest beside her royal predecessors.

A deep sigh rippled through the crowd as the old Hawaiian caretaker finally closed the door of the sacred tomb and on the golden-mantled pageantry of the kings and queens who had cherished the dream of Kamehameha the Great. It had been a long and colorful procession, fusing the past with the present. But in the heart of old Hawaii, Kamehameha is yet King. He still reigns.

GLOSSARY

AIKANAKA
A high chief and aide to Kamehameha I. Grandfather of Kalakaua and Liliuokalani.

Akua
A god who presided over the occupation or profession of old Hawaiians.

ALAPAINUI
King of Hawaii. Uncle of Kekuiapoiwa, who was the mother of Kamehameha I.

ALEXANDER LIHOLIHO
Ruled as Kamehameha IV.

Alii
Hawaiian nobility.

ARMSTRONG, REV. RICHARD
A missionary who served as Minister of Public Instruction under Kamehameha III.

ARMSTRONG, R. G.
Son of Rev. Richard Armstrong. Hawaiian Consul to London under Kalakaua.

ARMSTRONG, WILLIAM
Son of the Rev. Richard Armstrong. A member of Kalakaua's cabinet. Accompanied Kalakaua around the world as Minister of State and Royal Commissioner of Immigration.

AUHEA
Pet name for Kekauluohi, premier or *kuhina-nui* to Kamehameha III.

BACHELOT, FATHER
Leader of the first group of Catholic priests to arrive in Hawaii.

BANDMAN, DANIEL
English actor, friend of Kamehameha V and Lunalilo.

BARONOV, ALEXANDER
Governor of the Russian - American Co. in Alaska.

BERGER, HENRY
Founder of the Royal Hawaiian Band under Kamehameha V.

BINGHAM, REV. HIRAM
One of the first Christian missionaries to arrive in Hawaii aboard the *Thaddeus* in 1820.

BISHOP, CHARLES R.
Husband of Bernice Pauahi, great-granddaughter of Kamehameha I.

BLOUNT, COL. JAMES H.
Emissary of President Cleveland to investigate the overthrow of Queen Liliuokalani.

BOKI
Governor of Oahu, and close friend of Liholiho.

BRINTNALL, CAPT.
Commander of the *Triumph,* on which Obookiah and Thomas Hopoo sailed to New England.

BYNG, HON. FREDERICK
Sponsor of the Royal party when Liholiho visited England.

BYRON, LORD
Cousin of the poet. Captain of the *Blonde,* which returned the bodies of Liholiho and Kamamalu to Hawaii from England.

CAMPBELL, ARCHIBALD
World traveler and visitor to Hawaii in Kamehameha I's day.

CHAMBERLAIN, DANIEL
A farmer aboard the *Thaddeus* when it brought the first Christian missionaries to Hawaii in 1820.

CHAMISSO, ADELBERT VON
Naturalist with the Russian vessel *Rurik.*

CHARLTON, RICHARD
English consul in Hawaii.

CHORIS, LOUIS
Artist with the Russian vessel *Rurik.*

CLEGHORN, A. S.
A Scottish businessman in Honolulu, husband of Likelike.

COOK, CAPT. JAMES
British explorer. Re-discovered the Hawaiian Islands in 1778.

DAVIES, THEOPHILUS H.
British Vice Consul to Hawaii who, despite his business interests in the Islands, sided with the monarchy in the Revolution of 1893.

DAVIS, ISAAC
A British sailor. Friend of Kamehameha I and of John Young.

DE TROMELIN,
    ADMIRAL LEGOARANT
A French admiral who threatened the independence of the Hawaiian Islands in 1849.

DILLON, G. P.
French consul under Kamehameha III. Caused France to take over the Hawaiian Islands in 1849 with the aid of Admiral de Tromelin.

DOLE, SANFORD B.
Head of the Provisional Government of Hawaii, first president of the Republic, and first governor of the Territory of Hawaii. A leader in the movement to dethrone Queen Liliuokalani.

DOMINIS, JOHN
Husband of Liliuokalani, last queen of Hawaii.

DWIGHT, EDWARD
A student at Yale and tutor to Obookiah.

ELLIOT, JOHN
An adventurous sailor who became surgeon to Kamehameha I.

EMMA
Granddaughter of John Young and queen of Kamehameha IV.

HAALILIO
A Hawaiian diplomat under Kamehameha III.

Hale-o-keawe
Mausoleum of the Hawaiian kings at Honaunau on the big island of Hawaii.

Hamakua
A district on the big island of Hawaii.

Hana
A district on Maui. Birthplace of Kaahumanu.

Haystack Band
A group of students at Williams College who, in the early 19th century, took an active part in the great revival of religion.

Heiau
A religious temple.

Hilo
A district on the big island of Hawaii.

HOLMAN, DR. THOMAS
Physician aboard the *Thaddeus* when

it brought the first Christian missionaries to Hawaii in 1820.

Honaunau
Burial place of the kings of old Hawaii.

Hookupu
The presentation of gifts to a high chief.

HOPOO, THOMAS
A Hawaiian youth who accompanied Obookiah on his trip to New England.

HUBBARD, RUSSELL
Friend of Obookiah who taught him the English alphabet.

Iao
A valley on the island of Maui, site of one of Kamehameha I's greatest battles.

JUDD, DR. GERRIT
Medical missionary. Held many diplomatic posts and was one of the most influential foreigners, particularly during the reign of Kamehameha III.

KAAHUMANU
Favorite queen of Kamehameha I.

KAEO
King of Kauai and Niihau.

KAHEKILI
King of Maui, Molokai, Oahu and Lanai. Believed by many to be the true father of Kamehameha I.

Kahili
A tall, feathered standard symbolic of Hawaiian nobility.

Kahu
A teacher, instructor or guardian.

Kahuna
A prophet, priest, or professional person.

KAIANA
Son of the king of Maui. Traitor to Kamehameha I.

KALAKAUA
A high chief, and the penultimate ruler of Hawaii. Ascended the throne by election after death of Lunalilo.

KALAMA
A lesser chieftess, wife of Kamehameha III.

KALANIKUPULE
Son of Kahekili and ruling chief of Oahu.

KALANIMOKU
Premier of Hawaii under Kaahumanu.

KALANIOPUU
King of Hawaii. Half-uncle of Kamehameha I.

KAMAKAU
A chief of the South Kona district of the big island of Hawaii under High Chieftess Kapiolani.

KAMAMALU
Half-sister and favorite queen of Liholiho.

KAMEHAMEHA I (THE GREAT)
A high chief of the island of Hawaii. Brought all of the Hawaiian Islands under one (his) rule. Founder of the Kamehameha dynasty.

KANE
The god of light and life.

KAPAAKA
A high chief, and father of Kalakaua and Liliuokalani.

KAPIHE
Advisor to Liholiho.

KAPIOLANI
A high chieftess of South Kona on the big island of Hawaii. Defied the goddess Pele in an attempt to supplant the religion of old Hawaii with Christianity.

KAPIOLANI, QUEEN
Consort to Kalakaua.

Kau
A district on the big island of Hawaii.

KAUIKEAOULI
Younger brother of Liholiho and heir-presumptive to the throne. Ruled as Kamehameha III.

Kaumakapili Church
The second Hawaiian Christian church in Honolulu. Used for mass meetings, and is often referred to as the Faneuil Hall of Hawaii.

KAUMUALII
A king of Kauai.

KAUMUALII, GEORGE
Son of the king of Kauai. Student at Cornwall with Obookiah. Came to Hawaii with the first missionaries to act as interpreter.

Kawaiahao Church
The "Old Stone Church" in Hono-

lulu, still standing at King and Punchbowl Streets.

Kawaihae
Site of Kamehameha I's *heiau* on the big island of Hawaii.

Kealakekua Bay
A harbor on the big island of Hawaii. Site of Capt. Cook's death.

KEAWE-A-HEULU
A warrior chief and councilor to Kamehameha I. Great-grandfather of Kalakaua and Liliuokalani.

KEAWEMAUHILI
A high chief and ruler of the Hilo district on the big island of Hawaii. Brother to Kalaniopuu and uncle of Kamehameha I. Father of Kapiolani.

KEEAUMOKU
Husband of Namahana and father of Kaahumanu. One of the five chiefs who made Kamehameha I king of Hawaii.

KEKAULUOHI
A noble chieftess. Mother of Lunalilo, and premier of the kingdom under Kamehameha III following Kinau. Known also by her pet name of Auhea.

KEKUANAOA
A high chief, father of Kamehameha IV and Kamehameha V.

KEKUAOKALANI
Cousin of Liholiho. Keeper of the ancient war god and last defender of the old religion.

KEKUIAPOIWA
High chieftess of Hawaii. Mother of Kamehameha I.

KENDRICK, CAPT. JOHN
Commander of the *Lady Washington*, an American ship.

KEOHOKALOLOE
A high chieftess and councilor to Kamehameha III. Mother of Kalakaua and Liliuokalani.

KEOPUOLANI
Queen and sacred wife of Kamehameha I. Mother of Liholiho (Kamehameha II) and Kauikeaouli (Kamehameha III).

KEOUA
High chief of Hawaii. Father of Kamehameha I.

KEOUA KUAHUULA
Son of Kalaniopuu and younger brother of Kiwalao. Later king of the district of Kau on the big island of Hawaii.

Kiheki
Scarf-like piece of *tapa* thrown across the shoulder.

Kilauea
A volcano on the big island of Hawaii.

KINAU
A daughter of Kamehameha I. Premier during the reign of Kamehameha III.

KING, LT.
An officer aboard Capt. Cook's ship.

KIWALAO
Son of Kalaniopuu, and heir-presumptive to the throne of the big island of Hawaii.

Koa
A native tree, whose hard wood is used extensively.

Kohala
A district on the big island of Hawaii.

Kokoiki
A star, possibly Halley's comet, known to have passed the sun in late 1758 or early 1759.

Kona
A district on the big island of Hawaii.

KONIA
Granddaughter of Kamehameha I. Mother of Bernice Pauahi and foster mother of Liliuokalani.

KOTZEBUE, OTTO VON
Captain of the Russian vessel *Rurik,* seeking a passage from the Pacific to the Atlantic.

KUAKINI
A brother of Kaahumanu. A governor of Maui, for which he took the name of "Governor Adams."

Kuhina-nui
A high chieftess acting as premier of the kingdom.

KUKAILIMOKU
War god of the kings of the big island of Hawaii.

Kukui
A nut-bearing tree.

Kuleana
A parcel of land.

Lanai
A porch.

Lauhala
The leaves of the *hala* tree, used for making mats.

Lei
A garland of flowers or feathers.

LELEIOHOKU
Younger brother and heir apparent of Kalakaua.

LIHOLIHO
Son of Kamehameha the Great. Ruled as Kamehameha II.

LIKELIKE
Sister of Kalakaua and Liliuokalani and wife of A. S. Cleghorn, businessman.

LILIHA
Wife of Boki, who later took his place as governor of Oahu.

LILIUOKALANI
Sister of Kalakaua and his heir apparent after the death of their younger brother, Leleiohoku. Deposed in 1893.

LISIANSKY, CAPT.
Commander of a Russian exploring expedition. Captain of the Russian vessel *Neva.*

LONO
Polynesian god of agriculture and peace.

LOOMIS, ELISHA
A printer aboard the *Thaddeus* when it brought the first Christian missionaries to Hawaii in 1820.

LOT KAMEHAMEHA
Brother of Alexander Liholiho. Succeeded him to rule as Kamehameha V.

LUNALILO
A high chief of Hawaii, and the first king to be elected to office in the Islands. He succeeded Kamehameha V.

Mahele
A land division.

Maile
A sweet-smelling vine.

Malo
A garment worn by men about their loins.

MALO, DAVID
A Hawaiian historian.

Mamo
A Hawaiian bird, now extinct. Some of its feathers were used in making the feather capes, helmets, and leis worn by Hawaiian royalty.

MARIN, DON FRANCISCO
An early Spanish immigrant to Hawaii. Friend of Kamehameha I. An agriculturalist who imported many new plants to the Islands.

Mauna Loa
A mountain on the big island of Hawaii.

Mele
A song or chant.

METCALF, CAPT. SIMON
American fur trader. Captain of the *Eleanora,* of which John Young was boatswain.

MILLS, SAMUEL J., JR.
Friend of Obookiah. A leader of the Haystack Band. Obookiah lived with his family at Torringford.

NAEOLE
High chief of Hawaii, to whom the baby Kamehameha I was entrusted.

NAHAOLELU
Governor of Maui under Kamehameha V.

NAHIENAENA
Sister of Kamehameha III.

NAIHE
Orator of Kamehameha I.

NAMAHANA
Former queen of Maui, and mother of Kaahumanu.

Nei
Translated, "All of this, time or place."

NEILSON, H. A.
Secretary to Kamehameha IV.

NOLWEIN, SAMUEL
A leader of the insurgents who, along with Robert Wilcox, tried to overthrow the Republic of Hawaii and restore the monarchy in 1895.

Nuuanu
A valley on Oahu, site of Kamehameha I's greatest battle.

OBOOKIAH
The first Hawaiian Christian convert. Largely responsible for the coming of the Christian missionaries to Hawaii in 1820.

Ohelo
A native berry sacred to the goddess Pele.

Ohia
A native tree.

OLOHANA
Hawaiian name for John Young.

PAKI
A high chief, and father of Bernice Pauahi.

Pali
A cliff or steep place.

PARKER, JOHN
New England sailor who settled on the big island of Hawaii. Friend and advisor to Kamehameha I, who gave him a large grant of land which is today the famed Parker Ranch.

Pa-u
A woman's garment with a long, flowing skirt. Used largely for riding horseback.

PAUAHI, BERNICE
Great-granddaughter of Kamehameha I. She married Charles R. Bishop and refused the throne when Kamehameha V died.

PAULET, LORD GEORGE
Commander of the frigate *Carysfort,* who attempted to take over the Hawaiian Islands in the name of the British crown.

PELE
The goddess of fire and volcanoes.

Poi
A pasty native food, pounded from the *taro* root.

Poi-dog
A dog of mixed breed, used as the meat course in ancient days at feasts.

PRINCE OF HAWAII
Albert Edward Kauikeaouli Leiopapa A Kamehameha, only child of Kamehameha IV and Queen Emma.

RICHARDS, WILLIAM
A missionary who became advisor to Kamehameha III and Kamehameha IV.

RUGGLES, SAMUEL
A teacher aboard the *Thaddeus* when it brought the first Christian missionaries to Hawaii in 1820.

SANDWICH, EARL
    Patron of Capt. Cook, after whom
    Cook named the Hawaiian Islands.

STEVENS, JOHN L.
    U. S. minister to Hawaii. Landed a
    force from the *U.S.S. Boston* to pro-
    tect Americans at the time of the
    Revolution of 1893.

STONE, REV. TIMOTHY
    Friend of Obookiah. It was in the
    Stone home in Cornwall, Conn., that
    Obookiah died.

Tabu
    Forbidden, sacred.

Tapa
    A cloth made from the beaten bark
    of the mulberry tree.

Taro
    A plant from whose roots is pounded
    poi, the staff of the Hawaiians' diet.

THOMAS, ADMIRAL RICHARD
    British admiral who restored Ha-
    waiian independence in 1843.

THURSTON, REV. ASA
    One of the first Christian mission-
    aries to arrive in Hawaii aboard the
    Thaddeus in 1820.

THURSTON, LORRIN A.
    A grandson of one of the first Chris-
    tian missionaries to Hawaii. A leader
    in the revolution against Liliuokalani.

Ukeke
    A reed flute.

VANCOUVER, CAPT. GEORGE
    British explorer, friend of Kameha-
    meha I.

VICTORIA KAMAMALU
    KAAHUMANU
    A Hawaiian princess, sister of Ka-
    mehameha IV and Kamehameha V.

Waialae Bay
    A bay on the island of Oahu.

Waipio
    A valley on the big island of Hawaii,
    scene of one of Kamehameha I's
    greatest battles.

WHITNEY, SAMUEL
    A teacher aboard the *Thaddeus* when
    it brought the first Christian mission-
    aries to Hawaii in 1820.

WILCOX, ROBERT W.
    A leader in the insurrections of 1889
    and 1895 to make "Hawaii for the
    Hawaiians." On this slogan, he was
    later elected delegate to Congress.

WILLIS, ALBERT S.
    Appointed U. S. Minister to Hawaii,
    replacing John L. Stevens, to nego-
    tiate with Liliuokalani.

WINSHIP, CAPT. NATHAN
    Skipper of the *Albatross*, friend of
    Don Marin.

WYLLIE, ROBERT C.
    Foreign minister under Kamehameha
    III.

YOUNG, JAMES
    Son of John Young and friend of
    Liholiho.

YOUNG, JOHN
    A British sailor, friend of Kameha-
    meha I. Known also in Hawaiian as
    Olohana.

YOUNG, JOHN, JR.
    A son of John Young, and a friend
    of Kamehameha IV.

INDEX